taste of home
30-MINUTE HEALTHY COOKING

taste of home
BOOKS

taste of home
30-MINUTE
HEALTHY COOKING

EDITORIAL

EDITOR-IN-CHIEF	Catherine Cassidy
CREATIVE DIRECTOR	Howard Greenberg
EDITORIAL SERVICES MANAGER	Kerri Balliet
MANAGING EDITOR/PRINT & DIGITAL BOOKS	Mark Hagen
ASSOCIATE CREATIVE DIRECTOR	Edwin Robles Jr.
EDITOR	Michelle Rozumalski
ART DIRECTOR	Jessie Sharon
CONTRIBUTING LAYOUT DESIGNER	Matt Fukuda
EDITORIAL PRODUCTION MANAGER	Dena Ahlers
COPY CHIEF	Deb Warlaumont Mulvey
COPY EDITOR	Mary C. Hanson
CHIEF FOOD EDITOR	Karen Berner
FOOD EDITORS	James Schend; Peggy Woodward, RD
ASSOCIATE FOOD EDITOR	Krista Lanphier
ASSOCIATE EDITOR/FOOD CONTENT	Annie Rundle
RECIPE EDITORS	Mary King; Jenni Sharp, RD; Irene Yeh
CONTENT OPERATIONS MANAGER	Colleen King
TEST KITCHEN AND FOOD STYLING MANAGER	Sarah Thompson
TEST KITCHEN COOKS	Alicia Rooker, RD (lead); Holly Johnson; Jimmy Cababa
PREP COOKS	Matthew Hass (lead), Nicole Spohrleder, Lauren Knoelke
FOOD STYLISTS	Kathryn Conrad (senior), Shannon Roum, Leah Rekau
GROCERY COORDINATOR	Molly McCowan
PHOTO DIRECTOR	Dan Bishop
PHOTOGRAPHERS	Dan Roberts, Grace Natoli Sheldon, Jim Wieland
SET STYLING MANAGER	Stephanie Marchese
SET STYLISTS	Melissa Haberman, Dee Dee Jacq

BUSINESS

VICE PRESIDENT, PUBLISHER	Jan Studin, jan_studin@rd.com
GENERAL MANAGER, TASTE OF HOME COOKING SCHOOLS	Erin Puariea
VICE PRESIDENT, BRAND MARKETING	Jennifer Smith
VICE PRESIDENT, CIRCULATION AND CONTINUITY MARKETING	Dave Fiegel

READER'S DIGEST NORTH AMERICA

VICE PRESIDENT, BUSINESS DEVELOPMENT	Jonathan Bigham
PRESIDENT, BOOKS AND HOME ENTERTAINING	Harold Clarke
CHIEF FINANCIAL OFFICER	Howard Halligan
VICE PRESIDENT, GENERAL MANAGER, READER'S DIGEST MEDIA	Marilynn Jacobs
CHIEF MARKETING OFFICER	Renee Jordan
VICE PRESIDENT, CHIEF SALES OFFICER	Mark Josephson
GENERAL MANAGER, MILWAUKEE	Frank Quigley
VICE PRESIDENT, CHIEF CONTENT OFFICER	Liz Vaccariello

THE READER'S DIGEST ASSOCIATION, INC.

PRESIDENT AND CHIEF EXECUTIVE OFFICER	Robert E. Guth

COVER PHOTOGRAPHY

PHOTOGRAPHER	Dan Roberts
FOOD STYLIST	Shannon Roum
SET STYLIST	Dee Dee Jacq

© 2013 Reiman Media Group, Inc.
5400 S. 60th St., Greendale WI 53129

INTERNATIONAL STANDARD BOOK NUMBER (13):	978-1-61765-185-4
LIBRARY OF CONGRESS CONTROL NUMBER:	2012949323
COMPONENT NUMBER:	116000198H00

Printed in U.S.A.
1 3 5 7 9 10 8 6 4 2

PICTURED ON THE FRONT COVER: Loaded Mexican Pizza (p. 109).
PICTURED ON THE BACK COVER: Clockwise from top left: Heavenly Filled Strawberries (p. 221), Makeover Tuna Melt Bites (p. 75), Italian Spinach and Chicken Skillet (p. 181), Turkey Stir-Fry with Cabbage (p. 114), Italian Steaks (p. 158) and O'Larry's Skillet Potatoes (p. 93).

TABLE OF CONTENTS

Eat Better and Sooner with
30-Minute Healthy Cooking

Yes, you can have it all! Just take a look inside this exciting, one-of-a-kind new cookbook compiled by the pros at *Taste of Home*.

In *30-Minute Healthy Cooking,* you'll enjoy 308 tasty recipes shared by busy but health-conscious cooks just like you. Each scrumptious sensation is not only quick to fix, but also a lighter option for menus. So you don't have to choose between eating right and getting food on the table fast.

From savory main courses and fun party appetizers to heartwarming soups and delectable desserts, every mouthwatering dish can be prepared from start to finish in just 30 minutes—or less! Plus, each includes complete Nutrition Facts and Diabetic Exchanges (where applicable), giving you the dietary information you need at a glance.

All of the dishes in this special cookbook have been approved as healthier options by *Taste of Home's* team of registered dietitians and recommended as swift-and-easy choices by families like yours. No matter what you decide to make for your loved ones, you can rest assured it will fit both your diet-minded lifestyle and your hectic schedule.

Nine big chapters give you everything you need for weekday dinners, busy-morning breakfasts, speedy lunches, holiday feasts and more. We've also included a gorgeous color photo with each recipe, so you can see exactly what your finished creation will look like.

Want help locating the kinds of dishes you have in mind? Just use the convenient Alphabetical Index and General Recipe Index in the back of the book. And look for handy hints and tips scattered throughout each chapter.

Whether you're cooking to suit a special diet or just want to eat lighter, *30-Minute Healthy Cooking* serves up family-pleasing fare in a snap!

Here's just a sampling of what you'll find in each chapter:

APPETIZERS & SNACKS

Party guests will love these extra-special munchies! You'll also appreciate the selection of snacks that will tide the whole family over until dinner.

TRY: Tortellini with Roasted Red Pepper Dip (p. 14), Chili-Cheese Wonton Cups (p. 28), Crab Asparagus Quesadillas (p. 8) and Crescent Samosas (p. 21).

BREAKFAST & BRUNCH

Start the day with bright delights your gang will jump out of bed for. These sunrise sensations are perfect both for busy weekdays and lazy weekends.

TRY: Sausage and Egg Pizza (p. 47), Cherry-Almond Drop Scones (p. 52), A.M. Rush Espresso Smoothie (p. 35) and Strawberry Puff Pancake (p. 44).

SOUPS & SANDWICHES

Whether for a casual lunch or quick dinner, the popular combo of a steaming bowl of soup and a piled-high sandwich is hard to beat. You won't want to miss the recipes here!

TRY: Salsa Black Bean Burgers (p. 66), Toasted Clubs with Dill Mayo (p. 60), Makeover Cream of Tomato Soup (p. 68) and Hearty Vegetarian Chili (p. 67).

SIDES, SALADS & BREADS

Round out a memorable meal with the standout selections from this chapter. It's jam-packed with scrumptious accompaniments that suit a wide variety of menus.

TRY: Grilled Portobellos with Mozzarella Salad (p. 103), Buttermilk Mashed Potatoes (p. 88), Honey-Orange Broccoli Slaw (p. 84) and Maple Syrup Corn Bread (p. 94).

EVERYDAY ENTREES

These mouthwatering main courses are a breeze to prepare any day of the week. Choose from savory beef, pork, chicken, turkey, fish, seafood and meatless options.

TRY: Ranch Ham 'n' Cheese Pasta (p. 137), Spicy Mango Scallops (p. 127), Bow Ties with Walnut-Herb Pesto (p. 113) and Skewerless Stovetop Kabobs (p. 121).

MEALTIME MENUS

Create a complete meal—main course, side dish and sweet treat—using these convenient menus. Every recipe comes together in just 30 minutes or less!

TRY: Italian Steaks (p. 158), Mediterranean Shrimp and Linguine (p. 163), Gingered Green Bean Salad (p. 150) and No-Bake Peanut Butter Treats (p. 153).

ALL-IN-ONE DINNERS

When you have time to prepare only one dish for dinner, turn to this chapter. Each rave-winning recipe makes a wholesome, satisfying meal all by itself.

TRY: Beef 'n' Asparagus Pasta (p. 187), Fettuccine with Mushrooms and Tomatoes (p. 179), Easy Chicken and Dumplings (p. 177) and Sausage Zucchini Skillet (p. 169).

DECADENT DESSERTS

Why skip dessert when you have luscious options like these? You'll want to surprise your family with these delights on special occasions, weeknights... any time at all.

TRY: Chocolate Mousse with Strawberries (p. 207), Double-Decker Banana Cups (p. 205), Makeover Nutty Monkey Malts (p. 212) and Lemon Burst Tartlets (p. 215).

HOLIDAYS & PARTIES

Celebrations call for festive specialties your loved ones will long remember. From entrees and sides to appetizers and desserts, they're all here!

TRY: Autumn Turkey Tenderloins (p. 218) Orange-Glazed Sweet Potatoes (p. 237), Smoked Salmon Tomato Cups (p.237) and Fruit-Filled Angel Food Torte (p. 231).

9

16

15

Appetizers & Snacks

❝This unique, warm and savory treat is sure to be a hit with any hungry crowd. For special occasions, I serve the tortellini with fancy, frilled party picks.❞

MICHELLE BOUCHER MILFORD, NEW HAMPSHIRE
about her recipe, Tortellini with Roasted Red Pepper Dip, on page 14

Chipotle Pea Spread

I've always enjoyed cooking but wanted a new challenge in the kitchen. It took a few experiments to come up with a distinctive spread my friends and family love. Just add veggies or crackers!

—FRANCES "KAY" BOUMA TRAIL, BRITISH COLUMBIA

PREP/TOTAL TIME: 20 MINUTES **MAKES:** 1½ CUPS

- 2 **cups frozen peas**
- ⅓ **cup grated Parmesan cheese**
- 3 **cooked bacon strips, chopped**
- ¼ **cup reduced-fat sour cream**
- 2 **tablespoons olive oil**
- 1 **tablespoon lime juice**
- 2 **garlic cloves**
- 1 **to 2 teaspoons minced chipotle pepper in adobo sauce**
- ¼ **teaspoon pepper**
  Assorted fresh vegetables or crackers

1. In a small saucepan, bring 4 cups water to a boil. Add peas; cover and cook for 1 minute. Drain and immediately place peas in ice water. Drain and pat dry.

2. Place peas in a food processor; add the cheese, bacon, sour cream, oil, lime juice, garlic, chipotle pepper and pepper. Cover and process until smooth. Serve with vegetables or crackers.

Nutrition Facts: ¼ cup (calculated without vegetables) equals 129 calories, 8 g fat (2 g saturated fat), 11 mg cholesterol, 207 mg sodium, 8 g carbohydrate, 2 g fiber, 6 g protein. **Diabetic Exchanges:** 1½ fat, ½ starch.

Crab Asparagus Quesadillas

Here's a deliciously different appetizer that gives fresh asparagus and crabmeat a bit of south-of-the-border flair. The quesadillas can also be served as a side dish or main course.

—CURTIS GUNNARSON SYCAMORE, ILLINOIS

PREP/TOTAL TIME: 20 MINUTES **MAKES:** 6 SERVINGS

- 4 **flour tortillas (8 inches)**
- 2 **cups (8 ounces) shredded reduced-fat Mexican cheese blend**
- 1 **cup chopped fresh asparagus, cooked**
- ½ **cup chopped imitation crabmeat**
- 2 **tablespoons plus ¾ cup picante sauce, divided**
- 2 **teaspoons canola oil**
- 6 **tablespoons fat-free sour cream**
- 12 **large ripe olives, sliced**

1. On two tortillas, layer each with ½ cup cheese, ½ cup asparagus, ¼ cup crab, 1 tablespoon picante sauce and remaining cheese. Top with the remaining tortillas; press down lightly.

2. In a small skillet coated with cooking spray, cook one quesadilla at a time in oil for 2 minutes on each side or until cheese is melted. Cut each into six wedges. Serve with sour cream, olives and remaining picante sauce.

Nutrition Facts: 2 wedges equals 280 calories, 13 g fat (4 g saturated fat), 31 mg cholesterol, 778 mg sodium, 28 g carbohydrate, 1 g fiber, 17 g protein. **Diabetic Exchanges:** 2 starch, 2 lean meat, 1 fat.

Mini Spinach Frittatas

PREP/TOTAL TIME: 30 MINUTES **MAKES:** 2 DOZEN

- 1 cup ricotta cheese
- ¾ cup grated Parmesan cheese
- ⅔ cup chopped fresh mushrooms
- 1 package (10 ounces) frozen chopped spinach, thawed and squeezed dry
- 1 egg
- ½ teaspoon dried oregano
- ¼ teaspoon salt
- ¼ teaspoon pepper
- 24 slices pepperoni

1. In a small bowl, combine the first eight ingredients. Place a slice of pepperoni in each of 24 greased miniature muffin cups. Fill muffin cups three-fourths full with cheese mixture.

2. Bake at 375° for 20-25 minutes or until completely set. Carefully run a knife around edges of muffin cups to loosen. Serve warm.

Nutrition Facts: *3 mini frittatas equals 128 calories, 9 g fat (5 g saturated fat), 50 mg cholesterol, 396 mg sodium, 4 g carbohydrate, 1 g fiber, 10 g protein.*

“These mini frittatas are a cinch to make. Plus, the recipe doubles easily for a crowd and even freezes well for added convenience.”

—**NANCY STATKEVICUS** TUCSON, ARIZONA

Calico Corn Salsa

A friend introduced me to this refreshing medley...and when I took it to a luncheon, everyone raved about it. With a big bowl of tortilla chips on the side, the colorful salsa is irresistible.

—**JENNIFER GARDNER** SANDY, UTAH

PREP/TOTAL TIME: 25 MINUTES **MAKES:** 4 CUPS

- 1½ cups frozen corn, thawed
- 1 cup frozen peas, thawed
- ½ teaspoon ground cumin
- ⅛ teaspoon dried oregano
- 1 tablespoon olive oil
- 1 can (15 ounces) black beans, rinsed and drained
- 1 medium tomato, chopped
- ⅓ cup chopped red onion
- ¼ cup lime juice
- 1 tablespoon Dijon mustard
- 1 garlic clove, minced
- ½ teaspoon salt
- 2 tablespoons minced fresh cilantro
  Tortilla chips

1. In a large bowl, combine the corn and peas. In a nonstick skillet, cook cumin and oregano in oil over medium heat for 2 minutes. Pour over corn mixture; stir to coat evenly. Stir in the beans, tomato and onion.

2. In a small bowl, whisk the lime juice, mustard, garlic and salt. Stir in cilantro. Pour over corn mixture and stir to coat. Serve with tortilla chips. Refrigerate leftovers.

Nutrition Facts: *½ cup salsa (calculated without chips) equals 107 calories, 2 g fat (trace saturated fat), 0 cholesterol, 317 mg sodium, 18 g carbohydrate, 4 g fiber, 5 g protein.* **Diabetic Exchanges:** *1 starch, ½ fat.*

Sunny Asparagus Tapenade

I use fresh asparagus from the farmers market to make this better-for-you spread. I like to serve the tapenade with veggies, crackers or bread for family gatherings.

—**KATHY PATALSKY** NEW YORK, NEW YORK

PREP/TOTAL TIME: 30 MINUTES
MAKES: 2 CUPS

- ¾ pound fresh asparagus, chopped
- ¾ cup packed fresh parsley sprigs
- ⅓ cup unsalted sunflower kernels
- ¼ cup lemon juice
- ¼ cup orange juice
- 1 tablespoon olive oil
- 2 teaspoons maple syrup
- 1 small garlic clove, chopped
- ½ teaspoon salt
- ½ teaspoon crushed red pepper flakes
- 1 teaspoon pepper
  Additional sunflower kernels, optional
  Assorted fresh vegetables, crackers and/or toasted French bread baguette

1. In a large saucepan, bring ½ in. of water to a boil. Add asparagus; cover and cook for 3-5 minutes or until tender. Drain and immediately place asparagus in ice water. Drain and pat dry.
2. Place in a food processor; add the parsley, sunflower kernels, lemon juice, orange juice, oil, syrup, garlic, salt, pepper flakes and pepper. Cover and process until desired consistency.
3. Transfer to a small bowl; sprinkle with additional sunflower kernels if desired. Serve at room temperature or chilled with the dippers of your choice.
Nutrition Facts: *¼ cup (calculated without dippers or additional sunflower kernels) equals 64 calories, 4 g fat (1 g saturated fat), 0 cholesterol, 154 mg sodium, 5 g carbohydrate, 1 g fiber, 2 g protein.* **Diabetic Exchange:** *1 fat.*

Apricot-Ricotta Stuffed Celery

The wholesome, protein-rich filling I stuff into celery can double as a dip for sliced apples. I often prepare it ahead of time so it's ready as a spur-of-the-moment snack.

—**DOROTHY REINHOLD** MALIBU, CALIFORNIA

PREP/TOTAL TIME: 15 MINUTES **MAKES:** ABOUT 2 DOZEN

- 3 dried apricots
- ½ cup part-skim ricotta cheese
- 2 teaspoons brown sugar
- ¼ teaspoon grated orange peel
- ⅛ teaspoon salt
- 5 celery ribs, cut into 1½ inch pieces

1. Place apricots in a food processor. Cover and process until finely chopped. Add the ricotta cheese, brown sugar, orange peel and salt; cover and process until blended. Stuff or pipe into celery. Chill until serving.
Nutrition Facts: *1 piece equals 12 calories, trace fat (trace saturated fat), 2 mg cholesterol, 25 mg sodium, 1 g carbohydrate, trace fiber, 1 g protein.* **Diabetic Exchange:** *Free food.*

top tip Grating Orange Peel

I've found that grating fresh orange peel is much easier when I place the orange in the freezer the night before. I also wear a pair of clean gloves to avoid cutting my fingertips on the grater.
—**JENNIFER BENSON** SHEBOYGAN, WISCONSIN

Spinach Feta Pizza

My husband and I love this pizza, which makes a quick yet hearty dinner for us on busy work nights. We're eating more vegetarian entrees now, and this certainly fills the bill! I buy packaged baby spinach and use the extra greens in a warm salad later in the week.

—CONNIE CLEGG FREDERICK, MARYLAND

PREP/TOTAL TIME: 30 MINUTES **MAKES:** 12 PIECES

 1 tube (13.8 ounces) refrigerated pizza crust
 1 tablespoon olive oil
 1 teaspoon minced garlic
 1 can (15 ounces) pizza sauce
 2 cups chopped fresh spinach
 ¾ cup sliced red onion, separated into rings
 1 cup sliced fresh mushrooms
 1 cup (4 ounces) shredded part-skim mozzarella cheese
 ½ cup crumbled feta cheese
 1 teaspoon dried basil
 1 teaspoon Italian seasoning
   Crushed red pepper flakes, optional

1. Unroll crust into a greased 15-in. x 10-in. x 1-in. baking pan; flatten dough and build up edges slightly. Brush with oil; sprinkle with garlic. Spread with pizza sauce.

2. Layer with spinach, onion, mushrooms and cheeses. Sprinkle with basil, Italian seasoning and pepper flakes if desired. Bake at 400° for 15-18 minutes or until golden brown.

Nutrition Facts: *1 serving (1 piece) equals 122 calories, 4 g fat (1 g saturated fat), 7 mg cholesterol, 366 mg sodium, 15 g carbohydrate, 1 g fiber, 6 g protein.* **Diabetic Exchanges:** *1 starch, ½ lean meat.*

Cinnamon Chips 'n' Dip

I received a recipe for cinnamon-spiced chips with a creamy dip from a friend. We lightened it up a bit to create a healthier yet yummy treat that's a great addition to Southwestern menus.

—KRISTA FRANK RHODODENDRON, OREGON

PREP/TOTAL TIME: 20 MINUTES **MAKES:** 8 SERVINGS

 4 flour tortillas (8 inches)
   Refrigerated butter-flavored spray
 1 tablespoon sugar
 1 teaspoon ground cinnamon
DIP
 4 ounces reduced-fat cream cheese
 ¾ cup (6 ounces) vanilla yogurt
 4½ teaspoons sugar
 ½ teaspoon ground cinnamon

1. For chips, spritz tortillas with butter-flavored spray; cut each into eight wedges. Place on ungreased baking sheets. Combine sugar and cinnamon; sprinkle over tortillas. Bake at 350° for 7-9 minutes or just until crisp.

2. Meanwhile, for dip, in a small bowl, beat the cream cheese, yogurt, sugar and cinnamon until smooth. Serve with cinnamon chips.

Nutrition Facts: *1 serving (2 tablespoons) equals 146 calories, 5 g fat (3 g saturated fat), 12 mg cholesterol, 198 mg sodium, 20 g carbohydrate, trace fiber, 5 g protein.* **Diabetic Exchanges:** *1 starch, 1 fat.*

Fruity Horseradish Cream Cheese

Typically called Jezebel Sauce, this sweet, fruity topping has an underlying bite from horseradish. It pairs well with cream cheese, but try it over grilled pork and chicken, too.

—**RITA REIFENSTEIN** EVANS CITY, PENNSYLVANIA

PREP/TOTAL TIME: 10 MINUTES **MAKES:** 1⅓ CUPS

- 1 package (8 ounces) fat-free cream cheese
- ⅓ cup apple jelly, warmed
- 1 tablespoon prepared horseradish
- 1½ teaspoons ground mustard
- ⅓ cup apricot spreadable fruit
  Assorted crackers

1. Place cream cheese on a serving plate. In a small microwave-safe bowl, heat jelly until warmed. Stir in horseradish and mustard until blended. Stir in spreadable fruit; spoon over cream cheese. Serve with crackers. Refrigerate leftovers.

Nutrition Facts: *1 serving (2 tablespoons) equals 73 calories, trace fat (trace saturated fat), 2 mg cholesterol, 128 mg sodium, 14 g carbohydrate, trace fiber, 3 g protein.* **Diabetic Exchange:** *1 starch.*

Chicken Turnovers

Here's a terrific way to use up any leftover cooked chicken in the fridge. I sometimes serve the turnovers with a fresh fruit salad for a delicious, light meal for up to four people.

—**SANDRA LEE HERR** STEVENS, PENNSYLVANIA

PREP/TOTAL TIME: 30 MINUTES **MAKES:** 8 SERVINGS

- 1 cup diced cooked chicken breast
- 1 cup (4 ounces) shredded reduced-fat cheddar cheese
- ¼ cup chopped celery
- 1 tablespoon finely chopped onion
- ¼ teaspoon salt
- ¼ teaspoon pepper
- 1 tube (8 ounces) refrigerated reduced-fat crescent rolls

1. In a small bowl, combine the chicken, cheese, celery, onion, salt and pepper. Separate crescent dough into eight triangles; top each with chicken mixture. Fold dough over and seal edges.
2. Place on an ungreased baking sheet. Bake at 375° for 13-17 minutes or until golden brown. Serve warm.

Nutrition Facts: *1 turnover equals 169 calories, 8 g fat (3 g saturated fat), 24 mg cholesterol, 338 mg sodium, 13 g carbohydrate, trace fiber, 11 g protein.*

? Did you know?

Neufchatel cheese is a soft unripened cheese that originates in France. The American version, which is similar to cream cheese, is made from pasteurized milk and cream. American Neufchatel is slightly lower in calories than cream cheese and has slightly more moisture. Regular cream cheese can be substituted for Neufchatel cheese, especially in recipes for dips and spreads, with good results. You may notice a slightly different texture in cooked products.

Tortellini with Roasted Red Pepper Dip

PREP/TOTAL TIME: 25 MINUTES
MAKES: 10 SERVINGS

- 1 package (19 ounces) frozen cheese tortellini
- 1 jar (7 ounces) roasted sweet red peppers, drained
- 3 garlic cloves, minced
- ½ cup fat-free mayonnaise
- ½ teaspoon balsamic vinegar
- ¼ teaspoon salt
- ⅛ teaspoon pepper
- 1 tablespoon olive oil
- 1 large zucchini, cut into strips

1. Prepare tortellini according to the package directions. Meanwhile, place red peppers and garlic in a food processor; cover and process until combined. Add the mayonnaise, vinegar, salt and pepper; cover and process until blended. Transfer to a small bowl.

2. Drain tortellini; toss with oil. Serve with zucchini strips and red pepper dip.

Nutrition Facts: *14 tortellini and 4 zucchini strips with 4½ teaspoons dip equals 142 calories, 5 g fat (2 g saturated fat), 10 mg cholesterol, 333 mg sodium, 19 g carbohydrate, 1 g fiber, 6 g protein.* **Diabetic Exchanges:** *1 starch, 1 lean meat.*

This unique, warm and savory treat is sure to be a hit with any hungry crowd. For special occasions, I serve the tortellini with fancy, frilled party picks.
—**MICHELLE BOUCHER** MILFORD, NEW HAMPSHIRE

Did you know?

With all of the different olive oils on grocery store shelves today, choosing one can be confusing. But it may help to know that olive oils are graded according to acidity. Extra-virgin olive oil is the top grade and is extremely low in acidity (1%). It is produced by the first crushing and pressing of tree-ripened olives and has a deep color and intense olive flavor. Virgin olive oil also comes from the first pressing but has a slightly higher acidity (2%), lighter color and less fruity flavor. Both of these oils are best used in dishes where their stronger flavors can be appreciated.

Cranberry Chili Meatballs

I save time in the kitchen using packaged meatballs, and they're just as tasty as the homemade kind when I prepare them this way. My friends really look forward to these appetizers at our holiday gatherings—there are never any leftovers! The sauce is tangy yet sweet, and the festive color is perfect for parties.

—**AMY SCAMERHORN** INDIANAPOLIS, INDIANA

PREP/TOTAL TIME: 30 MINUTES **MAKES:** ABOUT 6 DOZEN

- 1 can (14 ounces) jellied cranberry sauce
- 1 bottle (12 ounces) chili sauce
- ¾ cup packed brown sugar
- ½ teaspoon chili powder
- ½ teaspoon ground cumin
- ¼ teaspoon cayenne pepper
- 1 package (32 ounces) frozen fully cooked homestyle meatballs, thawed

1. In a large saucepan over medium heat, combine the first six ingredients; stir until the brown sugar is dissolved. Add the meatballs; cook for 20-25 minutes or until heated through, stirring occasionally.

Nutrition Facts: *1 meatball equals 51 calories, 2 g fat (1 g saturated fat), 12 mg cholesterol, 80 mg sodium, 6 g carbohydrate, trace fiber, 2 g protein.* **Diabetic Exchanges:** *½ starch, ½ lean meat.*

Shrimp Bites

Living near the coast, I have a great advantage when it comes to getting fresh seafood. Phyllo tart shells make fun little "bowls" for shrimp mixed with cheese, sour cream and seasonings.

—**ROBERT LOGAN** CLAYTON, CALIFORNIA

PREP/TOTAL TIME: 25 MINUTES **MAKES:** 2½ DOZEN

- 6 ounces reduced-fat cream cheese
- 2 tablespoons fat-free sour cream
- 2 tablespoons minced fresh parsley
- 2 teaspoons dried minced onion
- ½ teaspoon Worcestershire sauce
- ¼ teaspoon seafood seasoning
- 1 cup finely chopped cooked peeled shrimp
- ½ cup shredded part-skim mozzarella cheese
- 2 packages (1.9 ounces each) frozen miniature phyllo tart shells

1. In a small bowl, beat the cream cheese and sour cream until blended. Add the parsley, minced onion, Worcestershire sauce and seafood seasoning; mix well. Stir in shrimp and mozzarella cheese.

2. Spoon filling into tart shells. Place on an ungreased baking sheet. Bake at 350° for 8-12 minutes or until shells are lightly browned. Serve warm or cold.

Nutrition Facts: *1 appetizer equals 48 calories, 3 g fat (1 g saturated fat), 16 mg cholesterol, 63 mg sodium, 3 g carbohydrate, trace fiber, 3 g protein.*

Mini BBQ Chicken Pizzas

My miniature pizzas make a hearty, satisfying snack any time of day. Or turn them into a quick weeknight dinner by adding a salad.

—DEBORAH FORBES FORT WORTH, TEXAS

PREP/TOTAL TIME: 25 MINUTES **MAKES:** 1 DOZEN

- 1 medium onion, chopped
- 2 teaspoons olive oil
- 1½ cups shredded cooked chicken
- ⅔ cup barbecue sauce
- 1 can (4 ounces) chopped green chilies
- 1½ teaspoons garlic powder
- ¼ teaspoon pepper
- 1 package (13 ounces) whole wheat English muffins, split
- 1½ cups (6 ounces) shredded part-skim mozzarella cheese

1. In a large nonstick skillet, saute onion in oil until tender. Stir in the chicken, barbecue sauce, chilies, garlic powder and pepper. Spread over cut sides of muffins; sprinkle with cheese.
2. Place on baking sheets; broil 4-6 in. from the heat for 2-3 minutes or until cheese is melted.

Nutrition Facts: *1 pizza equals 157 calories, 5 g fat (2 g saturated fat), 24 mg cholesterol, 428 mg sodium, 16 g carbohydrate, 3 g fiber, 12 g protein.*

On-The-Go Snack Mix

This no-bake finger food is really simple to fix. Plus, it's packed with wholesome ingredients that deliver protein and a few vitamins and minerals. Go ahead and munch guilt-free!

—LEAH FIRESTONE SCOTTDALE, PENNSYLVANIA

PREP/TOTAL TIME: 10 MINUTES **MAKES:** 7 CUPS

- 3 cups Wheat Chex
- ½ cup blanched almonds
- ½ cup unsalted peanuts
- ½ cup lightly salted cashews
- ½ cup chopped pecans
- ½ cup fat-free miniature pretzels
- ½ cup raisins
- ½ cup milk chocolate M&M's
- ¼ cup dried banana chips
- ¼ cup dried cranberries

1. In a large bowl, combine all ingredients. Store in an airtight container.

Nutrition Facts: *½ cup equals 217 calories, 13 g fat (3 g saturated fat), 1 mg cholesterol, 93 mg sodium, 23 g carbohydrate, 3 g fiber, 5 g protein.*

Deviled Eggs with Dill

These change-of-pace deviled eggs boast a hint of Worcestershire sauce in addition to the slight tang from mustard. Try using Dijon mustard for an extra layer of flavor.

—**MARY PRIOR** RUSH CITY, MINNESOTA

PREP/TOTAL TIME: 20 MINUTES **MAKES:** 1 DOZEN

- 6 hard-cooked eggs
- 2 tablespoons reduced-fat mayonnaise
- 1½ teaspoons cider vinegar
- ¾ teaspoon prepared mustard
- ¼ teaspoon Worcestershire sauce
- ¼ teaspoon salt
  Dash pepper
- 12 fresh dill sprigs

1. Cut eggs in half lengthwise. Remove yolks; set aside egg whites and four yolks (discard remaining yolks or save for another use).

2. In a large bowl, mash reserved yolks. Stir in the mayonnaise, vinegar, mustard, Worcestershire sauce, salt

and pepper. Stuff or pipe into egg whites. Garnish with dill. Refrigerate until serving.

Nutrition Facts: *2 egg halves equals 74 calories, 5 g fat (1 g saturated fat), 144 mg cholesterol, 207 mg sodium, 1 g carbohydrate, trace fiber, 5 g protein.* **Diabetic Exchanges:** *1 lean meat, ½ fat.*

Refried Bean Nachos

Cumin and cayenne pepper spice up homemade chips to create extra-special yet no-fuss nachos. Loaded with beans, cheese, tomato, onions and salsa, they'll turn snacktime into a fiesta!

—**TASTE OF HOME TEST KITCHEN**

PREP/TOTAL TIME: 25 MINUTES **MAKES:** 4 SERVINGS

- 4 flour tortillas (8 inches)
  Refrigerated butter-flavored spray
- ½ teaspoon ground cumin
- ¼ teaspoon ground coriander
- ¼ teaspoon chili powder
- ⅛ teaspoon cayenne pepper
- 1 can (16 ounces) vegetarian refried beans
- ½ cup shredded reduced-fat cheddar cheese
- 1 large tomato, chopped
- 4 green onions, chopped
- ½ cup salsa

1. Spritz one side of each tortilla with refrigerated butter-flavored spray. Combine the cumin, coriander, chili powder and cayenne; sprinkle over tortillas. Cut each into 12 wedges.

2. Place in a single layer in ungreased 15-in. x 10-in. x 1-in. baking pans. Bake at 425° for 5-7 minutes or until lightly browned.

3. Meanwhile, in a microwave-safe bowl, heat the refried beans on high for 1-2 minutes or until warm. Arrange baked tortillas on serving plates; top with the beans, cheese, tomato and onions. Serve with salsa.

Nutrition Facts: *1 serving equals 310 calories, 7 g fat (2 g saturated fat), 10 mg cholesterol, 959 mg sodium, 47 g carbohydrate, 8 g fiber, 14 g protein.* **Diabetic Exchanges:** *3 starch, 1 lean meat, 1 vegetable, ½ fat.*

? Did you know?

As an egg ages, the yolk moves more freely and can become displaced as the white thins out. Using fresh eggs will reduce the chance of having off-centered yolks, but fresh hard-cooked eggs are hard to peel. To have centered yolks in eggs that are still easy to peel, use eggs that have been refrigerated for a week to 10 days. Researchers have also found that eggs stored on their sides have the most consistently centered yolks. Secure the carton of eggs closed with a rubber band, and turn the carton on its side in the refrigerator for up to 24 hours before cooking.

Pineapple Salsa

PREP/TOTAL TIME: 20 MINUTES **MAKES:** 3½ CUPS

- 2 cups diced fresh pineapple
- 2 medium tomatoes, seeded and chopped
- ¾ cup chopped sweet onion
- ¼ cup minced fresh cilantro
- 1 jalapeno pepper, seeded and chopped
- 1 tablespoon olive oil
- 1 teaspoon ground coriander
- ¾ teaspoon ground cumin
- ½ teaspoon salt
- ½ teaspoon minced garlic
  Tortilla chips

1. In a large bowl, combine the first 10 ingredients. Cover and refrigerate until serving. Serve with tortilla chips.

Editor's Note: *Wear disposable gloves when cutting hot peppers; the oils can burn skin. Avoid touching your face.*

Nutrition Facts: *¼ cup (calculated without chips) equals 29 calories, 1 g fat (trace saturated fat), 0 cholesterol, 87 mg sodium, 5 g carbohydrate, 1 g fiber, trace protein.* **Diabetic Exchange:** *Free food.*

❝This mouthwatering salsa features fresh pineapple and a handful of seasonings. Serve it with tortilla chips or even grilled chicken or fish for a jazzed-up meal.❞

—**SUZI LAPAR** WAHIAWA, HAWAII

Makeover Hot Pizza Dip

Lighten up pepperoni pizza dip so that it has fewer calories and less than half the saturated fat of the original recipe. After just one taste, you and your guests will be glad you did!

—**TRISHA KRUSE** EAGLE, IDAHO

PREP/TOTAL TIME: 25 MINUTES **MAKES:** ABOUT 4 CUPS

- 1 package (8 ounces) fat-free cream cheese
- 1½ teaspoons Italian seasoning
- 1 cup (4 ounces) shredded part-skim mozzarella cheese, divided
- ½ cup grated Parmigiano-Reggiano cheese, divided
- 1 small sweet red pepper, chopped
- ¼ cup chopped sweet onion
- 1 teaspoon olive oil
- 1 garlic clove, minced
- 1 can (8 ounces) pizza sauce
- 4 ounces sliced turkey pepperoni, chopped
- 1 can (2¼ ounces) sliced ripe olives, drained
- 1 French bread baguette (10½ ounces), cut into ¼-inch slices, toasted

1. In a small bowl, beat cream cheese and Italian seasoning until smooth; spread into a 9-in. microwave-safe pie plate. Sprinkle with ½ cup mozzarella cheese and ¼ cup Parmigiano-Reggiano cheese.

2. In a small nonstick skillet, saute pepper and onion in oil until tender. Add garlic; cook 1 minute longer. Spoon over cheeses. Spread pizza sauce over pepper mixture. Sprinkle with remaining cheeses, pepperoni and olives.

3. Microwave, uncovered, at 70% power for 5-7 minutes or until cheese is melted. Serve with toasted baguette slices.

Editor's Note: *This recipe was tested in a 1,100-watt microwave.*

Nutrition Facts: *¼ cup dip with 4 baguette slices equals 154 calories, 6 g fat (2 g saturated fat), 16 mg cholesterol, 466 mg sodium, 17 g carbohydrate, 2 g fiber, 9 g protein.*

With convenient frozen phyllo shells, this impressive starter is surprisingly easy to prepare. The tartlets are especially good with fresh-from-the-garden tomatoes.
—**AMY GOLDEN** EAST AURORA, NEW YORK

Mozzarella Tomato Tartlets

PREP/TOTAL TIME: 20 MINUTES
MAKES: 2 DOZEN

1 garlic clove, minced
1 tablespoon olive oil
1½ cups seeded chopped tomatoes
¾ cup shredded part-skim mozzarella cheese
½ teaspoon dried basil
 Pepper to taste
24 frozen miniature phyllo tart shells
6 pitted ripe olives, quartered
 Grated Parmesan cheese

1. In a small skillet, saute garlic in oil for 1 minute. Add the tomatoes; cook until liquid has evaporated. Remove from the heat; stir in the mozzarella cheese, basil and pepper.

2. Spoon 1 teaspoonful into each tart shell. Top each with an olive piece; sprinkle with Parmesan cheese. Place on an ungreased baking sheet. Bake at 450° for 5-8 minutes or until bubbly.

Nutrition Facts: *1 tart (calculated without Parmesan cheese) equals 40 calories, 2 g fat (trace saturated fat), 2 mg cholesterol, 37 mg sodium, 3 g carbohydrate, trace fiber, 1 g protein.*

top tip Seeding Tomatoes

It's usually not necessary to remove the seeds from tomatoes before using them. But for some recipes, seeding the tomatoes can improve the dish's appearance or eliminate excess moisture. For example, it's not important to seed tomatoes for a tossed salad. But it's nice to remove the seeds when making a creamy soup to ensure a smooth texture. And using seeded tomatoes for a casserole can prevent it from becoming watery. To remove the seeds from a tomato, cut it in half horizontally and remove the stem. Holding a tomato half over a bowl or sink, scrape out the seeds with a small spoon or squeeze the tomato to force out the seeds. Then slice or dice as directed in the recipe.

Crescent Samosas

With a delicious potato filling and creamy sauce for dipping, these tender, buttery crescents are always popular. And no one ever guesses that they're light!

—JENNIFER KEMP
GROSSE POINTE PARK, MICHIGAN

PREP/TOTAL TIME: 30 MINUTES
MAKES: 16 APPETIZERS (¾ CUP SAUCE)

- 1 can (14½ ounces) diced new potatoes, drained
- 1 tablespoon olive oil
- ¼ cup chopped green chilies
- 1 garlic clove, minced
- 1 cup frozen peas, thawed
- 1½ teaspoons lemon juice
- 1 teaspoon curry powder
  Dash pepper
- 2 tubes (8 ounces each) refrigerated reduced-fat crescent rolls

SAUCE
- ¾ cup reduced-fat plain yogurt
- 2 tablespoons minced fresh cilantro
- 1 garlic clove, minced
- ½ teaspoon ground cumin
  Dash pepper

1. In a large nonstick skillet, saute potatoes in oil until lightly browned. Add chilies and garlic; saute 1 minute longer. Stir in the peas, lemon juice, curry powder and pepper. Transfer to a large bowl and coarsely mash.

2. Separate the crescent dough into 16 triangles. Place 1 tablespoon potato mixture on the wide end of each triangle; roll up from the wide end. Place the point side down 2 in. apart on ungreased baking sheets; curve the ends to form crescent shapes.

3. Bake at 375° for 10-12 minutes or until golden brown. Meanwhile, in a small bowl, combine sauce ingredients. Serve with warm samosas.

Nutrition Facts: *1 appetizer with about 2 teaspoons sauce equals 140 calories, 6 g fat (1 g saturated fat), 1 mg cholesterol, 316 mg sodium, 18 g carbohydrate, 1 g fiber, 4 g protein.*

Greek Sandwich Bites

Here's an appetizer that tastes like traditional spanakopita but takes much less time and effort to make. Cut the sandwiches into quarters for the perfect party starters.

—LYNN SCULLY RANCHO SANTA FE, CALIFORNIA

PREP/TOTAL TIME: 25 MINUTES **MAKES:** 16 APPETIZERS

- 1 medium onion, finely chopped
- 1 tablespoon olive oil
- 2 garlic cloves, minced
- 1 pound fresh baby spinach
- 1 cup (4 ounces) crumbled feta cheese
- ¼ cup pine nuts, toasted
- ¼ teaspoon salt
- ¼ teaspoon pepper
- ⅛ teaspoon ground nutmeg
- 8 slices Italian bread (½ inch thick)
- 4 teaspoons butter, softened

1. In a large nonstick skillet, saute onion in oil until tender. Add garlic; cook 1 minute longer. Stir in the spinach; cook and stir until wilted. Drain. Stir in the feta, pine nuts, salt, pepper and nutmeg.

2. Spread over four bread slices; top with remaining bread. Spread outsides of sandwiches with butter. Grill, uncovered, over medium heat for 3-4 minutes or until bread is browned and cheese is melted, turning once. Cut each sandwich into quarters.

Nutrition Facts: *1 appetizer equals 87 calories, 5 g fat (2 g saturated fat), 6 mg cholesterol, 200 mg sodium, 8 g carbohydrate, 1 g fiber, 4 g protein.* **Diabetic Exchanges:** *1 fat, ½ starch.*

Quick Corn Dip

When a friend gave me her favorite corn dip recipe, I substituted as much as I could with fat-free ingredients. The result was lighter but still delectable!

—MONICA CHILDS OLATHE, KANSAS

PREP/TOTAL TIME: 15 MINUTES
MAKES: 4 CUPS

- 1 can (11 ounces) white corn, drained
- 1 can (11 ounces) Mexicorn, drained
- 1 cup (4 ounces) shredded fat-free cheddar cheese
- 4 green onions, chopped
- ½ cup fat-free sour cream
- ½ cup fat-free mayonnaise
- 1 can (4 ounces) chopped green chilies
- ¼ teaspoon garlic powder
- ¼ teaspoon seasoned salt
- ⅛ teaspoon chili powder
  Baked tortilla chip scoops

1. In a large bowl, combine the first nine ingredients; sprinkle with chili powder. Refrigerate until serving. Serve with tortilla chips.

Nutrition Facts: *¼ cup (calculated without chips) equals 58 calories, trace fat (trace saturated fat), 3 mg cholesterol, 327 mg sodium, 11 g carbohydrate, 1 g fiber, 4 g protein.* **Diabetic Exchange:** *1 starch.*

top tip
Popcorn Pointer
Don't pre-salt the kernels—this toughens the popcorn. If desired, salt the corn after it's popped.

Tex-Mex Popcorn

Southwest seasoning turns plain popcorn into a special snack that's ideal for any fiesta. Serve a big bowlful for your next movie night or when the big game is on TV.

—KATIE ROSE PEWAUKEE, WISCONSIN

PREP/TOTAL TIME: 15 MINUTES **MAKES:** 4 QUARTS

- ½ cup popcorn kernels
- 3 tablespoons canola oil
- ½ teaspoon cumin seeds
  Refrigerated butter-flavored spray
- ¼ cup minced fresh cilantro
- 1 teaspoon salt
- 1 teaspoon chili powder
- ½ teaspoon garlic powder
- ⅛ teaspoon smoked paprika

1. In a Dutch oven over medium heat, cook popcorn kernels, oil and cumin seeds until oil begins to sizzle. Cover and shake for 2-3 minutes or until popcorn stops popping.
2. Transfer to a large bowl; spritz with butter-flavored spray. Add remaining ingredients and toss to coat. Continue spritzing and tossing until popcorn is coated.

Nutrition Facts: *1 cup equals 44 calories, 3 g fat (trace saturated fat), 0 cholesterol, 150 mg sodium, 5 g carbohydrate, 1 g fiber, 1 g protein.*

Stuffed Mushrooms

PREP/TOTAL TIME: 15 MINUTES
MAKES: 8 APPETIZERS

- ¼ cup shredded Swiss cheese
- 1 hard-cooked egg, finely chopped
- 4½ teaspoons seasoned bread crumbs
- 2 tablespoons butter, melted, divided
- ¼ teaspoon minced garlic
- ⅛ teaspoon salt
- 8 large fresh mushrooms

1. In a small bowl, combine the cheese, egg, bread crumbs, 1 tablespoon butter, garlic and salt; set aside. Remove stems from mushrooms. Place mushroom caps, hollow side down, on a baking sheet coated with cooking spray. Brush with remaining butter.

2. Broil 4 in. from the heat for 4-5 minutes or just until tender. Turn over; stuff with cheese mixture. Broil 2-3 minutes longer or until lightly browned and heated through.

Nutrition Facts: *1 stuffed mushroom equals 59 calories, 5 g fat (3 g saturated fat), 37 mg cholesterol, 95 mg sodium, 2 g carbohydrate, trace fiber, 3 g protein.*
Diabetic Exchange: *1 fat.*

If you like mushrooms, you'll love this broiled appetizer. The tasty filling is easy to prepare and stuff into the large mushroom caps. —KELLI EGBERT IDAHO FALLS, IDAHO

top tip

Preparing Mushrooms for Stuffing

To prepare mushrooms for stuffing, hold the mushroom cap in one hand and grab the stem with the other hand. Twist to snap off the stem; place the caps on a greased baking sheet. Mince or finely chop the stems.

Gouda Bites

I use just three ingredients—refrigerated crescent dough, garlic powder and cheese—to create little golden bites everyone enjoys.

—**PHYLLIS BEHRINGER** DEFIANCE, OHIO

PREP/TOTAL TIME: 25 MINUTES **MAKES:** 2 DOZEN

- 1 tube (8 ounces) refrigerated reduced-fat crescent rolls
- ½ teaspoon garlic powder
- 5 ounces Gouda cheese, cut into 24 pieces

1. Unroll crescent dough into one long rectangle; seal seams and perforations. Sprinkle with garlic powder. Cut into 24 pieces; lightly press onto the bottom and up the sides of ungreased miniature muffin cups.

2. Bake at 375° for 3 minutes. Place a piece of cheese in each cup. Bake 8-10 minutes longer or until golden brown and cheese is melted. Serve warm.

Nutrition Facts: *2 bites equals 110 calories, 6 g fat (3 g saturated fat), 13 mg cholesterol, 252 mg sodium, 8 g carbohydrate, trace fiber, 4 g protein.* **Diabetic Exchanges:** *1½ fat, ½ starch.*

Makeover Spinach Artichoke Spread

My original recipe for spinach artichoke spread was absolutely delicious—but also a diet-buster! This just-as-yummy makeover boasts 60% less fat and about half of the calories. It's a guilt-free way to indulge, and I never feel deprived.

—**SUSANNE NONEKOWSKI** OREGON, OHIO

PREP/TOTAL TIME: 30 MINUTES **MAKES:** 5 CUPS

- 1 package (16 ounces) soft tofu, drained
- 2 cups grated Parmesan cheese
- 1 cup reduced-fat mayonnaise
- 1 can (14 ounces) water-packed artichoke hearts, rinsed, drained and chopped
- 2 packages (10 ounces each) frozen chopped spinach, thawed and squeezed dry
- 3 garlic cloves, minced

1. In a large bowl, combine all ingredients. Spoon into an ungreased 9-in. deep-dish pie plate. Bake, uncovered, at 350° for 20-25 minutes or until heated through. Serve warm.

Nutrition Facts: *¼ cup equals 109 calories, 8 g fat (2 g saturated fat), 11 mg cholesterol, 317 mg sodium, 4 g carbohydrate, 1 g fiber, 7 g protein.* **Diabetic Exchanges:** *1½ fat, ½ starch.*

Grilled Feta Quesadillas

I like to serve my grilled cheese quesadillas when I'm having friends and family over for a barbecue. I sampled a similar appetizer at a Memorial Day picnic and enjoyed the flavor so much, I decided to re-create it using reduced-fat ingredients.

—JACQUELINE CORREA
LANDING, NEW JERSEY

PREP/TOTAL TIME: 20 MINUTES
MAKES: 12 WEDGES

- 3 ounces fat-free cream cheese
- ½ cup shredded reduced-fat Mexican cheese blend
- ⅓ cup crumbled feta cheese
- ½ teaspoon dried oregano
- 4 flour tortillas (6 inches), warmed
- ¼ cup chopped pitted ripe olives
- 2 tablespoons diced pimientos
- 1 green onion, chopped

1. In a small bowl, beat the cheeses with oregano until blended. Spread 3 tablespoons of cheese mixture over half of each tortilla; top with olives, pimientos and onion. Fold tortillas over.
2. Using long-handled tongs, moisten a paper towel with cooking oil and lightly coat the grill rack. Grill quesadillas, uncovered, over medium heat or broil 4 in. from the heat for 1-2 minutes on each side or until golden brown. Cut each quesadilla into three wedges. Serve warm.

Nutrition Facts: *1 wedge equals 62 calories, 3 g fat (1 g saturated fat), 6 mg cholesterol, 198 mg sodium, 5 g carbohydrate, trace fiber, 4 g protein.*
Diabetic Exchanges: *½ starch, ½ fat.*

Easy Buffalo Chicken Dip

Guys and gals of all ages will devour this savory, delicious dip. Loaded with shredded chicken and punched up with hot sauce, it's the perfect snack for game day!

—JANICE FOLTZ HERSHEY, PENNSYLVANIA

PREP/TOTAL TIME: 30 MINUTES **MAKES:** 4 CUPS

- 1 package (8 ounces) reduced-fat cream cheese
- 1 cup (8 ounces) reduced-fat sour cream
- ½ cup Louisiana-style hot sauce
- 3 cups shredded cooked chicken breast
  Assorted crackers

1. In a large bowl, beat the cream cheese, sour cream and hot sauce until smooth; stir in chicken.
2. Transfer to an 8-in. square baking dish coated with cooking spray. Cover and bake at 350° for 18-22 minutes or until heated through. Serve warm with crackers.

Nutrition Facts: *3 tablespoons (calculated without crackers) equals 77 calories, 4 g fat (2 g saturated fat), 28 mg cholesterol, 71 mg sodium, 1 g carbohydrate, trace fiber, 8 g protein.*

Scissors-Cut Green Onions

When a recipe calls for green onions, I find it easier and faster to cut them with a kitchen scissors than with a knife. If the recipe calls for quite a few onions, grab a bunch at one time and snip away. You're done before you know it, and this saves you from washing a cutting board.

—LOUISE B.
COLUMBIA, SOUTH CAROLINA

Chili-Cheese Wonton Cups

In just 30 minutes, I can have a delicious, warm-from-the-oven appetizer to serve friends and family. Baked in miniature muffin cups, the wonton wrappers form fun little cups for a filling of cheese, green chilies, chives, ripe olives and seasonings.

—LYN RENWICK CHARLOTTE, NORTH CAROLINA

PREP/TOTAL TIME: 30 MINUTES **MAKES:** 2 DOZEN

- 24 wonton wrappers
-     Refrigerated butter-flavored spray
- 1 cup (4 ounces) shredded reduced-fat cheddar cheese
- ½ cup reduced-fat ricotta cheese
- 1 can (4 ounces) chopped green chilies, well drained
- 1 tablespoon minced chives
- ¼ teaspoon salt
- ¼ teaspoon ground cumin
- 3 tablespoons sliced ripe olives

1. Press the wonton wrappers into miniature muffin cups coated with cooking spray, forming a cup. Spritz with butter-flavored spray. Bake at 350° for 8-9 minutes or until the edges are golden.

2. In a small bowl, combine the cheeses, chilies, chives, salt and cumin. Spoon into cups. Top with olives. Bake for 10 minutes longer or until golden brown and bubbly. Serve warm.

Nutrition Facts: *2 wonton cups equals 229 calories, 4 g fat (2 g saturated fat), 14 mg cholesterol, 542 mg sodium, 38 g carbohydrate, trace fiber, 10 g protein.* **Diabetic Exchanges:** *2 starch, 1 fat, ½ lean meat.*

Little Mexican Pizzas

PREP/TOTAL TIME: 25 MINUTES **MAKES:** 1 DOZEN

- 1 package (13 ounces) whole wheat English muffins, split
- ¾ cup fat-free refried beans
- ¾ cup salsa
- ⅓ cup sliced ripe olives
- 2 green onions, chopped
- 2 tablespoons canned chopped green chilies
- 1½ cups (6 ounces) shredded part-skim mozzarella cheese

1. Spread cut sides of muffins with refried beans; top with salsa, olives, onions, chilies and cheese.

2. Place on baking sheets; broil 4-6 in. from the heat for 2-3 minutes or until cheese is melted.

Nutrition Facts: *1 pizza equals 129 calories, 3 g fat (2 g saturated fat), 8 mg cholesterol, 368 mg sodium, 17 g carbohydrate, 2 g fiber, 7 g protein.* **Diabetic Exchanges:** *1 starch, 1 lean meat.*

❝These mini pizzas are perfect for snacktime or even lunch. Whole wheat English muffins offer more fiber than a regular pizza crust.❞

—LINDA EGGERS ALBANY, CALIFORNIA

Spinach & Crab Dip

I lightened up my dip recipe considerably without sacrificing flavor, and no one can tell the difference. If you have leftovers, try spooning them onto baked potatoes.

—SANDIE HEINDEL LIBERTY, MISSOURI

PREP/TOTAL TIME: 25 MINUTES
MAKES: 4 CUPS

- 1 package (10 ounces) frozen chopped spinach, thawed and squeezed dry
- 1 package (8 ounces) reduced-fat cream cheese, cubed
- 1 cup (8 ounces) plain yogurt
- ½ cup grated Parmesan cheese
- ½ cup Miracle Whip Light
- 2 garlic cloves, minced
- 1 teaspoon crushed red pepper flakes
- ¼ teaspoon salt
- ¼ teaspoon pepper
- 1 can (6 ounces) lump crabmeat, drained
  Assorted crackers or baked tortilla chip scoops

1. In a large saucepan over low heat, combine the first nine ingredients. Cook and stir until cream cheese is melted. Stir in crab; heat through.

2. Transfer to a serving bowl; serve with crackers. Refrigerate leftovers.

Nutrition Facts: *¼ cup (calculated without crackers) equals 89 calories, 6 g fat (3 g saturated fat), 26 mg cholesterol, 256 mg sodium, 3 g carbohydrate, 1 g fiber, 6 g protein.*

39

38

42

Breakfast & Brunch

"Keep 'em going right through to lunchtime with this quick and easy breakfast idea. It turns frozen waffles into a hot, hearty egg sandwich featuring bacon and cheese."

MICHELE MCHENRY BELLINGHAM, WASHINGTON
about her recipe, Waffle Sandwich, on page 36

Savory Apple-Chicken Sausage

These easy, healthier-for-you sausages taste great, require only five basic ingredients and make a special brunch choice. The recipe is also very versatile—it can be doubled or tripled for a crowd, and the sausage freezes well whether cooked or raw.

—**ANGELA BUCHANAN** LONGMONT, COLORADO

PREP/TOTAL TIME: 25 MINUTES   **MAKES:** 8 PATTIES

- 1 **large tart apple, peeled and diced**
- 2 **teaspoons poultry seasoning**
- 1 **teaspoon salt**
- ¼ **teaspoon pepper**
- 1 **pound ground chicken**

1. In a large bowl, combine the apple, poultry seasoning, salt and pepper. Crumble chicken over mixture and mix well. Shape into eight 3-in. patties.

2. In a large skillet coated with cooking spray, cook patties over medium heat for 5-6 minutes on each side or until a thermometer reads 165° and juices run clear.

Nutrition Facts: *1 sausage patty equals 92 calories, 5 g fat (1 g saturated fat), 38 mg cholesterol, 328 mg sodium, 4 g carbohydrate, 1 g fiber, 9 g protein.* **Diabetic Exchange:** *1 medium-fat meat.*

Roasted Red Pepper Omelets

Take ordinary omelets up a notch by tossing in roasted sweet red peppers, Muenster cheese and green onions. It's a combination that brings vibrant flavor and color to a breakfast favorite.

—**TASTE OF HOME TEST KITCHEN**

PREP/TOTAL TIME: 20 MINUTES   **MAKES:** 2 SERVINGS

- 3 **eggs**
- 3 **tablespoons water**
- ¼ **teaspoon salt**
- ⅛ **teaspoon pepper**
- ½ **cup chopped roasted sweet red peppers**
- ¼ **cup shredded Muenster cheese**
- 2 **green onions, chopped**

1. Coat an 8-in. nonstick skillet with cooking spray and place over medium heat. In a small bowl, whisk the eggs, water, salt and pepper. Add half of egg mixture to skillet (mixture should set immediately at edges).

2. As eggs set, push cooked edges toward the center, letting uncooked portion flow underneath. When the eggs are set, add half of the red peppers, cheese and onions on one side; fold other side over filling. Slide omelet onto a plate. Repeat.

Nutrition Facts: *1 omelet equals 185 calories, 12 g fat (5 g saturated fat), 331 mg cholesterol, 714 mg sodium, 4 g carbohydrate, trace fiber, 13 g protein.*

Makeover British Scones

I wanted to lighten up my original version of a British tearoom mainstay. The slimmed-down result has 54 fewer calories and 75% less saturated fat per serving, but it doesn't sacrifice a single tender, flaky, mouthwatering bite. I love it!

—CAROLE JASLER LECANTO, FLORIDA

PREP/TOTAL TIME: 30 MINUTES **MAKES:** 8 SCONES

- 1¼ cups all-purpose flour
- 1 cup cake flour
- 2 tablespoons brown sugar
- 1½ teaspoons baking powder
- ½ teaspoon salt
- ¼ teaspoon baking soda
- 3 tablespoons cold butter
- 1 egg, lightly beaten
- ⅓ cup buttermilk
- 2 tablespoons canola oil
- ½ teaspoon vanilla extract
- 1 tablespoon 2% milk
- 1 teaspoon sugar

1. In a large bowl, combine the flours, brown sugar, baking powder, salt and baking soda. Cut in butter until mixture resembles coarse crumbs. Combine the egg, buttermilk, oil and vanilla; add to crumb mixture and stir until a soft dough forms. Turn onto a floured surface; gently knead 6-8 times.
2. Pat the dough into a 6-in. circle. Cut into eight wedges. Separate wedges and place 1 in. apart on an ungreased baking sheet. Brush tops with milk; sprinkle with sugar. Bake at 400°

for 12-14 minutes or until lightly browned. Remove to a wire rack. Serve warm.
Nutrition Facts: *1 scone equals 219 calories, 9 g fat (3 g saturated fat), 39 mg cholesterol, 343 mg sodium, 30 g carbohydrate, 1 g fiber, 4 g protein.* **Diabetic Exchanges:** *2 starch, 1½ fat.*

Berry Best Smoothies

Here's a wonderful way to use up over-ripened bananas while helping your family get five daily servings of fruits and veggies. The smoothies are simple to fix, and my kids consider them a treat.

—PAMELA KLIM BETTENDORF, IOWA

PREP/TOTAL TIME: 10 MINUTES **MAKES:** 3 SERVINGS

- 3 tablespoons orange juice concentrate
- 3 tablespoons fat-free half-and-half
- 12 ice cubes
- 1 cup fresh strawberries, hulled
- 1 medium ripe banana, cut into chunks
- ½ cup fresh or frozen blueberries
- ½ cup fresh or frozen raspberries

1. In a blender, combine all ingredients; cover and process for 30-45 seconds or until smooth. Stir if necessary. Pour into chilled glasses; serve immediately.
Nutrition Facts: *1 cup equals 108 calories, 1 g fat (trace saturated fat), 0 cholesterol, 14 mg sodium, 26 g carbohydrate, 4 g fiber, 2 g protein.* **Diabetic Exchange:** *1½ fruit.*

Iced Coffee

When my sister introduced me to iced coffee drinks, I wasn't convinced I'd like them. Not only did I like them, but I decided I wanted to make my own! This fast-to-fix blend is refreshing and a guilt-free way to indulge. Plus, it's less expensive than buying a beverage at a coffeehouse—and saves me the wait at the drive-thru.

—**JENNY REECE** LOWRY, MINNESOTA

PREP/TOTAL TIME: 5 MINUTES
MAKES: 2 CUPS

- 4 **teaspoons instant coffee granules**
- 1 **cup boiling water**
  Sugar substitute equivalent to 4 teaspoons sugar, optional
- 1 **cup fat-free milk**
- 4 **teaspoons chocolate syrup**
- ⅛ **teaspoon vanilla extract**
  Ice cubes

1. In a large bowl, dissolve the instant coffee granules in boiling water. Add sweetener if desired. Stir in the milk, chocolate syrup and vanilla; mix well. Serve over ice.

Editor's Note: *This recipe was tested with Splenda no-calorie sweetener.*

Nutrition Facts: *1 cup (calculated without sugar substitute) equals 79 calories, 0.55 g fat (0 saturated fat), 2 mg cholesterol, 76 mg sodium, 15 g carbohydrate, 0 fiber, 5 g protein.* **Diabetic Exchanges:** *½ starch, ½ fat-free milk.*

Want an early morning pick-me-up that's also good for you? Fruit and flaxseed give this sweet espresso a nutritious twist. —AIMEE WILSON CLOVIS, CALIFORNIA

A.M. Rush Espresso Smoothie

PREP/TOTAL TIME: 10 MINUTES
MAKES: 1 SERVING

- ½ cup cold fat-free milk
- 1 tablespoon vanilla flavoring syrup
- 1 cup ice cubes
- ½ medium banana, cut up
- 1 to 2 teaspoons instant espresso powder
- 1 teaspoon ground flaxseed
- 1 teaspoon baking cocoa

1. In a blender, combine all the ingredients; cover and process for 1-2 minutes or until blended. Pour into a chilled glass; serve immediately.

Editor's Note: *This recipe was tested with Torani brand flavoring syrup. Look for it in the coffee section.*

Nutrition Facts: *1½ cups equals 148 calories, 2 g fat (trace saturated fat), 2 mg cholesterol, 54 mg sodium, 31 g carbohydrate, 3 g fiber, 6 g protein.*

Did you know?

Milled flaxseed is packed with heart-healthy oils and is a good source of fiber. It not only can be sprinkled on cereal or blended into smoothies, but also can be used as a substitute for some of the fat in breads and muffins. Try adding 3 tablespoons of milled flaxseed instead of 1 tablespoon butter or oil called for in a recipe. Be sure to use the milled or ground flaxseed to enjoy all of its wholesome benefits.
—KAREN K., NEW BERLIN, PENNSYLVANIA

Black Forest Crepes

Cherries and chocolate naturally taste great together, but the combination is even better when enhanced by tender crepes and a smooth, creamy filling.

—MARY RELYEA CANASTOTA, NEW YORK

PREP/TOTAL TIME: 20 MINUTES **MAKES:** 8 SERVINGS

- 1 **package (8 ounces) reduced-fat cream cheese, softened**
- ½ **cup reduced-fat sour cream**
- ½ **teaspoon vanilla extract**
- ⅔ **cup confectioners' sugar**
- 8 **prepared crepes (9 inches)**
- 1 **can (20 ounces) reduced-sugar cherry pie filling, warmed**
- ¼ **cup chocolate syrup**

1. In a small bowl, beat the cream cheese, sour cream and vanilla until smooth. Gradually beat in confectioners' sugar. Spread about 3 tablespoons over each crepe to within ½ in. of edges and roll up.

2. Arrange in an ungreased 13-in. x 9-in. baking dish. Bake, uncovered, at 350° for 5-7 minutes or until warm. To serve, top each crepe with ¼ cup pie filling and drizzle with 1½ teaspoons chocolate syrup.

Nutrition Facts: *1 filled crepe equals 256 calories, 9 g fat (6 g saturated fat), 31 mg cholesterol, 222 mg sodium, 39 g carbohydrate, 1 g fiber, 6 g protein.* **Diabetic Exchanges:** *2½ starch, 1½ fat.*

Waffle Sandwich

Keep 'em going right through to lunchtime with this quick and easy breakfast idea. It turns frozen waffles into a hot, hearty egg sandwich featuring bacon and cheese.

—MICHELE MCHENRY
BELLINGHAM, WASHINGTON

PREP/TOTAL TIME: 20 MINUTES
MAKES: 1 SERVING

- 1 **slice Canadian bacon**
- 1 **egg**
- 1 **green onion, chopped**
- 2 **frozen low-fat multigrain waffles**
- 1 **tablespoon shredded reduced-fat cheddar cheese**

1. In a small nonstick skillet coated with cooking spray, cook bacon for 1-2 minutes on each side or until lightly browned. Remove and keep warm.

2. Whisk egg and green onion. In the same skillet, add egg mixture. Cook and stir until completely set.

3. Meanwhile, prepare the waffles according to the package directions. Place one waffle on a plate. Layer with the bacon, egg mixture, cheese and remaining waffle.

Nutrition Facts: *1 sandwich equals 261 calories, 10 g fat (3 g saturated fat), 223 mg cholesterol, 733 mg sodium, 30 g carbohydrate, 3 g fiber, 16 g protein.* **Diabetic Exchanges:** *2 starch, 2 medium-fat meat.*

Did you know?

Closer to ham than bacon, Canadian bacon usually is derived from a loin cut and is leaner and meatier than conventional bacon. Canadian bacon is cured, smoked and fully cooked, and needs only to be warmed. It's ideal for breakfast dishes such as Waffle Sandwich (recipe above).

Blueberry Orange Smoothies

PREP/TOTAL TIME: 10 MINUTES **MAKES:** 4 SERVINGS

- 2 **medium navel oranges**
- 1 **cup fat-free plain yogurt**
- ¼ **cup fat-free milk**
- ⅔ **cup fresh or frozen blueberries**
- 4 **teaspoons sugar**
- 1 **to 1⅓ cups ice cubes**

1. Peel and remove the white pith from oranges; separate into sections. Place in a blender; add the yogurt, milk, blueberries and sugar. Cover and process until smooth. Add ice; cover and process until smooth. Pour into chilled glasses; serve immediately.

Nutrition Facts: *1 serving (1 cup) equals 92 calories, trace fat (trace saturated fat), 2 mg cholesterol, 43 mg sodium, 21 g carbohydrate, 2 g fiber, 4 g protein.* **Diabetic Exchange:** *1½ fruit.*

❝I love to start my day with a refreshing, low-fat smoothie. To complete the meal in a healthy way, just add a whole-grain muffin, bagel or slice of toast.❞

—**NELLA PARKER** HERSEY, MICHIGAN

Pumpkin Pancakes

Savor the harvest of fall with pumpkin-flavored pancakes spiced with cinnamon, nutmeg and ginger. They're great not only for breakfast, but also as a change-of-pace, meatless dinner.

—**VICKI FLODEN** STORY CITY, IOWA

PREP/TOTAL TIME: 20 MINUTES **MAKES:** 6 SERVINGS

- 1½ **cups all-purpose flour**
- ½ **cup whole wheat flour**
- 2 **tablespoons brown sugar**
- 2 **teaspoons baking powder**
- 1 **teaspoon ground cinnamon**
- ½ **teaspoon salt**
- ½ **teaspoon ground ginger**
- ½ **teaspoon ground nutmeg**
- 2 **cups fat-free milk**
- ½ **cup canned pumpkin**
- 1 **egg white, lightly beaten**
- 2 **tablespoons canola oil**

1. In a large bowl, combine the first eight ingredients. In a small bowl, combine the milk, pumpkin, egg white and oil; stir into dry ingredients just until moistened.

2. Pour batter by ¼ cupfuls onto a hot griddle coated with cooking spray; turn when bubbles form on top. Cook until second side is golden brown.

Nutrition Facts: *2 pancakes equals 240 calories, 5 g fat (1 g saturated fat), 1 mg cholesterol, 375 mg sodium, 41 g carbohydrate, 3 g fiber, 8 g protein.* **Diabetic Exchanges:** *2½ starch, 1 fat.*

Morning Cinnamon Rolls

Convenient crescent roll dough speeds up these delectable rolls. I discovered the recipe in a cookbook and have prepared it many times since. Pop a batch in the freezer to enjoy later in the week.

—HELEN LIPKO MARTINSBURG, PENNSYLVANIA

PREP/TOTAL TIME: 25 MINUTES **MAKES:** 8 SERVINGS

> 1 tube (8 ounces) refrigerated reduced-fat crescent rolls
> ½ teaspoon ground cinnamon
>   Sugar substitute equivalent to ½ cup sugar, divided
> ¼ cup confectioners' sugar
> 1 tablespoon fat-free milk

1. Unroll crescent dough into a rectangle; seal seams and perforations. Combine the cinnamon and half of the sugar substitute; sprinkle over dough. Roll up jelly-roll style, starting with a long side; seal edge. Cut into eight slices.

2. Place rolls cut side down in a 9-in. round baking pan coated with cooking spray. Bake at 375° for 12-15 minutes or until golden brown.

3. In a small bowl, combine the confectioners' sugar, milk and remaining sugar substitute; drizzle over the warm rolls. To freeze, cool the rolls. Wrap, unfrosted, in foil and freeze for up to 3 months.

To use frozen rolls: *Thaw at room temperature; warm if desired. Follow directions for icing.*

Editor's Note: *This recipe was tested with Splenda sugar blend.*

Nutrition Facts: *1 roll equals 123 calories, 5 g fat (1 g saturated fat), trace cholesterol, 234 mg sodium, 18 g carbohydrate, trace fiber, 2 g protein.* **Diabetic Exchanges:** *1 starch, 1 fat.*

Cafe Mocha Mini Muffins

Here's a good choice for many different occasions—including a quiet morning with a cup of coffee and the newspaper. The little chocolate-dotted muffins freeze well, so it's easy to keep some on hand. And they're just the right size for snacking!

—TINA SAWCHUK ARDMORE, ALBERTA

PREP/TOTAL TIME: 30 MINUTES **MAKES:** 1½ DOZEN

> 2 teaspoons instant coffee granules
> ⅓ cup boiling water
> ¼ cup quick-cooking oats
> 3 tablespoons butter, softened
> ¼ cup sugar
> 3 tablespoons brown sugar
> 1 egg yolk
> ½ teaspoon vanilla extract
> ½ cup all-purpose flour
> 1 tablespoon baking cocoa
> ½ teaspoon baking powder
> ⅛ teaspoon baking soda
> ⅛ teaspoon salt
> ½ cup miniature semisweet chocolate chips, divided

1. In a small bowl, dissolve coffee granules in water. Stir in the oats; set aside. In a small bowl, cream butter and sugars. Beat in egg yolk, vanilla and oat mixture. Combine the flour, cocoa, baking powder, baking soda and salt; add to oat mixture just until moistened. Stir in ⅓ cup chocolate chips.

2. Fill foil- or paper-lined miniature muffin cups three-fourths full. Sprinkle with remaining chips. Bake at 350° for 12-15 minutes or until a toothpick inserted near the center comes out clean. Cool for 5 minutes before removing from pans to wire racks.

Editor's Note: *Muffins may be frozen for up to 2 months.*

Nutrition Facts: *1 muffin equals 81 calories, 4 g fat (2 g saturated fat), 17 mg cholesterol, 53 mg sodium, 12 g carbohydrate, 1 g fiber, 1 g protein.* **Diabetic Exchanges:** *1 starch, ½ fat.*

Blueberry Orange Scones

PREP/TOTAL TIME: 30 MINUTES
MAKES: 8 SCONES

- 2 cups all-purpose flour
- 3 tablespoons sugar
- 2 teaspoons baking powder
- 2 teaspoons grated orange peel
- 1 teaspoon salt
- ¼ teaspoon baking soda
- ¼ teaspoon ground cloves
- ¼ cup cold butter
- ½ cup buttermilk
- ¼ cup orange juice
- ½ cup fresh or frozen unsweetened blueberries

1. In a large bowl, combine the first seven ingredients. Cut in butter until mixture resembles coarse crumbs. Stir in buttermilk and orange juice just until moistened. Gently fold in blueberries.

2. Turn the dough onto a floured surface; gently knead 10 times. Pat into an 8-in. circle. Cut into eight wedges. Separate wedges and place on a baking sheet coated with cooking spray. Bake at 425° for 10-12 minutes or until golden brown. Serve warm.

Editor's Note: *If using frozen blueberries, use without thawing to avoid discoloring the batter.*

Nutrition Facts: *1 scone equals 198 calories, 6 g fat (4 g saturated fat), 16 mg cholesterol, 509 mg sodium, 32 g carbohydrate, 1 g fiber, 4 g protein.* **Diabetic Exchanges:** *2 starch, 1 fat.*

It's hard to resist tender, flaky, buttery scones studded with blueberries. After enjoying one warm from the oven for breakfast, save another for your afternoon snack.
—**KATY RADTKE** APPLETON, WISCONSIN

top tip When a recipe instructs you to "cut in" butter, margarine or shortening, use two knives or a pastry blender—whichever tool you prefer—to break it down and distribute it into the flour mixture.

Baked Eggs with Cheddar and Bacon

These individual-serving egg bakes are super-easy to make and perfect for a special breakfast—or even a casual weekday dinner. Smoked cheddar cheese adds a whole new level of flavor.

—**CATHERINE WILKINSON** DEWEY, ARIZONA

PREP/TOTAL TIME: 25 MINUTES **MAKES:** 4 SERVINGS

  4 **eggs**
  4 **tablespoons fat-free milk, divided**
  2 **tablespoons shredded smoked cheddar cheese**
  2 **teaspoons minced fresh parsley**
  ¼ **teaspoon salt**
  ⅛ **teaspoon pepper**
  2 **bacon strips**

1. Coat four 4-oz. ramekins with cooking spray; break an egg into each dish. Spoon 1 tablespoon milk over each egg. Combine the cheddar cheese, parsley, salt and pepper; sprinkle over tops.

2. Bake, uncovered, at 325° for 12-15 minutes or until whites are completely set and yolks begin to thicken but are not firm.

3. Meanwhile, in a small skillet, cook bacon over medium heat until crisp. Remove to paper towels to drain. Crumble bacon and sprinkle over eggs.

Nutrition Facts: *1 serving equals 107 calories, 7 g fat (3 g saturated fat), 219 mg cholesterol, 319 mg sodium, 1 g carbohydrate, trace fiber, 9 g protein.* **Diabetic Exchange:** *1 medium-fat meat.*

Omelet Tortilla Wrap

Here's a hearty, better-for-you breakfast that can be eaten out of hand and on your way out the door. Kids just love it!

—**INGRID PARKER** HATTIESBURG, MISSISSIPPI

PREP/TOTAL TIME: 25 MINUTES **MAKES:** 1 SERVING

  1 **egg**
  2 **egg whites**
  2 **tablespoons finely chopped fully cooked lean ham**
  1 **green onion, thinly sliced**
  1 **tablespoon chopped sweet red pepper**
  1 **tablespoon fat-free milk**
  2 **teaspoons chopped seeded jalapeno pepper**
  ⅛ **teaspoon pepper**
     Dash hot pepper sauce, optional
  2 **tablespoons shredded reduced-fat Monterey Jack cheese or Mexican cheese blend**
  1 **whole wheat tortilla (8 inches), warmed**

1. In a small bowl, whisk the egg, egg whites, ham, onion, red pepper, milk, jalapeno, pepper and pepper sauce if desired. Coat a small nonstick skillet with cooking spray and place over medium heat. Add egg mixture to skillet (mixture should set immediately at edges).

2. As eggs set, push cooked edges toward the center, letting uncooked portion flow underneath. When the eggs are set, remove from the heat; sprinkle with cheese. Slide omelet onto tortilla; roll up tightly.

Editor's Note: *Wear disposable gloves when cutting hot peppers; the oils can burn skin. Avoid touching your face.*

Nutrition Facts: *1 wrap equals 322 calories, 12 g fat (4 g saturated fat), 229 mg cholesterol, 701 mg sodium, 26 g carbohydrate, 3 g fiber, 25 g protein.*

Puffy Apple Omelet

Here's one omelet you won't soon forget! The spiced, apple-topped treat is especially yummy on a cool autumn morning.

—MELISSA DAVENPORT
CAMPBELL, MINNESOTA

PREP/TOTAL TIME: 30 MINUTES
MAKES: 2 SERVINGS

- 3 tablespoons all-purpose flour
- ¼ teaspoon baking powder
- 2 eggs, separated
- 3 tablespoons fat-free milk
- 1 tablespoon lemon juice
- 3 tablespoons sugar

TOPPING
- 1 large tart apple, peeled and thinly sliced
- 1 teaspoon sugar
- ¼ teaspoon ground cinnamon

1. In a small bowl, combine the flour and baking powder. In a small bowl, whisk the egg yolks, milk and lemon juice. Stir into dry ingredients and mix well; set aside.

2. In another small bowl, beat egg whites on medium speed until soft peaks form. Gradually beat in the sugar 1 tablespoon at a time, on high until stiff peaks form. Fold into yolk mixture.

3. Pour into a shallow 1½-qt. baking dish coated with cooking spray. Arrange apple slices on top. Combine sugar and cinnamon; sprinkle over apples.

4. Bake, uncovered, at 375° for 18-20 minutes or until a knife inserted near the center comes out clean. Cut in half.

Nutrition Facts: *1 serving equals 249 calories, 5 g fat (2 g saturated fat), 212 mg cholesterol, 130 mg sodium, 44 g carbohydrate, 2 g fiber, 9 g protein.* **Diabetic Exchanges:** *2 starch, 1 lean meat, 1 fruit.*

Spicy Scrambled Egg Sandwiches

Family breakfasts are well in hand with these energy-building muffins-to-go. They're packed with wholesome vegetables for a burst of great-tasting nutrition.

—HELEN VAIL GLENSIDE, PENNSYLVANIA

PREP/TOTAL TIME: 30 MINUTES **MAKES:** 4 SERVINGS

- ⅓ cup chopped green pepper
- ¼ cup chopped onion
- 3 eggs
- 4 egg whites
- 1 tablespoon water
- ¼ teaspoon salt
- ¼ teaspoon ground mustard
- ⅛ teaspoon pepper
- ⅛ teaspoon hot pepper sauce
- ⅓ cup fresh or frozen corn, thawed
- ¼ cup real bacon bits
- 4 English muffins, split and toasted

1. In a 10-in. skillet coated with cooking spray, cook green pepper and onion over medium heat until tender, about 8 minutes.

2. In a large bowl, whisk the eggs, egg whites, water, salt, mustard, pepper and hot pepper sauce. Pour into skillet. Add corn and bacon; cook and stir until the eggs are completely set. Spoon onto English muffin bottoms; replace tops. Serve immediately.

Nutrition Facts: *1 sandwich equals 248 calories, 6 g fat (2 g saturated fat), 164 mg cholesterol, 739 mg sodium, 31 g carbohydrate, 2 g fiber, 16 g protein.* **Diabetic Exchanges:** *2 starch, 2 lean meat.*

top tip

Separating an Egg

Place an egg separator over a custard cup and crack the egg into the separator. As each egg is separated, place the yolk in another bowl and empty the egg whites into a mixing bowl. Keep in mind that it's easier to separate eggs when they are cold.

Strawberry Puff Pancake

I've cut this recipe to 2 eggs and ½ cup milk for my husband and me, and it still works well. The oven-baked pancake is so yummy with fresh strawberries and a sprinkling of sugar. You could even add a dollop of whipped topping for a light dessert.

—**BRENDA MORTON** HALE CENTER, TEXAS

PREP/TOTAL TIME: 30 MINUTES **MAKES:** 4 SERVINGS

- 2 **tablespoons butter**
- 3 **eggs**
- ¾ **cup fat-free milk**
- 1 **teaspoon vanilla extract**
- ¾ **cup all-purpose flour**
- ⅛ **teaspoon salt**
- ⅛ **teaspoon ground cinnamon**
- ¼ **cup sugar**
- 1 **tablespoon cornstarch**
- ½ **cup water**
- 1 **cup sliced fresh strawberries**
  Confectioners' sugar

1. Place butter in a 9-in. pie plate; place in a 400° oven for 4-5 minutes or until melted. Meanwhile, in a small bowl, whisk the eggs, milk and vanilla. In another small bowl, combine the flour, salt and cinnamon; whisk into egg mixture until blended.
2. Pour into prepared pie plate. Bake for 15-20 minutes or until sides are crisp and golden brown.
3. In a small saucepan, combine sugar and cornstarch. Stir in water until smooth; add strawberries. Cook and stir over medium heat until thickened. Coarsely mash strawberries. Serve with pancake. Dust with confectioners' sugar.

Nutrition Facts: *1 slice with ⅓ cup sauce (calculated without confectioners' sugar) equals 277 calories, 10 g fat (5 g saturated fat), 175 mg cholesterol, 187 mg sodium, 38 g carbohydrate, 2 g fiber, 9 g protein.* **Diabetic Exchanges:** *2½ starch, 1 medium-fat meat, 1 fat.*

Sweet Berry Bruschetta

I've made my berry bruschetta by toasting the bread on a grill at cookouts instead of broiling it. No matter how I prepare the sweet slices, I never have a crumb left over!

—**PATRICIA NIEH** PORTOLA VALLY, CALIFORNIA

PREP/TOTAL TIME: 20 MINUTES **MAKES:** 10 PIECES

- 10 **slices French bread (½ inch thick)**
  Cooking spray
- 5 **teaspoons sugar, divided**
- 6 **ounces fat-free cream cheese**
- ½ **teaspoon almond extract**
- ¾ **cup fresh blackberries**
- ¾ **cup fresh raspberries**
- ¼ **cup slivered almonds, toasted**
- 2 **teaspoons confectioners' sugar**

1. Place bread on an ungreased baking sheet; lightly coat with cooking spray. Sprinkle with 2 teaspoons sugar. Broil 3-4 in. from the heat for 1-2 minutes or until lightly browned.
2. In a small bowl, combine the cream cheese, extract and remaining sugar. Spread over toasted bread. Top with berries and almonds; dust with confectioners' sugar. Serve immediately.

Nutrition Facts: *1 piece equals 92 calories, 2 g fat (trace saturated fat), 1 mg cholesterol, 179 mg sodium, 14 g carbohydrate, 2 g fiber, 4 g protein.* **Diabetic Exchanges:** *1 starch, ½ fat.*

Sunrise Slushies

My teenage daughters are often on a diet, so I sometimes worried about their nutrition. Then I came up with this frosty, blended beverage that just bursts with wholesome fruit, and they love it.

—**LINDA EVANCOE-COBLE** LEOLA, PENNSYLVANIA

PREP/TOTAL TIME: 10 MINUTES   **MAKES:** 8 SERVINGS

- 2 **cups orange juice**
- 1 **cup reduced-calorie reduced-sugar cranberry juice**
- 1 **medium tart apple, chopped**
- ½ **cup cubed peeled mango**
- 2 **kiwifruit, peeled, sliced and quartered**
- 2 **cups halved fresh strawberries**
- 8 **to 10 ice cubes**

1. In a blender, place half of each ingredient; cover and process until smooth. Pour into chilled glasses. Repeat with remaining ingredients. Serve immediately.

Nutrition Facts: *1 serving (1 cup) equals 73 calories, trace fat (trace saturated fat), 0 cholesterol, 2 mg sodium, 18 g carbohydrate, 2 g fiber, 1 g protein.* **Diabetic Exchange:** *1 fruit.*

Easy Breakfast Quesadillas

PREP/TOTAL TIME: 20 MINUTES   **MAKES:** 6 SERVINGS

- 4 **eggs**
- 1 **cup egg substitute**
- 6 **whole wheat tortillas (8 inches)**
- 1 **cup (4 ounces) shredded reduced-fat cheddar cheese**
- 3 **turkey bacon strips, diced and cooked**
- 6 **tablespoons salsa**
- 6 **tablespoons fat-free sour cream**

1. In a small bowl, whisk eggs and egg substitute. Coat a large skillet with cooking spray. Add egg mixture; cook and stir over medium heat until completely set.

2. Heat another large nonstick skillet coated with cooking spray; add one tortilla. Top with ⅓ cup cheddar cheese, scant 2 tablespoons bacon, 1 cup egg mixture and one tortilla. Cook over medium heat for 2-3 minutes on each side or until lightly browned.

3. Repeat with remaining tortillas, cheese, bacon and eggs, spraying pan as needed. Cut each quesadilla into six wedges. Serve with salsa and sour cream.

Nutrition Facts: *3 wedges with 1 tablespoon salsa and 1 tablespoon sour cream equals 299 calories, 12 g fat (4 g saturated fat), 164 mg cholesterol, 588 mg sodium, 27 g carbohydrate, 2 g fiber, 19 g protein.*

❝These cheesy, hearty quesadillas were my attempt at preparing Mexican food for breakfast. When my children ate every last bite, I knew I was successful!❞

—**JUDY PARKER** MOORE, OKLAHOMA

Makeover Hash and Eggs

Loaded with red potatoes and deli corned beef, this lightened-up take on corned beef hash delivers fresh flavors and a dose of fiber. It's so close to the classic version, you'll swear you're in a diner!

—TASTE OF HOME TEST KITCHEN

PREP/TOTAL TIME: 30 MINUTES
MAKES: 4 SERVINGS

- 1 large onion, chopped
- 1 tablespoon canola oil
- 6 medium red potatoes (about 1½ pounds), cut into ½-inch cubes
- ¼ cup water
- 3 packages (2 ounces each) thinly sliced deli corned beef, coarsely chopped
- ¼ teaspoon pepper
- 4 eggs

1. In a large nonstick skillet, saute onion in oil until tender. Stir in potatoes and water. Bring to a boil. Reduce heat; cover and simmer for 15-20 minutes or until potatoes are tender. Stir in corned beef and pepper; heat through.

2. Meanwhile, in a large nonstick skillet coated with cooking spray, fry eggs as desired. Serve with corned beef hash.

Nutrition Facts: *1 cup corned beef hash with 1 egg equals 301 calories, 12 g fat (3 g saturated fat), 239 mg cholesterol, 652 mg sodium, 31 g carbohydrate, 4 g fiber, 18 g protein.*

Sausage and Egg Pizza

Using turkey sausage, fat-free cheddar cheese, egg substitute and reduced-fat crescent rolls really reduced the fat and calories in my hearty breakfast pizza.

—VICKI MEYERS CASTALIA, OHIO

PREP/TOTAL TIME: 30 MINUTES **MAKES:** 6 SLICES

- 1 tube (8 ounces) refrigerated reduced-fat crescent rolls
- ½ pound Italian turkey sausage links, casings removed
- 1¾ cups sliced fresh mushrooms
- 1¼ cups frozen shredded hash brown potatoes
- ¼ teaspoon garlic salt
- ¼ teaspoon pepper
- 2 green onions, chopped
- 2 tablespoons finely chopped sweet red pepper
- ½ cup shredded fat-free cheddar cheese
- ¾ cup egg substitute

1. Separate crescent dough into eight triangles; place on an ungreased 12-in. pizza pan with points toward the center. Press onto the bottom and up the sides of pan to form a crust; seal perforations. Bake at 375° for 8 minutes.

2. Meanwhile, crumble sausage into a large nonstick skillet coated with cooking spray. Add mushrooms; cook and stir over medium heat until meat is no longer pink. Drain and set aside. In the same skillet, cook the potatoes, garlic salt and pepper over medium heat until browned.

3. Sprinkle sausage mixture over crust. Layer with potatoes, onions, red pepper and cheese; pour egg substitute over the top. Bake for 10-12 minutes or until egg is set and cheese is melted.

Nutrition Facts: *1 slice equals 241 calories, 10 g fat (2 g saturated fat), 24 mg cholesterol, 744 mg sodium, 22 g carbohydrate, 1 g fiber, 16 g protein.* **Diabetic Exchanges:** *2 lean meat, 1½ starch, ½ fat.*

Removing Onion Odors

Need to chop, slice or dice onions? When you're finished, sprinkle your hands with table salt, rub them together for a few moments and then wash them as usual. Presto—no more onion smell on your hands!

—CONNIE S., AMHERST, OHIO

Coconut-Glazed Orange Scones

Escape to a tropical paradise with these warm-from-the-oven goodies. Guaranteed to brighten up any gloomy autumn or winter day, they offer a refreshing burst of orange and coconut flavor. A confectioners' sugar glaze is the perfect finishing touch.

—TASTE OF HOME TEST KITCHEN

PREP/TOTAL TIME: 30 MINUTES **MAKES:** 1½ DOZEN

3¾ cups self-rising flour
¼ cup sugar
2 teaspoons baking powder
½ cup cold butter
2 eggs
1 cup plus 1 to 2 tablespoons fat-free milk, divided
1 teaspoon grated orange peel
½ cup confectioners' sugar
¼ teaspoon coconut extract

1. In a large bowl, combine the flour, sugar and baking powder. Cut in butter until mixture resembles coarse crumbs. In a small bowl, whisk eggs, 1 cup milk and orange peel; stir into crumb mixture just until moistened. Turn onto a floured surface; knead 10 times.

2. Roll into a 14-in. x 8-in. rectangle. Using a floured pizza cutter, cut widthwise into 2-in. strips, then cut diagonally into 2-in. strips, forming diamond shapes. Place 2 in. apart on baking sheets coated with cooking spray.

3. Bake at 400° for 8-10 minutes or until lightly browned. Remove to wire racks.

4. For the glaze, in a small bowl, combine the confectioners' sugar, coconut extract and enough remaining milk to achieve the desired consistency; drizzle over scones. Serve warm.

Editor's Note: *As a substitute for self-rising flour, place 5½ teaspoons baking powder and 1¾ teaspoons salt in a measuring cup. Add all-purpose flour to measure 1 cup. Add another 2¾ cups all-purpose flour to the bowl.*

Nutrition Facts: *1 scone equals 165 calories, 6 g fat (3 g saturated fat), 38 mg cholesterol, 410 mg sodium, 25 g carbohydrate, trace fiber, 4 g protein.* **Diabetic Exchanges:** *1½ starch, 1 fat.*

French Toast with Apple Topping

You'll start the morning off right when you sit down to golden-brown French toast topped with sauteed, spiced apples. Yum!

—JANIS SCHARNOTT FONTANA, WISCONSIN

PREP/TOTAL TIME: 20 MINUTES
MAKES: 2 SERVINGS

1 medium apple, peeled and thinly sliced
1 tablespoon brown sugar
¼ teaspoon ground cinnamon
2 tablespoons reduced-fat butter, divided
1 egg
¼ cup 2% milk
1 teaspoon vanilla extract
4 slices French bread (½ inch thick)
Maple syrup, optional

1. In a large skillet, saute apple, brown sugar and cinnamon in 1 tablespoon butter until apple is tender.

2. In a shallow bowl, whisk the egg, milk and vanilla. Dip both sides of bread in egg mixture.

3. In a large skillet, melt remaining butter over medium heat. Cook bread on both sides until golden brown. Serve with apple mixture and syrup if desired.

Editor's Note: *This recipe was tested with Land O'Lakes light stick butter.*

Nutrition Facts: *2 slices with ¼ cup apple mixture (calculated without syrup) equals 219 calories, 10 g fat (5 g saturated fat), 113 mg cholesterol, 279 mg sodium, 29 g carbohydrate, 2 g fiber, 6 g protein.* **Diabetic Exchanges:** *1½ starch, 1½ fat, ½ fruit.*

French Bread Slices

We found it difficult to prevent a loaf of French bread from becoming hard before we used it. Now I slice the loaf, return it to its original wrapper and place it in a plastic bag in the freezer. To use the loaf, I dampen a microwave-safe paper towel, wrap it around the number of slices I'd like and warm them in the microwave for 30 seconds. They taste just like fresh! Then I simply return the rest of the loaf to the freezer.

—CAROLYN DE WALT
FORT WORTH, TEXAS

Makeover Waffles

PREP/TOTAL TIME: 25 MINUTES
MAKES: 10 WAFFLES

- 1¾ cups all-purpose flour
- 3 teaspoons baking powder
- ½ teaspoon salt
- 2 egg yolks
- 1¾ cups fat-free milk
- ¼ cup canola oil
- ¼ cup unsweetened applesauce
- 2 egg whites

1. In a large bowl, combine the flour, baking powder and salt. In a small bowl, whisk the egg yolks, milk, oil and applesauce. Stir into dry ingredients just until moistened.

2. In another small bowl, beat egg whites until stiff peaks form. Fold into batter. Bake in a preheated waffle iron according to manufacturer's directions until golden brown.

Nutrition Facts: *2 waffles equals 321 calories, 13 g fat (2 g saturated fat), 84 mg cholesterol, 538 mg sodium, 39 g carbohydrate, 1 g fiber, 10 g protein.*

These trimmed-down waffles taste every bit as good as the original recipe—with only half the fat. So dust off that waffle iron and enjoy a breakfast treat anytime!
—CAROL BURGER PHILLIPS, WISCONSIN

top tip

On Saturday mornings, I like to mix up a big batch of pancakes or waffles. What our family doesn't eat for breakfast that day, I store in the freezer to use throughout the week. It's a breeze to heat up individual servings in the toaster for quick but filling meals on weekdays when everyone's in a hurry.
—JENNIFER P.
HAVELOCK, NORTH CAROLINA

Honey Wheat Pancakes

I put healthy whole wheat flour and wheat germ in my pancakes, and even my children rave about them. The thick, tender flapjacks have a delightful hint of honey and cinnamon.

—**MARTINA BIAS** BELLEVILLE, ILLINOIS

PREP: 10 MINUTES **COOK:** 5 MINUTES/BATCH
MAKES: 12 PANCAKES

  1½ cups reduced-fat biscuit/baking mix
  ½   cup whole wheat flour
  ¼   cup wheat germ
  1   teaspoon baking powder
  1   teaspoon ground cinnamon
  2   eggs, lightly beaten
  1½ cups buttermilk
  1   medium ripe banana, mashed
  2   tablespoons honey
      Assorted fresh fruit and/or maple syrup, optional

1. In a small bowl, combine the first five ingredients. Combine the eggs, buttermilk, banana and honey; add to dry ingredients just until moistened.
2. Pour batter by ¼ cupfuls onto a hot griddle coated with cooking spray; turn when bubbles form on top. Cook until the second side is golden brown. Serve with fruit and/or maple syrup if desired.

Nutrition Facts: *2 pancakes (calculated without optional toppings) equals 253 calories, 5 g fat (1 g saturated fat), 73 mg cholesterol, 502 mg sodium, 44 g carbohydrate, 3 g fiber, 9 g protein.* **Diabetic Exchanges:** *3 starch, ½ fat.*

Tropical Yogurt

Plain yogurt becomes a flavorful sensation with help from coconut extract, pineapple bits and a burst of lime. Try it and see!

—**TASTE OF HOME TEST KITCHEN**

PREP/TOTAL TIME: 5 MINUTES **MAKES:** 4 SERVINGS

  2   cups (16 ounces) reduced-fat plain yogurt
  1   can (8 ounces) unsweetened crushed pineapple, drained
  2   teaspoons sugar
  ¼   teaspoon coconut extract
  ¼   teaspoon grated lime peel

1. In a small bowl, combine all ingredients. Chill until serving.

Nutrition Facts: *½ cup equals 121 calories, 2 g fat (1 g saturated fat), 7 mg cholesterol, 86 mg sodium, 20 g carbohydrate, trace fiber, 7 g protein.* **Diabetic Exchanges:** *1 reduced-fat milk, ½ fruit.*

Cherry-Almond Drop Scones

These golden goodies are studded with dried cherries and crunchy slivered almonds. Pair a warm scone with a cup of steaming coffee, cocoa or tea for a special treat.

—HELEN PHILLIPS EATON, COLORADO

PREP/TOTAL TIME: 30 MINUTES   **MAKES:** 14 SCONES

- 2¼ cups all-purpose flour
- 2 tablespoons sugar
- 2¼ teaspoons baking powder
- ½ teaspoon baking soda
- ½ teaspoon salt
- 1 cup vanilla yogurt
- ¼ cup butter, melted
- 1 egg, lightly beaten
- ¼ teaspoon almond extract
- ½ cup dried cherries, chopped
- ½ cup slivered almonds

1. In a large bowl, combine the flour, sugar, baking powder, baking soda and salt. In another bowl, combine the yogurt, butter, egg and extract. Stir into dry ingredients just until moistened. Fold in cherries and almonds.

2. Drop by heaping tablespoonfuls 2 in. apart onto a baking sheet coated with cooking spray. Bake at 400° for 15-18 minutes or until lightly browned. Remove to wire racks. Serve warm.

Nutrition Facts: *1 scone equals 166 calories, 6 g fat (2 g saturated fat), 25 mg cholesterol, 243 mg sodium, 24 g carbohydrate, 1 g fiber, 4 g protein.* **Diabetic Exchanges:** *1 starch, 1 fat, ½ fruit.*

Bird's Nest Breakfast Cups

Here's a lightened-up version of an original recipe that called for regular bacon and eggs. Everyone enjoys the cute little cups, and they couldn't be easier to make.

—ARIS GONZALEZ DELTONA, FLORIDA

PREP/TOTAL TIME: 30 MINUTES
MAKES: 6 SERVINGS

- 12 turkey bacon strips
- 1½ cups egg substitute
- 6 tablespoons shredded reduced-fat Mexican cheese blend
- 1 tablespoon minced fresh parsley

1. In a large skillet, cook bacon over medium heat for 2 minutes on each side or until partially set but not crisp. Coat six muffin cups with cooking spray; wrap two bacon strips around the inside of each cup. Fill each with ¼ cup egg substitute; top with cheese.

2. Bake at 350° for 18-20 minutes or until set. Cool for 5 minutes before removing from pan. Sprinkle with parsley.

Nutrition Facts: *1 breakfast cup equals 120 calories, 7 g fat (2 g saturated fat), 30 mg cholesterol, 515 mg sodium, 2 g carbohydrate, trace fiber, 12 g protein.* **Diabetic Exchange:** *2 lean meat.*

Keeping Parsley Fresh

To keep fresh parsley in the refrigerator for several weeks, wash the entire bunch in warm water, shake off all excess moisture, wrap it in a paper towel and seal it in a plastic bag. If you need more storage time, remove the paper towel and place the sealed bag in the freezer. Then simply break off and crumble the amount of parsley you need for dishes such as Bird's Nest Breakfast Cups (recipe above).

56

60

66

Soups &
Sandwiches

66 This south-of-the-border soup is one of my husband's wintertime favorites. It's quick to make but tastes like it simmered all day. What a delicious way to use up those last tortilla chips in the bag! 99

LINDA LASHLEY REDGRANITE, WISCONSIN
about her recipe, Zippy Chicken Soup, on page 73

Spicy Chicken Tomato Pitas

PREP/TOTAL TIME: 30 MINUTES
MAKES: 4 SERVINGS

TOMATO RELISH

- 4 medium tomatoes, seeded and chopped
- 1 small onion, chopped
- ¼ cup minced fresh parsley
- ¼ cup lemon juice
- 1 tablespoon olive oil
- 1 teaspoon ground coriander
- 1 teaspoon ground cumin
- ¼ teaspoon crushed red pepper flakes

CHICKEN PITAS

- 1 tablespoon ground cumin
- 1 tablespoon paprika
- 1½ teaspoons dried oregano
- 1½ teaspoons ground coriander
- ½ teaspoon crushed red pepper flakes
- ¼ teaspoon salt
- 4 boneless skinless chicken breast halves (4 ounces each)
- 8 whole wheat pita pocket halves

1. Combine the relish ingredients; chill until serving.

2. Combine cumin, paprika, oregano, coriander, pepper flakes and salt; rub over both sides of chicken. Grill chicken, covered, over medium heat or broil 4 in. from the heat for 4-7 minutes on each side or until juices run clear.

3. Slice chicken. Fill each pita half with chicken and tomato relish.

Nutrition Facts: *2 filled pita halves equals 383 calories, 9 g fat (2 g saturated fat), 63 mg cholesterol, 558 mg sodium, 47 g carbohydrate, 9 g fiber, 32 g protein.*

Easy Tortellini Soup

Simple and colorful, this recipe makes a cozy menu addition—or even a light lunch all by itself. The cheese tortellini are filling, and veggies provide plenty of nutrition.
—GAYE THOMPSON ST. CHARLES, MISSOURI

PREP/TOTAL TIME: 30 MINUTES **MAKES:** 6 SERVINGS

- 1 medium onion, chopped
- 1 teaspoon olive oil
- 1 garlic clove, minced
- 2 cans (14½ ounces each) reduced-sodium chicken broth
- 1 can (14½ ounces) diced tomatoes, undrained
- 1 package (9 ounces) refrigerated cheese tortellini or tortellini of your choice
- 3 cups chopped fresh spinach
- 1 tablespoon balsamic vinegar
- ¼ teaspoon pepper
    Shredded Parmesan cheese, optional

1. In a Dutch oven, saute onion in oil until tender. Add garlic; cook 1 minute longer. Stir in chicken broth and tomatoes. Bring to a boil. Reduce heat; simmer, uncovered, for 10 minutes, stirring occasionally.

2. Add the tortellini; cook for 7-9 minutes or until tender. Stir in the spinach, vinegar and pepper. Cook and stir until heated through and spinach is wilted. Sprinkle with Parmesan cheese.

Nutrition Facts: *1 cup (calculated without cheese) equals 178 calories, 4 g fat (2 g saturated fat), 18 mg cholesterol, 652 mg sodium, 27 g carbohydrate, 3 g fiber, 9 g protein.* **Diabetic Exchanges:** *1 starch, 1 lean meat, 1 vegetable.*

? Did you know?
Cooking times should be the same for gas or charcoal grills. When a recipe says to cook over medium coals, use the medium heat setting on your gas grill.

"Here's a real crowd pleaser! The whole wheat pitas pack the spicy taste of the Southwest and a bright splash of lemon. They go together quickly, too, which is always a big bonus."

—CORI COOPER BOISE, IDAHO

Chicken Lettuce Wraps

Filled with chicken, mushrooms, water chestnuts and carrots, my lettuce wraps are both wholesome and delicious. The gingerroot, rice wine vinegar and teriyaki sauce give them a touch of Asian flair.

—KENDRA DOSS KANSAS CITY, MISSOURI

PREP/TOTAL TIME: 25 MINUTES
MAKES: 6 SERVINGS

- 1½ **pounds boneless skinless chicken breasts, cubed**
- 1 **tablespoon plus 1½ teaspoons peanut oil, divided**
- ¾ **cup chopped fresh mushrooms**
- 1 **can (8 ounces) water chestnuts, drained and diced**
- 1 **tablespoon minced fresh gingerroot**
- 2 **tablespoons rice vinegar**
- 2 **tablespoons reduced-sodium teriyaki sauce**
- 1 **tablespoon reduced-sodium soy sauce**
- ½ **teaspoon garlic powder**
- ¼ **teaspoon crushed red pepper flakes**
- 1½ **cups shredded carrots**
- ½ **cup julienned green onions**
- 12 **Bibb or Boston lettuce leaves**
- ⅓ **cup sliced almonds, toasted**

1. In a large nonstick skillet coated with cooking spray, cook the chicken in 1 tablespoon oil for 3 minutes; drain. Add the mushrooms, water chestnuts and ginger; cook 4-6 minutes longer or until the chicken is no longer pink. Drain and set aside.

2. In a small bowl, whisk the vinegar, teriyaki sauce, soy sauce, garlic powder, red pepper flakes and remaining oil. Stir in the carrots, onions and chicken mixture.

3. Spoon onto lettuce leaves; sprinkle with almonds. If desired, fold sides of lettuce over filling and roll up.

Nutrition Facts: *2 wraps equals 230 calories, 9 g fat (2 g saturated fat), 63 mg cholesterol, 278 mg sodium, 12 g carbohydrate, 3 g fiber, 26 g protein.*
Diabetic Exchanges: *3 lean meat, 2 vegetable, 1 fat.*

My husband is diabetic, and I'm watching my weight. This broccoli-cheese blend fits our diets perfectly. And no one would guess it takes just 15 minutes to make!
—**CAROL COLVIN** DERBY, NEW YORK

Broccoli Cheese Soup

PREP/TOTAL TIME: 15 MINUTES
MAKES: 8 SERVINGS

- 1 can (10¾ ounces) reduced-fat reduced-sodium condensed cream of celery soup, undiluted
- 1 can (10¾ ounces) reduced-fat reduced-sodium condensed cream of chicken soup, undiluted
- 3 cups fat-free milk
- 1 tablespoon dried minced onion
- 1 teaspoon dried parsley flakes
- ½ teaspoon garlic powder
- ¼ teaspoon pepper
- 3 cups frozen chopped broccoli, thawed
- 1 can (14½ ounces) sliced potatoes, drained
- ½ cup shredded reduced-fat cheddar cheese

1. In a large saucepan, combine the soups, milk, onion, parsley, garlic powder and pepper. Stir in broccoli and potatoes; heat through. Just before serving, sprinkle with cheese.

Nutrition Facts: *1 cup equals 135 calories, 3 g fat (2 g saturated fat), 11 mg cholesterol, 521 mg sodium, 19 g carbohydrate, 3 g fiber, 8 g protein.* **Diabetic Exchanges:** *1½ starch, ½ fat.*

top tip

Storing Garlic & Onion Powders

Garlic and onion powders tend to absorb moisture from the air, especially during warm weather months. Store garlic and onion powders in airtight spice jars to keep them as free from moisture and humidity as possible.

Toasted Clubs with Dill Mayo

Try a bistro-style sandwich that's simple to prepare, eye-appealing and loaded with flavor. You'll be glad you did!

—**JENNY FLAKE** NEWPORT BEACH, CALIFORNIA

PREP/TOTAL TIME: 20 MINUTES **MAKES:** 2 SERVINGS

- 2 **tablespoons fat-free mayonnaise**
- ¼ **teaspoon dill weed**
- ¾ **teaspoon lemon juice, divided**
- ⅛ **teaspoon pepper**
- 4 **slices whole wheat bread, toasted**
- 4 **thin slices deli roast beef**
- 4 **thin slices deli ham**
- 2 **slices reduced-fat provolone cheese**
- 2 **Bibb lettuce leaves**
- 2 **slices tomato**
- 2 **center-cut bacon strips, cooked and crumbled**
- ¼ **cup alfalfa sprouts**
- ¼ **medium ripe avocado, peeled and sliced**

1. In a small bowl, combine the mayonnaise, dill, ¼ teaspoon lemon juice and pepper; spread over toast. Layer two slices with beef, ham, cheese, lettuce, tomato, bacon and sprouts.

2. Drizzle avocado with remaining lemon juice; place over sprouts. Top with remaining toast. Secure with toothpicks.

Nutrition Facts: *1 sandwich equals 328 calories, 13 g fat (4 g saturated fat), 47 mg cholesterol, 1,056 mg sodium, 29 g carbohydrate, 6 g fiber, 26 g protein.*

Veggie Chowder

My vegetable-packed chowder combines a variety of wholesome ingredients—potatoes, mushrooms, carrots and more. Enjoy a bowlful as a meal or pair it with your favorite salad.

—**VICKI KERR** PORTLAND, MAINE

PREP/TOTAL TIME: 30 MINUTES **MAKES:** 7 SERVINGS

- 2 **cups reduced-sodium chicken broth**
- 2 **cups cubed peeled potatoes**
- 1 **cup chopped carrots**
- ½ **cup chopped onion**
- 1 **can (14¾ ounces) cream-style corn**
- 1 **can (12 ounces) fat-free evaporated milk**
- ¾ **cup shredded reduced-fat cheddar cheese**
- ½ **cup sliced fresh mushrooms**
- ¼ **teaspoon pepper**
- 2 **tablespoons real bacon bits**

1. In a large saucepan, combine the broth, potatoes, carrots and onion. Bring to a boil. Reduce heat; simmer, uncovered, for 10-15 minutes or until vegetables are tender.

2. Add the corn, milk, cheese, mushrooms and pepper. Cook and stir 4-6 minutes longer or until heated through. Sprinkle with bacon.

Nutrition Facts: *1 cup equals 178 calories, 3 g fat (2 g saturated fat), 12 mg cholesterol, 554 mg sodium, 29 g carbohydrate, 2 g fiber, 11 g protein.* **Diabetic Exchanges:** *2 starch, ½ fat.*

Buffalo Turkey Burgers

There's nothing bland or boring about juicy turkey burgers spiced with chili powder and cumin. Celery and blue cheese salad dressing help tame the hot sauce in this recipe. For an even skinnier version, skip the bun and add sliced onion and chopped tomato.

—**MARY PAX-SHIPLEY** BEND, OREGON

PREP/TOTAL TIME: 25 MINUTES   **MAKES:** 4 SERVINGS

- 2 **tablespoons Louisiana-style hot sauce, divided**
- 2 **teaspoons ground cumin**
- 2 **teaspoons chili powder**
- 2 **garlic cloves, minced**
- ½ **teaspoon salt**
- ⅛ **teaspoon pepper**
- 1 **pound lean ground turkey**
- 4 **whole wheat hamburger buns, split**
- 1 **cup shredded lettuce**
- 2 **celery ribs, chopped**
- 2 **tablespoons fat-free blue cheese salad dressing**

1. In a large bowl, combine 1 tablespoon hot sauce, cumin, chili powder, garlic, salt and pepper. Crumble turkey over mixture and mix well. Shape into four patties.

2. In a large nonstick skillet coated with cooking spray, cook patties over medium heat for 4-5 minutes on each side or until a thermometer reads 165° and juices run clear.

3. Serve on buns with lettuce, celery, blue cheese dressing and remaining hot sauce.

Nutrition Facts: *1 burger equals 312 calories, 12 g fat (3 g saturated fat), 90 mg cholesterol, 734 mg sodium, 28 g carbohydrate, 5 g fiber, 24 g protein.* **Diabetic Exchanges:** *3 lean meat, 2 starch, ½ fat.*

Italian BLTs

Toasting Italian-style BLTs in a coating of crispy crumbs transforms ordinary sandwiches. They go from satisfying to spectacular!

—**JOYCE MOUL** YORK HAVEN, PENNSYLVANIA

PREP/TOTAL TIME: 20 MINUTES   **MAKES:** 2 SERVINGS

- 2 **turkey bacon strips, diced**
- 4 **slices Italian bread (½ inch thick)**
- 2 **slices reduced-fat provolone cheese**
- 2 **lettuce leaves**
- 1 **small tomato, sliced**
- 4 **teaspoons fat-free Italian salad dressing**
- ⅓ **cup panko (Japanese) bread crumbs**
  Butter-flavored cooking spray
- ½ **teaspoon olive oil**

1. In a small skillet, cook bacon over medium heat until crisp. Layer two bread slices with cheese, bacon, lettuce and tomato; top with remaining bread.

2. Brush outsides of sandwiches with salad dressing. Place bread crumbs in a shallow bowl. Coat sandwiches with bread crumbs; spray with butter-flavored cooking spray.

3. In a large skillet over medium heat, toast sandwiches in oil for 2-3 minutes on each side or until bread is lightly browned.

Nutrition Facts: *1 sandwich equals 272 calories, 11 g fat (4 g saturated fat), 25 mg cholesterol, 761 mg sodium, 30 g carbohydrate, 2 g fiber, 13 g protein.* **Diabetic Exchanges:** *2 starch, 2 lean meat.*

My husband enjoys my Pasta Fagioli Soup so much, he doesn't order it at restaurants anymore. The hearty blend of spinach, macaroni and Italian sausage makes a satisfying meal. —**BRENDA THOMAS** SPRINGFIELD, MISSOURI

Pasta Fagioli Soup

PREP/TOTAL TIME: 30 MINUTES
MAKES: 5 SERVINGS

- ½ pound Italian turkey sausage links, casings removed, crumbled
- 1 small onion, chopped
- 1½ teaspoons canola oil
- 1 garlic clove, minced
- 2 cups water
- 1 can (15½ ounces) great northern beans, rinsed and drained
- 1 can (14½ ounces) diced tomatoes, undrained
- 1 can (14½ ounces) reduced-sodium chicken broth
- ¾ cup uncooked elbow macaroni
- ¼ teaspoon pepper
- 1 cup fresh spinach leaves, cut into strips
- 5 teaspoons shredded Parmesan cheese

1. In a large saucepan, cook sausage over medium heat until no longer pink; drain and set aside. In the same pan, saute onion in oil until tender. Add garlic; saute 1 minute longer.

2. Add the water, beans, tomatoes, broth, macaroni and pepper; bring to a boil. Cook, uncovered, for 8-10 minutes or until macaroni is tender.

3. Reduce heat to low; stir in sausage and spinach. Cook for 2-3 minutes or until spinach is wilted. Garnish with Parmesan cheese.

Nutrition Facts: *1⅓ cups equals 228 calories, 7 g fat (1 g saturated fat), 29 mg cholesterol, 841 mg sodium, 27 g carbohydrate, 6 g fiber, 16 g protein.*

Chopping an Onion

To quickly chop an onion, peel and cut it in half from the root to the top. Leaving the root attached, place the flat side down on a work surface. Cut vertically through the onion, leaving the root end uncut.

Barbecue Beef Sandwiches

A quick, lip-smacking sauce gives these family-pleasing sandwiches lots of zip. I've had the recipe for years and have given it out so many times, I've lost count.

—SHARON ZAGAR GARDNER, ILLINOIS

PREP/TOTAL TIME: 30 MINUTES   **MAKES:** 6 SERVINGS

- 1½ pounds lean ground beef (90% lean)
- 2 celery ribs, sliced
- 1 large onion, chopped
- 1 can (8 ounces) tomato sauce
- ¼ cup ketchup
- 2 tablespoons brown sugar
- 2 tablespoons barbecue sauce
- 1 tablespoon prepared mustard
- 1 tablespoon Worcestershire sauce
- 6 hamburger buns, split

1. In a large nonstick skillet, cook the beef, celery and onion over medium heat until meat is no longer pink; drain.

2. Stir in the tomato sauce, ketchup, brown sugar, barbecue sauce, mustard and Worcestershire sauce. Bring to a boil. Reduce heat; simmer, uncovered, for 10-15 minutes to allow flavors to blend. Spoon ¾ cup onto each bun.

Nutrition Facts: *1 sandwich equals 348 calories, 11 g fat (4 g saturated fat), 56 mg cholesterol, 719 mg sodium, 35 g carbohydrate, 2 g fiber, 27 g protein.* **Diabetic Exchanges:** *3 lean meat, 2 starch.*

Lasagna Soup

Bring all the wonderful ingredients of classic lasagna together in a heartwarming, filling meal-in-a-bowl. You'll love it!

—**SHERYL OLENICK** DEMAREST, NEW JERSEY

PREP/TOTAL TIME: 30 MINUTES
MAKES: 8 SERVINGS

- 1 **pound lean ground beef (90% lean)**
- 1 **large green pepper, chopped**
- 1 **medium onion, chopped**
- 2 **garlic cloves, minced**
- 2 **cans (14½ ounces each) reduced-sodium beef broth**
- 2 **cans (14½ ounces each) diced tomatoes**
- 1 **can (8 ounces) tomato sauce**
- 1 **cup frozen corn**
- ¼ **cup tomato paste**
- 2 **teaspoons Italian seasoning**
- ¼ **teaspoon pepper**
- 2½ **cups uncooked spiral pasta**
- ½ **cup shredded Parmesan cheese**

1. In a large saucepan, cook the beef, green pepper and onion over medium heat until meat is no longer pink. Add garlic; cook 1 minute longer. Drain.

2. Stir in the broth, tomatoes, tomato sauce, corn, tomato paste, Italian seasoning and pepper. Bring to a boil. Stir in the spiral pasta. Return to a boil. Reduce heat; cover and simmer for 10-12 minutes or until pasta is tender. Sprinkle with cheese.

Nutrition Facts: *1⅓ cups equals 280 calories, 7 g fat (3 g saturated fat), 41 mg cholesterol, 572 mg sodium, 35 g carbohydrate, 4 g fiber, 20 g protein.*
Diabetic Exchanges: *2 lean meat, 2 vegetable, 1½ starch.*

top tip For handy premeasured tomato paste, freeze a 6-ounce can, open both ends and push the frozen paste out onto a cutting board. Cut the roll into six slices (approximately 1 tablespoon each). Quickly refreeze them in a resealable freezer bag to use as needed.

—**BOBBIE L.** KAPAA, HAWAII

Pastrami Deli Wraps

I sometimes add horseradish when I assemble these deli wraps for my husband. The spinach tortillas add a little extra flair.
—**NILA GRAHL** GURNEE, ILLINOIS

PREP/TOTAL TIME: 20 MINUTES **MAKES:** 4 SERVINGS

- ¼ cup reduced-fat spreadable cream cheese
- ¼ cup coarsely chopped roasted sweet red pepper
- 4 spinach tortillas (8 inches), warmed
- 4 lettuce leaves
- 4 slices deli pastrami
- 4 slices reduced-fat provolone cheese
- ¼ cup thinly sliced red onion
- 1 small sweet red pepper, julienned
- ½ cup chopped cucumber

1. Place cream cheese and roasted pepper in a small food processor. Cover and process until blended. Spread over tortillas. Layer with remaining ingredients; roll up. Secure with toothpicks.

Nutrition Facts: *1 wrap equals 271 calories, 10 g fat (4 g saturated fat), 29 mg cholesterol, 697 mg sodium, 29 g carbohydrate, 1 g fiber, 15 g protein.* **Diabetic Exchanges:** *2 medium-fat meat, 1½ starch, 1 vegetable, 1 fat.*

Family-Pleasing Sloppy Joes

My grandmother gave me her sloppy joe recipe years ago, and I made a few changes to give it a little more pizzazz.
—**JILL ZOSEL** SEATTLE, WASHINGTON

PREP/TOTAL TIME: 30 MINUTES **MAKES:** 6 SERVINGS

- 1 pound lean ground turkey
- ½ cup chopped onion
- 2 garlic cloves, minced
- 1 tablespoon sugar
- 1 tablespoon all-purpose flour
- ¼ teaspoon pepper
- 1 cup ketchup
- 1 tablespoon prepared mustard
- 1 tablespoon barbecue sauce
- 1 tablespoon Worcestershire sauce
- 6 sandwich buns, split

1. In a large nonstick skillet, cook the turkey and onion over medium heat until turkey is no longer pink; drain if necessary. Add garlic; cook for 1-2 minutes or until tender.

2. Stir in the sugar, flour and pepper. Add the ketchup, mustard, barbecue sauce and Worcestershire sauce. Bring to a boil. Reduce heat; cover and simmer for 5-10 minutes or until heated through. Serve on buns.

Nutrition Facts: *1 sandwich equals 388 calories, 11 g fat (4 g saturated fat), 60 mg cholesterol, 969 mg sodium, 52 g carbohydrate, 3 g fiber, 22 g protein.* **Diabetic Exchanges:** *3½ starch, 2 lean meat.*

Salsa Black Bean Burgers

Meatless meals can be terrific when hearty bean burgers are on the menu. Guacamole and sour cream make decadent toppings.

—JILL REICHARDT ST. LOUIS, MISSOURI

PREP/TOTAL TIME: 30 MINUTES **MAKES:** 4 SERVINGS

- 1 **can (15 ounces) black beans, rinsed and drained**
- ⅔ **cup dry bread crumbs**
- 1 **small tomato, seeded and finely chopped**
- 1 **jalapeno pepper, seeded and finely chopped**
- 1 **egg**
- 1 **teaspoon minced fresh cilantro**
- 1 **garlic clove, minced**
- 1 **tablespoon olive oil**
- 4 **whole wheat hamburger buns, split**
    Reduced-fat sour cream and guacamole, optional

1. Place beans in a food processor; cover and process until blended. Transfer to a large bowl. Add the bread crumbs, tomato, jalapeno, egg, cilantro and garlic. Mix until combined. Shape into four patties.

2. In a large nonstick skillet, cook patties in oil in batches over medium heat for 4-6 minutes on each side or until lightly browned. Serve on buns. Top with sour cream and guacamole if desired.

Editor's Note: *Wear disposable gloves when cutting hot peppers; the oils can burn skin. Avoid touching your face.*

Nutrition Facts: *1 burger (calculated without optional ingredients) equals 323 calories, 8 g fat (1 g saturated fat), 53 mg cholesterol, 557 mg sodium, 51 g carbohydrate, 9 g fiber, 13 g protein.*

Makeover Creamy Seafood Soup

Here's a slimmed-down version of a rich seafood soup that has only half the cholesterol, a fourth of the fat and half the calories of the original recipe. Go ahead—indulge guilt-free!

—MILDRED FASIG STEPHENS CITY, VIRGINIA

PREP/TOTAL TIME: 30 MINUTES **MAKES:** 6 SERVINGS

- ½ **pound uncooked medium shrimp, peeled and deveined**
- ½ **pound bay scallops**
- 2 **tablespoons butter, divided**
- 2 **celery ribs, thinly sliced**
- 1 **medium sweet red pepper, finely chopped**
- 1 **medium onion, finely chopped**
- ¼ **cup all-purpose flour**
- 2 **cups fat-free milk**
- 2 **cups half-and-half cream**
- ¼ **cup sherry or reduced-sodium chicken broth**
- 1 **tablespoon minced fresh thyme or 1 teaspoon dried thyme**
- ½ **teaspoon salt**
- ¼ **teaspoon cayenne pepper**
- ⅛ **teaspoon ground nutmeg**

1. In a Dutch oven, saute shrimp and scallops in 1 tablespoon butter until shrimp turn pink. Remove and set aside.

2. In the same pan, saute the celery, red pepper and onion in remaining butter until tender. Sprinkle with flour; stir until blended. Gradually stir in the remaining ingredients. Bring to a boil; cook and stir for 2 minutes or until thickened. Return seafood to the pan; heat through.

Nutrition Facts: *1 cup equals 274 calories, 13 g fat (8 g saturated fat), 120 mg cholesterol, 436 mg sodium, 16 g carbohydrate, 1 g fiber, 19 g protein.*

Hearty Vegetarian Chili

Rich and flavorful, this vegetarian chili is packed with portobello mushrooms, beans, sun-dried tomatoes and more. It's so delicious and satisfying, you'll fool any meat lover at the table.

—PAM IVBULS OMAHA, NEBRASKA

PREP/TOTAL TIME: 30 MINUTES
MAKES: 9 SERVINGS (2¼ QUARTS)

- 1¾ cups chopped baby portobello mushrooms
- 1 medium onion, finely chopped
- ½ cup chopped sun-dried tomatoes (not packed in oil)
- 2 tablespoons olive oil
- 2 garlic cloves, minced
- 1 package (12 ounces) frozen vegetarian meat crumbles
- 2 cans (16 ounces each) chili beans, undrained
- 2 cans (14½ ounces each) no-salt-added diced tomatoes
- ½ cup water
- ½ cup vegetable broth
- 4½ teaspoons chili powder
- 2 teaspoons brown sugar
- ½ teaspoon celery salt
- ½ teaspoon ground cumin
- 1 medium ripe avocado, peeled and finely chopped
- 9 tablespoons reduced-fat sour cream

1. In a Dutch oven, saute mushrooms, onion and sun-dried tomatoes in oil until tender. Add garlic; cook 1 minute longer. Add meat crumbles; heat through.

2. Stir in the chili beans, tomatoes, water, broth, chili powder, brown sugar, celery salt and cumin. Bring to a boil. Reduce heat; simmer, uncovered, for 10 minutes. Ladle chili into bowls. Top each with avocado and sour cream.

Editor's Note: *Vegetarian meat crumbles are a nutritious protein source made from soy. Look for them in the natural foods freezer section.*

Nutrition Facts: *1 cup equals 275 calories, 10 g fat (2 g saturated fat), 5 mg cholesterol, 768 mg sodium, 37 g carbohydrate, 12 g fiber, 17 g protein.* **Diabetic Exchanges:** *2 lean meat, 2 vegetable, 1½ starch, 1 fat.*

Makeover Cheesy Ham 'n' Potato Soup

What do you get when you combine chunks of lean ham, potatoes, fat-free milk and reduced-fat cheddar cheese? A better-for-you bowl of comfort food! Additional potatoes, along with dry milk powder, help create a thick, creamy texture.

—TASTE OF HOME TEST KITCHEN

PREP/TOTAL TIME: 30 MINUTES   **MAKES:** 7 SERVINGS

- 2¼ cups cubed potatoes
- 1½ cups water
- 1½ cups cubed fully cooked lean ham
- 1 large onion, chopped
- 2 teaspoons canola oil
- ¼ cup nonfat dry milk powder
- 3 tablespoons all-purpose flour
- ¼ teaspoon pepper
- 3 cups fat-free milk
- 1½ cups (6 ounces) finely shredded reduced-fat cheddar cheese
- 1 cup frozen broccoli florets, thawed and chopped

1. In a saucepan, bring potatoes and water to a boil. Cover and cook for 10-15 minutes or until tender. Drain, reserving 1 cup cooking liquid. In a blender or food processor, process reserved liquid and ¼ cup cooked potatoes until smooth; set aside. Set remaining potatoes aside.

2. In a large saucepan, saute the ham and onion in oil until the onion is tender. In a bowl, combine milk powder, flour, pepper, milk and processed potato mixture until smooth. Stir into ham and onion. Bring to a boil; cook and stir for 2 minutes or until thickened.

3. Reduce heat to low. Add the cheese, broccoli and reserved potatoes; cook and stir over low heat until cheese is melted and heated through. Serve immediately.

Nutrition Facts: *1 cup equals 228 calories, 8 g fat (4 g saturated fat), 36 mg cholesterol, 616 mg sodium, 21 g carbohydrate, 1 g fiber, 18 g protein.* **Diabetic Exchanges:** *2 lean meat, 1 starch, ½ fat-free milk.*

Makeover Cream of Tomato Soup

Although absolutely delicious and a surefire chill chaser, the original recipe for this soup had two major drawbacks—it was loaded with fat and sodium. This "makeover" version gives you the same creamy goodness but only half the fat and 367 fewer milligrams of sodium. For an extra treat, prepare the seasoned oyster crackers to sprinkle on top.

—LINDA PARKHURST BROOKLYN, MICHIGAN

PREP/TOTAL TIME: 30 MINUTES **MAKES:** 9 SERVINGS (3 CUPS CRACKERS)

- 1 can (14½ ounces) stewed tomatoes
- 4 ounces reduced-fat cream cheese, cubed
- 1 medium onion, chopped
- 2 tablespoons butter
- 2 garlic cloves, minced
- 3 cans (10¾ ounces each) reduced-sodium condensed tomato soup, undiluted
- 4 cans (5½ ounces each) reduced-sodium V8 juice
- 3 tablespoons tomato paste
- 1 cup fat-free half-and-half
- ½ teaspoon dried basil

SEASONED OYSTER CRACKERS
- 3 cups oyster crackers
- 2 tablespoons canola oil
- 1 tablespoon ranch salad dressing mix
- ½ teaspoon garlic powder
- ½ teaspoon dill weed
- 9 tablespoons shredded part-skim mozzarella cheese

1. In a food processor, combine stewed tomatoes and cream cheese; cover and process until smooth. Set aside.
2. In a large saucepan, saute onion in butter until crisp-tender. Add garlic; cook 1 minute longer. Whisk in tomato soup, V8 and tomato paste until blended. Gradually stir in cream cheese mixture, half-and-half and basil. Cook and stir until heated through (do not boil).
3. In a large bowl, combine the oyster crackers, oil, dressing mix, garlic powder and dill; toss to coat. Ladle soup into bowls; sprinkle with crackers and cheese.

Nutrition Facts: *1 cup soup with ⅓ cup oyster crackers equals 303 calories, 12 g fat (5 g saturated fat), 20 mg cholesterol, 893 mg sodium, 39 g carbohydrate, 3 g fiber, 8 g protein.*
Diabetic Exchanges: *2½ starch, 2 fat.*

Zesty Hamburger Soup

You won't get the mid-afternoon munchies when this filling burger-in-a-bowl is part of your lunch. Freeze the leftovers in small batches so you can enjoy them anytime.

—KELLY MILAN LAKE JACKSON, TEXAS

PREP/TOTAL TIME: 30 MINUTES
MAKES: 10 SERVINGS (3¾ QUARTS)

- 1 pound lean ground beef (90% lean)
- 2 cups sliced celery
- 1 cup chopped onion
- 2 teaspoons minced garlic
- 4 cups water
- 2 medium red potatoes, peeled and cubed
- 2 cups frozen corn
- 1½ cups uncooked small shell pasta
- 4 pickled jalapeno slices, chopped
- 4 cups V8 juice
- 2 cans (10 ounces each) diced tomatoes with green chilies
- 1 to 2 tablespoons sugar

1. In a Dutch oven, cook the beef, celery and onion over medium heat until the meat is no longer pink. Add garlic; cook 1 minute longer. Drain. Stir in the water, potatoes, corn, pasta and jalapeno.
2. Bring to a boil. Reduce heat; cover and simmer for 10-15 minutes or until the pasta is tender. Add the remaining ingredients; cook and stir until heated through.

Nutrition Facts: *1½ cups equals 222 calories, 5 g fat (2 g saturated fat), 28 mg cholesterol, 542 mg sodium, 33 g carbohydrate, 4 g fiber, 14 g protein.*
Diabetic Exchanges: *2 vegetable, 1½ starch, 1 lean meat.*

Storing Pasta

I store all my pastas in canning jars rather than the opened boxes. The pasta stays fresher, and the jars stack nicely, too, conserving pantry space. When I'm writing my grocery list, I just glance at the clear jars to see what I need.

—LAURIE S.
GETTYSBURG, PENNSYLVANIA

Chicken Sausage Gyros

PREP/TOTAL TIME: 20 MINUTES
MAKES: 4 SERVINGS

- 1 package (12 ounces) fully cooked spinach and feta chicken sausage links or flavor of your choice, cut into ¼-inch slices
- 1 cup (8 ounces) reduced-fat sour cream
- ¼ cup finely chopped cucumber
- 1½ teaspoons red wine vinegar
- 1½ teaspoons olive oil
- ½ teaspoon garlic powder
- 4 whole wheat pita breads (6 inches)
- 1 plum tomato, sliced
- ½ small onion, thinly sliced

1. In a large skillet coated with cooking spray, cook sausage over medium heat until heated through.

2. Meanwhile, in a small bowl, combine the sour cream, cucumber, vinegar, oil and garlic powder. Serve chicken sausage on pita breads with tomato, onion and cucumber sauce.

Nutrition Facts: *1 gyro with ¼ cup sauce equals 418 calories, 15 g fat (6 g saturated fat), 75 mg cholesterol, 873 mg sodium, 42 g carbohydrate, 5 g fiber, 27 g protein.*
Diabetic Exchanges: *3 starch, 3 lean meat, 1½ fat.*

Surprise your family after a busy day with this fast, filling meal in minutes. Casual yet hearty, the whole wheat pitas are packed with flavorful sausage and veggies.
—**KERRI GEORGE** BERNE, INDIANA

80

91

86

Sides, Salads & Breads

"My family loves this colorful Southwestern salad, and people always ask for the recipe when I bring it to potlucks. The spiced-up medley of crunchy veggies with beans is a winning combination."

GAIL PARK NEWPORT NEWS, VIRGINIA
about her recipe, Santa Fe Salad, on page 98

Black-Eyed Pea Salad

A homemade dressing spiced with cayenne pepper helps marry the flavors of this creamy salad. It's a popular contribution to spring luncheons or barbecue buffets in the summertime.

—**OLIVE FOEMMEL** CHILI, WISCONSIN

PREP/TOTAL TIME: 15 MINUTES   **MAKES:** 4 SERVINGS

- 1 can (15½ ounces) black-eyed peas, rinsed and drained
- 1 celery rib, chopped
- 1 tablespoon finely chopped onion
- 1 tablespoon canola oil
- 1 tablespoon cider vinegar
- 1 tablespoon reduced-fat mayonnaise
- ¼ teaspoon salt
   Dash cayenne pepper
- 1 medium tomato, chopped

1. In a large bowl, combine the peas, celery and onion. In a small bowl, whisk the oil, vinegar, mayonnaise, salt and cayenne. Stir into vegetable mixture. Cover and chill until serving. Stir in tomato just before serving.

Nutrition Facts: *¾ cup equals 133 calories, 5 g fat (trace saturated fat), 1 mg cholesterol, 321 mg sodium, 17 g carbohydrate, 3 g fiber, 6 g protein.* **Diabetic Exchanges:** *1 starch, 1 fat.*

Cheddar Dill Biscuits

My husband and I are always trying to eat in a healthful way, cutting fat and calories whenever possible. Reduced-fat biscuits are great for breakfast or paired with our entree for dinner.

—**CAROL BRALY** SOUTH FORK, COLORADO

PREP/TOTAL TIME: 30 MINUTES   **MAKES:** 1 DOZEN

- 2 cups all-purpose flour
- 2 teaspoons sugar
- 1 teaspoon dill weed
- ½ teaspoon baking soda
- ½ teaspoon cream of tartar
- ½ teaspoon salt
- ¼ cup cold butter, cubed
- ⅔ cup buttermilk
- ¼ cup egg substitute
- ½ cup shredded reduced-fat cheddar cheese

1. In a large bowl, combine the first six ingredients. Cut in butter until mixture resembles coarse crumbs. Combine buttermilk and egg substitute; stir into flour mixture just until moistened. Stir in cheese.

2. Turn onto a lightly floured surface; knead 8-10 times. Pat to ¾-in. thickness; cut with a floured 2½-in. biscuit cutter.

3. Place 1 in. apart on an ungreased baking sheet. Bake at 400° for 12-16 minutes or until golden brown. Serve warm.

Nutrition Facts: *1 biscuit equals 134 calories, 5 g fat (3 g saturated fat), 14 mg cholesterol, 245 mg sodium, 18 g carbohydrate, 1 g fiber, 4 g protein.* **Diabetic Exchanges:** *1 starch, 1 fat.*

Parmesan Sage Scones

PREP/TOTAL TIME: 25 MINUTES **MAKES:** 8 SCONES

- 2¼ cups biscuit/baking mix
- ¼ cup grated Parmesan cheese
- 1¾ teaspoons minced fresh sage
- ¼ teaspoon pepper
- ½ cup plus 1 tablespoon half-and-half cream, divided
- 8 fresh sage leaves

1. In a large bowl, combine the biscuit mix, cheese, minced sage and pepper. Stir in ½ cup cream. Turn onto a floured surface; knead 5 times.

2. Transfer dough to a baking sheet coated with cooking spray. Pat into a 6-in. circle. Cut into eight wedges, but do not separate. Brush remaining cream over dough. Press a sage leave onto the top of each wedge.

3. Bake at 375° for 10-15 minutes or until edges are golden brown. Serve warm.

Nutrition Facts: *1 scone equals 172 calories, 8 g fat (3 g saturated fat), 10 mg cholesterol, 480 mg sodium, 22 g carbohydrate, 1 g fiber, 4 g protein.*

❝The tops of these savory scones get dressed up with fresh sage leaves. Prepared with only a handful of basic ingredients, the delectable wedges are ideal alongside soup, pasta or even slices of oven-roasted turkey.❞

—TASTE OF HOME TEST KITCHEN

Southwest Iceberg Slaw

I often round out menus with a bowl of my south-of-the-border slaw. It's a cool, light and versatile side dish I created one day when I was trying to stretch my avocados. Friends give it rave reviews no matter what vegetables I toss into the mix!

—LEAH LYON ADA, OKLAHOMA

PREP/TOTAL TIME: 20 MINUTES **MAKES:** 6 SERVINGS

- ½ cup fat-free sour cream
- 3 tablespoons lime juice
- 2 tablespoons finely chopped onion
- 1 teaspoon finely chopped jalapeno pepper
- ¾ teaspoon salt
- ½ teaspoon pepper
- 6 cups shredded iceberg lettuce
- 1 cup cubed avocado
- ½ cup chopped plum tomatoes
- ¼ cup shredded carrot

1. In a small bowl, whisk the sour cream, lime juice, onion, jalapeno, salt and pepper. In a large bowl, combine the lettuce, avocado, tomatoes and carrot. Pour dressing over salad; toss to coat.

Editor's Note: *Wear disposable gloves when cutting hot peppers; the oils can burn skin. Avoid touching your face.*

Nutrition Facts: *1 cup equals 83 calories, 4 g fat (1 g saturated fat), 3 mg cholesterol, 322 mg sodium, 10 g carbohydrate, 3 g fiber, 3 g protein.* **Diabetic Exchanges:** *1 vegetable, 1 fat.*

top tip Try substituting other fresh vegetables in Southwest Iceberg Slaw (recipe above) or adding low-fat Mexican panela cheese.

Pear Cottage Cheese Salad

Perfect anytime, this quick-fix salad makes a great pack-along lunch. Plus, it requires just five simple ingredients.

—JEANNIE THOMAS DRY RIDGE, KENTUCKY

PREP/TOTAL TIME: 10 MINUTES
MAKES: 6 SERVINGS

- 2 **cups (16 ounces) 2% cottage cheese**
- 2 **medium pears, chopped**
- 2 **celery ribs, chopped**
- ⅓ **cup chopped pecans**
- ½ **teaspoon ground ginger**

1. In a large bowl, combine all ingredients. Chill until serving.

Nutrition Facts: ⅔ cup equals 135 calories, 6 g fat (1 g saturated fat), 9 mg cholesterol, 255 mg sodium, 14 g carbohydrate, 3 g fiber, 8 g protein. **Diabetic Exchanges:** 1 lean meat, 1 fat, ½ fruit.

Fettuccine with Asparagus and Peas

I discovered my fettuccine-and-veggies recipe years ago, and it's been a crowd pleaser ever since. I often prepare it using healthier-for-you whole wheat pasta.

—VICKI KAMSTRA SPOKANE, WASHINGTON

PREP/TOTAL TIME: 30 MINUTES **MAKES:** 6 SERVINGS

- 8 **ounces uncooked fettuccine**
- 2 **medium leeks (white portion only), sliced**
- 1 **tablespoon olive oil**
- 1 **pound fresh asparagus, trimmed and cut into 1-inch pieces**
- 2 **garlic cloves, minced**
- 1 **cup frozen peas, thawed**
- ½ **teaspoon salt**
- ¼ **teaspoon pepper**
- ½ **cup part-skim ricotta cheese**
- ¼ **cup plus 6 teaspoons grated Parmesan cheese, divided**
- 2 **tablespoons lemon juice**
- 1 **tablespoon grated lemon peel**

1. Cook fettuccine according to package directions. Meanwhile, in a large nonstick skillet coated with cooking spray, saute leeks in oil for 1 minute. Add asparagus and garlic; saute until asparagus is crisp-tender. Stir in the peas, salt and pepper.

2. Drain fettuccine, reserving ½ cup cooking liquid. Place ricotta cheese in a small bowl; whisk in reserved cooking liquid. Whisk in ¼ cup Parmesan cheese, lemon juice and peel. Add to the skillet; heat through.

3. Add fettuccine; toss to coat. Sprinkle with remaining Parmesan cheese.

Nutrition Facts: 1⅓ cups equals 250 calories, 7 g fat (2 g saturated fat), 10 mg cholesterol, 363 mg sodium, 38 g carbohydrate, 4 g fiber, 12 g protein. **Diabetic Exchanges:** 2 starch, 1 vegetable, 1 fat.

top tip Purchase pears that are firm, fragrant and free of blemishes and soft spots. To ripen pears, place them in a paper bag at room temperature for several days. When the pears give in slightly to pressure, store them in the refrigerator. To prevent pear slices from discoloring, toss them with a little lemon juice. Pears used for cooking should be a little more firm. Before cooking, use a vegetable peeler or paring knife to remove the skin, which turns dark and tough when exposed to heat. One pound of pears equals about 3 medium or 3 cups sliced.

Green Onion Biscuits

The zippy flavor of green onions comes through in these no-fuss but yummy drop biscuits. Featuring a crusty exterior and tender interior, they're best right out of the oven.

—TASTE OF HOME TEST KITCHEN

PREP/TOTAL TIME: 25 MINUTES **MAKES:** 16 BISCUITS

- 2 cups all-purpose flour
- 1 teaspoon baking powder
- ½ teaspoon salt
- ¼ teaspoon baking soda
- ¼ teaspoon onion powder
- 1 cup buttermilk
- ½ cup finely chopped green onions
- 3 tablespoons canola oil
  Refrigerated butter-flavored spray

1. In a large bowl, combine the first five ingredients. Combine the buttermilk, onions and oil; stir into dry ingredients just until moistened.

2. Drop by heaping teaspoonfuls 2 in. apart onto baking sheets coated with cooking spray. Spritz the tops with butter-flavored spray. Bake at 400° for 14-18 minutes or until golden brown. Serve warm.

Nutrition Facts: *1 biscuit equals 85 calories, 3 g fat (trace saturated fat), 1 mg cholesterol, 124 mg sodium, 12 g carbohydrate, 1 g fiber, 2 g protein.*

Honey-Orange Broccoli Slaw

When you need coleslaw quickly, look here. Honey, citrus, raisins and almonds all add up to a special yet light delight.

—DEBBIE CASSAR ROCKFORD, MICHIGAN

PREP/TOTAL TIME: 15 MINUTES **MAKES:** 6 SERVINGS

- 1 package (12 ounces) broccoli coleslaw mix
- ⅓ cup sliced almonds
- ⅓ cup raisins
- 2 to 3 tablespoons honey
- 2 tablespoons olive oil
- 2 tablespoons orange juice
- 4 teaspoons grated orange peel
- ¼ teaspoon salt

1. In a large bowl, combine the coleslaw mix, almonds and raisins. In a small bowl, whisk the remaining ingredients. Pour over salad; toss to coat.

Nutrition Facts: *⅔ cup equals 136 calories, 7 g fat (1 g saturated fat), 0 cholesterol, 103 mg sodium, 18 g carbohydrate, 3 g fiber, 3 g protein.* **Diabetic Exchanges:** *1½ fat, 1 starch.*

Savory 'n' Saucy Baked Beans

PREP/TOTAL TIME: 25 MINUTES   **MAKES:** 6 SERVINGS

- ½ cup chopped onion
- ½ cup chopped green pepper
- ½ cup chopped celery
- 1 can (28 ounces) vegetarian baked beans
- 1 can (14½ ounces) diced tomatoes, drained
- ½ teaspoon pepper
- ¼ teaspoon salt
- ¼ teaspoon garlic powder

1. In a large saucepan coated with cooking spray, cook the onion, green pepper and celery for 3 minutes or until tender. Stir in beans, tomatoes, pepper, salt and garlic powder. Bring to a boil. Reduce heat; simmer, uncovered, for 10-15 minutes.

Nutrition Facts: ¾ cup equals 148 calories, 1 g fat (trace saturated fat), 0 cholesterol, 648 mg sodium, 34 g carbohydrate, 7 g fiber, 7 g protein.

> ❝I dress up store-bought baked beans in a jiffy using green pepper, onion, celery and canned tomatoes. With just a hint of sweetness and a touch of garlic, this simple side dish is always a hit at potlucks and parties.❞
>
> —**A. G. STRICKLAND** MARIETTA, GEORGIA

Crunchy Apple Salad

If you're looking for a light but luscious fruit salad, look no further! The yummy dressing and crunchy walnuts make it special.

—**KATHY ARMSTRONG** POST FALLS, IDAHO

PREP/TOTAL TIME: 15 MINUTES   **MAKES:** 5 SERVINGS

- 6 tablespoons fat-free sugar-free vanilla yogurt
- 6 tablespoons reduced-fat whipped topping
- ¼ teaspoon plus ⅛ teaspoon ground cinnamon, divided
- 2 medium red apples, chopped
- 1 large Granny Smith apple, chopped
- ¼ cup dried cranberries
- 2 tablespoons chopped walnuts

1. In a large bowl, combine the yogurt, whipped topping and ¼ teaspoon cinnamon. Add apples and cranberries; toss to coat. Refrigerate until serving. Sprinkle with walnuts and remaining cinnamon before serving.

Nutrition Facts: ¾ cup equals 109 calories, 3 g fat (1 g saturated fat), trace cholesterol, 12 mg sodium, 22 g carbohydrate, 3 g fiber, 2 g protein. **Diabetic Exchanges:** 1 fruit, ½ starch, ½ fat.

Beans & Spinach

One of our favorite appetizers at a local restaurant is made with white beans and escarole. It's virtually impossible to find escarole where we live, so we tried substituting baby spinach—and were pleasantly surprised by the result. Enjoy!

—**PATRICK AND HELEN REDDY** WILMINGTON, NORTH CAROLINA

PREP/TOTAL TIME: 25 MINUTES   **MAKES:** 6 SERVINGS

- 4 **garlic cloves, sliced**
- 2 **tablespoons olive oil**
- 2 **large onions, chopped**
- 1 **pound fresh baby spinach**
- 1 **can (15 ounces) white kidney or cannellini beans, rinsed and drained**
- ½ **cup white wine or reduced-sodium chicken broth**
- ¾ **teaspoon salt**
- ¼ **teaspoon pepper**

1. In a large nonstick skillet, saute garlic in oil until tender. Remove garlic and discard. Add onions to pan; saute until crisp-tender.

2. Stir in the remaining ingredients. Cook and stir over medium heat for 10-12 minutes or until spinach is wilted. Serve with a slotted spoon.

Nutrition Facts: ¾ cup equals 138 calories, 5 g fat (1 g saturated fat), 0 cholesterol, 446 mg sodium, 17 g carbohydrate, 5 g fiber, 5 g protein. **Diabetic Exchanges:** 2 vegetable, 1 fat, ½ starch.

Speedy Spanish Rice

Mexican food is big with just about everyone in our family. One of my nephews loves Spanish rice so much that he always requests it as part of his special birthday dinner.

—**ANGIE RORICK** FORT WAYNE, INDIANA

PREP/TOTAL TIME: 25 MINUTES   **MAKES:** 4 SERVINGS

- 1½ **cups uncooked instant brown rice**
- 1 **medium onion, chopped**
- 1 **small green pepper, chopped**
- 1 **tablespoon butter**
- 1 **garlic clove, minced**
- 1½ **cups water**
- 1 **tablespoon minced fresh cilantro**
- 2 **teaspoons ground cumin**
- 1½ **teaspoons chicken bouillon granules**
- ¼ **teaspoon pepper**
- 1 **cup picante sauce**

1. In a large nonstick skillet, saute the rice, onion and green pepper in butter until rice is lightly browned and vegetables are crisp-tender. Add garlic; cook 1 minute longer. Stir in the water, cilantro, cumin, bouillon and pepper; bring to a boil. Reduce heat; cover and simmer for 5 minutes.

2. Remove from the heat; let stand for 5 minutes. Fluff with a fork. Stir in picante sauce.

Nutrition Facts: ¾ cup equals 201 calories, 4 g fat (2 g saturated fat), 8 mg cholesterol, 615 mg sodium, 35 g carbohydrate, 3 g fiber, 4 g protein. **Diabetic Exchanges:** 2 starch, 1 vegetable, 1 fat.

Italian Broccoli with Peppers

PREP/TOTAL TIME: 20 MINUTES
MAKES: 6 SERVINGS

- 6 cups water
- 4 cups fresh broccoli florets
- 1 medium sweet red pepper, julienned
- 1 medium sweet yellow pepper, julienned
- 1 tablespoon olive oil
- 1 garlic clove, minced
- 1 teaspoon dried oregano
- ½ teaspoon salt
- ¼ teaspoon pepper
- 1 medium ripe tomato, cut into wedges and seeded
- 1 tablespoon grated Parmesan cheese

1. In a large saucepan, bring the water to a boil. Add the broccoli; cover and boil for 3 minutes. Drain and immediately place the broccoli in ice water. Drain and pat dry.

2. In a large nonstick skillet, saute peppers in oil for 3 minutes or until crisp-tender. Add the broccoli, garlic, oregano, salt and pepper; cook 2 minutes longer. Add the tomato; heat through. Sprinkle with cheese.

Nutrition Facts: *¾ cup equals 55 calories, 3 g fat (1 g saturated fat), 1 mg cholesterol, 228 mg sodium, 7 g carbohydrate, 2 g fiber, 2 g protein.* **Diabetic Exchanges:** *1 vegetable, ½ fat.*

❝My husband, Larry, always uses fresh ingredients when he prepares his ever-popular O'Larry's Skillet Potatoes. The zippy, spiced spuds have colorful bits of red pepper.❞

—KERRY BARNETT-AMUNDSON

OCEAN PARK, WASHINGTON

O'Larry's Skillet Potatoes

PREP/TOTAL TIME: 30 MINUTES
MAKES: 10 SERVINGS

- 2 **pounds potatoes, cut into ½-inch cubes**
- 1 **medium onion, finely chopped**
- 1 **medium sweet red pepper, chopped**
- 1 **teaspoon Caribbean jerk seasoning**
- 1 **teaspoon salt**
- ¼ **cup olive oil**
- 2 **garlic cloves, minced**

1. Place potatoes in a large saucepan and cover with water. Bring to a boil. Reduce heat; cover and simmer for 5-10 minutes or until almost tender. Drain.

2. In a large skillet, saute the potatoes, onion, red pepper, jerk seasoning and salt in oil until potatoes are golden brown and vegetables are tender. Add garlic; cook 1 minute longer.

Nutrition Facts: *¾ cup equals 129 calories, 6 g fat (1 g saturated fat), 0 cholesterol, 271 mg sodium, 19 g carbohydrate, 2 g fiber, 2 g protein.*
Diabetic Exchanges: *1½ fat, 1 starch.*

Snow Pea & Carrot Saute

With bright carrot strips and snow peas, this honey-sweetened medley makes a wonderful side dish for any meal. Short on time? Purchase matchstick carrots at the grocery store.

—TASTE OF HOME TEST KITCHEN

PREP/TOTAL TIME: 20 MINUTES **MAKES:** 5 SERVINGS

- 1 **pound fresh snow peas**
- 1 **tablespoon butter**
- 2 **medium carrots, julienned**
- 1 **garlic clove, minced**
- 3 **tablespoons honey**
- ¼ **teaspoon salt**
- ⅛ **teaspoon pepper**

1. In a large skillet, saute the snow peas in butter for 3 minutes. Add the carrots and garlic; saute 1-2 minutes longer or until vegetables are crisp-tender. Add remaining ingredients; heat through.

Nutrition Facts: *¾ cup equals 108 calories, 3 g fat (1 g saturated fat), 6 mg cholesterol, 155 mg sodium, 20 g carbohydrate, 3 g fiber, 3 g protein.* **Diabetic Exchanges:** *2 vegetable, ½ starch.*

Maple Syrup Corn Bread

Here's a good-old New England recipe. Flavored with a hint of maple syrup, the golden corn bread makes the perfect companion for spicy chili or stew.

—ROGER HICKUM
PLYMOUTH, NEW HAMPSHIRE

PREP/TOTAL TIME: 30 MINUTES
MAKES: 12 SERVINGS

- 1¼ cups all-purpose flour
- 1 cup cornmeal
- 2 teaspoons baking powder
- 1 teaspoon salt
- 1 egg
- ¾ cup fat-free milk
- ½ cup maple syrup
- 3 tablespoons butter, melted

1. In a large bowl, combine the flour, cornmeal, baking powder and salt. In a small bowl, whisk together the egg, milk, syrup and butter; stir into dry ingredients just until moistened.
2. Pour into a 9-in. square baking pan coated with cooking spray. Bake at 400° for 15-20 minutes or until a toothpick inserted near the center comes out clean. Serve warm.

Nutrition Facts: *1 piece equals 161 calories, 4 g fat (2 g saturated fat), 26 mg cholesterol, 307 mg sodium, 29 g carbohydrate, 1 g fiber, 3 g protein.* **Diabetic Exchanges:** *2 starch, ½ fat.*

Strawberry Salad with Mojito Vinaigrette

Mojitos are a fun summertime drink and were the inspiration for this refreshing side salad. I didn't include any rum, but it certainly could be added to the vinaigrette.

—DONNA MARIE RYAN TOPSFIELD, MASSACHUSETTS

PREP/TOTAL TIME: 20 MINUTES **MAKES:** 5 SERVINGS

- ¼ cup white wine vinegar
- 4 fresh strawberries, hulled
- 2 tablespoons water
- 2 tablespoons lime juice
- 2 tablespoons coarsely chopped fresh mint
- 2 tablespoons honey
- ¼ teaspoon salt
  Dash pepper
- 2 tablespoons olive oil

SALAD
- 1 package (5 ounces) spring mix salad greens
- 2 cups fresh strawberries, hulled and sliced
- 1 small red onion, thinly sliced
- 3 ounces fresh goat cheese, crumbled
- ¼ cup chopped walnuts

1. In a blender, combine the first eight ingredients. While processing, gradually add oil in a steady stream. Set aside.
2. Divide salad greens among five salad plates; top with strawberries, onion, cheese and walnuts. Drizzle with vinaigrette.

Nutrition Facts: *1½ cups salad with 2 tablespoons vinaigrette equals 178 calories, 11 g fat (3 g saturated fat), 11 mg cholesterol, 195 mg sodium, 17 g carbohydrate, 3 g fiber, 4 g protein.* **Diabetic Exchanges:** *2 fat, 1 vegetable, ½ starch, ½ fruit.*

Did you know?

Nearly all baking powder available today is double-acting baking powder. This means it contains two different types of acids that react at different times. The first acid will react by creating gases when mixed with the liquid in the recipe. The second type will react by creating gases when the batter is exposed to oven heat. All of the recipes in this book were tested with double-acting baking powder, so use exactly the amount listed in the recipe.

Cheese Straws

PREP/TOTAL TIME: 30 MINUTES
MAKES: 4 DOZEN

- 1 **cup all-purpose flour**
- 1½ **teaspoons baking powder**
- ½ **teaspoon salt**
- ½ **cup shredded reduced-fat cheddar cheese**
- 2 **tablespoons plus 1½ teaspoons cold butter**
- ⅓ **cup fat-free milk**
- 2 **teaspoons paprika**

1. In a small bowl, combine the flour, baking powder and salt; stir in cheddar cheese. Cut in butter until the mixture resembles coarse crumbs. Gradually add milk, tossing with a fork until dough forms a ball.

2. On a lightly floured surface, roll dough into a 12-in. square. Cut in half lengthwise; cut each half widthwise into ½-in. strips. Sprinkle with paprika.

3. Place 1 in. apart on baking sheets coated with cooking spray. Bake at 425° for 6-8 minutes or until golden brown. Serve warm.

Zippy Cheese Straws: *Omit paprika. Add ¼ teaspoon cayenne pepper to flour mixture. Proceed as directed.*

Nutrition Facts: *1 cheese straw equals 19 calories, 1 g fat (1 g saturated fat), 2 mg cholesterol, 52 mg sodium, 2 g carbohydrate, trace fiber, 1 g protein.*

It's hard to eat just one of these cheesy, buttery treats. They make a fun appetizer or accompaniment for soups or salads. Twist the sticks to create an extra-fancy look.
—**ANN NACE** PERKASIE, PENNSYLVANIA

top tip
Preheating the Oven

It is important to preheat your oven before baking and roasting. Baked items depend on the correct oven temperature to help them rise and cook properly. All *Taste of Home* recipes are tested in preheated ovens. Place the oven racks at the proper levels first, then set the temperature stated in the recipe.

Sweet Potato Biscuits

Craving made-from-scratch biscuits? Whip up a batch in only 30 minutes and savor tender, golden goodies warm from the oven. Each bite bursts with flavor from sweet potatoes and honey.

—**DELYNNE RUTLEDGE** LOVELADY, TEXAS

PREP/TOTAL TIME: 30 MINUTES **MAKES:** 17 BISCUITS

- 2 **cups all-purpose flour**
- ⅓ **cup yellow cornmeal**
- 2½ **teaspoons baking powder**
- ½ **teaspoon salt**
- ⅓ **cup cold butter, cubed**
- 1 **cup mashed sweet potato**
- ½ **cup fat-free milk**
- 2 **tablespoons honey**

1. In a large bowl, combine the flour, cornmeal, baking powder and salt. Cut in butter until mixture resembles coarse crumbs. Stir in the sweet potato, milk and honey just until moistened. Turn onto a lightly floured surface; knead 5-8 times. Pat out to ½-in. thickness; cut with a floured 2-in. biscuit cutter.
2. Place 2 in. apart on an ungreased baking sheet. Bake at 400° for 14-18 minutes or until lightly browned. Serve warm.

Nutrition Facts: *1 biscuit equals 120 calories, 4 g fat (2 g saturated fat), 10 mg cholesterol, 162 mg sodium, 19 g carbohydrate, 1 g fiber, 2 g protein.* **Diabetic Exchanges:** *1 starch, 1 fat.*

Baked Veggie Chips

Try roasting colorful root vegetables as a side dish or snack. These perfectly seasoned chips are easy to fix and so tasty, they don't need dip. You'll never want store-bought versions again!

—**CHRISTINE SCHENHER** SAN CLEMENTE, CALIFORNIA

PREP/TOTAL TIME: 30 MINUTES **MAKES:** 7 SERVINGS

- ½ **pound fresh beets (about 2 medium)**
- 1 **medium potato**
- 1 **medium sweet potato**
- 1 **medium parsnip**
- 2 **tablespoons canola oil**
- 2 **tablespoons grated Parmesan cheese**
- ½ **teaspoon salt**
- ½ **teaspoon garlic powder**
- ½ **teaspoon dried oregano**
  Dash pepper

1. Peel vegetables and cut into ⅛-inch slices. Place in a large bowl. Drizzle with oil. Combine the remaining ingredients; sprinkle over vegetables and toss to coat.
2. Arrange in a single layer on racks in two ungreased 15-in. x 10-in. x 1-in. baking pans. Bake at 375° for 15-20 minutes or until golden brown, turning once.

Nutrition Facts: *½ cup equals 108 calories, 5 g fat (1 g saturated fat), 1 mg cholesterol, 220 mg sodium, 15 g carbohydrate, 2 g fiber, 2 g protein.* **Diabetic Exchanges:** *1 starch, 1 fat.*

Santa Fe Salad

My family loves this colorful Southwestern salad, and people always ask for the recipe when I bring it to potlucks. The spiced-up medley of crunchy vegetables with beans is a winning combination.

—**GAIL PARK** NEWPORT NEWS, VIRGINIA

PREP/TOTAL TIME: 30 MINUTES
MAKES: 10 SERVINGS

- 2½ cups cut fresh green beans
- 1 cup minced fresh cilantro
- ¼ cup fat-free sour cream
- 2 tablespoons lime juice
- 2 tablespoons balsamic vinegar
- 2 garlic cloves, minced
- 1½ teaspoons ground cumin
- ¼ teaspoon salt
  Dash cayenne pepper
- 2 cups frozen corn, thawed
- 1 can (15 ounces) pinto beans, rinsed and drained
- 1 can (15 ounces) black beans, rinsed and drained
- 1 small sweet red pepper, finely chopped
- 1 small red onion, chopped
- 1 can (4 ounces) chopped green chilies
- 1 can (2¼ ounces) sliced ripe olives, drained
- ½ cup shredded reduced-fat cheddar cheese

1. Place the green beans in a small saucepan and cover with water. Bring to a boil; cover and cook for 3-5 minutes or until crisp-tender. Drain and immediately place beans in ice water. Drain and pat dry.

2. For the dressing, in a small bowl, combine the cilantro, sour cream, lime juice, vinegar, garlic, cumin, salt and cayenne pepper.

3. In a large bowl, combine the green beans, corn, pinto beans, black beans, red pepper, onion, chilies and olives. Sprinkle with cheese. Pour the dressing over salad; toss gently to coat. Cover and refrigerate until serving.

Nutrition Facts: *¾ cup equals 151 calories, 2 g fat (1 g saturated fat), 5 mg cholesterol, 374 mg sodium, 26 g carbohydrate, 6 g fiber, 8 g protein.* **Diabetic Exchanges:** *1½ starch, ½ fat.*

Flavorful Summer Squash

I like to flavor sauteed yellow squash and zucchini with garlic, red onion and dried herbs for a bright side dish full of garden-fresh goodness. Sprinkled with a little mozzarella cheese, it's wonderful with a light main course in summer or any time at all.

—**ANDREA YACYK** BRIGANTINE, NEW JERSEY

PREP/TOTAL TIME: 25 MINUTES **MAKES:** 6 SERVINGS

- 3 medium yellow summer squash, sliced
- 2 medium zucchini, sliced
- 1 medium red onion, sliced and separated into rings
- 1 teaspoon minced garlic
- 1 tablespoon olive oil
- 1 teaspoon dried parsley flakes
- 1 teaspoon dried basil
- ½ teaspoon dried oregano
- ½ teaspoon dried thyme
- ¼ teaspoon salt
- ½ cup shredded part-skim mozzarella cheese

1. In a large nonstick skillet, saute the yellow squash, zucchini, onion and garlic in oil until crisp-tender, stirring occasionally.

2. Stir in the parsley, basil, oregano, thyme and salt. Remove from the heat. Sprinkle with cheese; cover and let stand until cheese is melted.

Nutrition Facts: *⅔ cup equals 83 calories, 4 g fat (1 g saturated fat), 5 mg cholesterol, 147 mg sodium, 9 g carbohydrate, 3 g fiber, 5 g protein.* **Diabetic Exchanges:** *2 vegetable, ½ fat.*

top tip

Trimming Green Beans
To trim fresh green beans quickly, simply line up the ends of the beans, then use a chef's knife to slice several at a time.

Creamy Noodles

Pasta lovers can't get enough of this creamy spaghetti. I like it best with grilled chicken, but it works well with just about any entree.

—BRENDA NOLEN FOLSOM, LOUISIANA

PREP/TOTAL TIME: 25 MINUTES   **MAKES:** 6 SERVINGS

- 8   **ounces uncooked thin spaghetti**
- 3   **garlic cloves, minced**
- 3   **tablespoons butter, divided**
- 6   **ounces fat-free cream cheese, cubed**
- 3   **tablespoons reduced-fat sour cream**
- 3   **tablespoons fat-free milk**
- ¾   **teaspoon salt**
- ½   **teaspoon onion powder**
- ¼   **teaspoon Cajun seasoning**
- ¼   **teaspoon white pepper**
- 4½ **teaspoons minced fresh parsley**

1. Cook the spaghetti according to the package directions. Meanwhile, in a large saucepan, saute garlic in 1 tablespoon butter for 1 minute. Add the cream cheese, sour cream, milk, salt, onion powder, Cajun seasoning, pepper and remaining butter. Cook and stir over low heat just until smooth (do not boil). Remove from the heat.

2. Drain the spaghetti; toss with the cream sauce. Sprinkle with parsley.

Nutrition Facts: *1 cup equals 234 calories, 7 g fat (4 g saturated fat), 20 mg cholesterol, 547 mg sodium, 32 g carbohydrate, 1 g fiber, 10 g protein.* **Diabetic Exchanges:** *2 starch, 1 lean meat, 1 fat.*

Roasted Parmesan Green Beans

I've never been a big fan of the traditional green bean casserole, so I came up with an oven-roasted alternative. It's so quick and easy to prepare, I add it to a wide variety of menus.

—CHRISTIE LADD MECHANICSBURG, PENNSYLVANIA

PREP/TOTAL TIME: 30 MINUTES   **MAKES:** 4 SERVINGS

- 1   **pound fresh green beans, trimmed**
- 2   **teaspoons olive oil**
- 1½ **teaspoons Greek seasoning**
- 2   **tablespoons shredded Parmesan cheese**

1. Place the green beans in a 15-in. x 10-in. x 1-in. baking pan coated with cooking spray. Drizzle with oil. Sprinkle with seasoning; stir to coat.

2. Bake, uncovered, at 425° for 12-15 minutes or until beans are tender, stirring once. Sprinkle with cheese.

Nutrition Facts: *⅔ cup equals 61 calories, 3 g fat (1 g saturated fat), 2 mg cholesterol, 410 mg sodium, 7 g carbohydrate, 3 g fiber, 3 g protein.* **Diabetic Exchanges:** *1 vegetable, ½ fat.*

> "Fun and flavorful, these rustic veggie cakes make a wonderfully versatile side dish. They're also the perfect solution when you have too much garden zucchini!"
>
> —DIANA JOHNSON AUBURN, WASHINGTON

Feta Zucchini Pancakes

PREP/TOTAL TIME: 25 MINUTES
MAKES: 8 PANCAKES

- 1 cup shredded zucchini
- ¼ cup panko (Japanese) bread crumbs
- 2 green onions, chopped
- 1 egg
- 3 tablespoons minced fresh parsley
- 1 tablespoon snipped fresh dill
- 1 garlic clove, minced
- ¼ cup crumbled feta cheese
- 3 teaspoons olive oil, divided

1. In a sieve or colander, drain zucchini, squeezing to remove excess liquid. Pat dry. In a small bowl, combine the zucchini, bread crumbs, onions, egg, parsley, dill, garlic and cheese.

2. Heat 1½ teaspoons oil in a large nonstick skillet over medium-low heat. Drop batter by heaping tablespoonfuls into oil; press lightly to flatten. Fry in batches until golden brown on both sides, using remaining oil as needed.

Nutrition Facts: *2 pancakes equals 91 calories, 6 g fat (2 g saturated fat), 57 mg cholesterol, 104 mg sodium, 5 g carbohydrate, 1 g fiber, 4 g protein.* **Diabetic Exchanges:** *1 fat, ½ starch.*

top tip

Zucchini from the Freezer

To freeze shredded zucchini to use later, first steam the shredded zucchini for 1 to 2 minutes or until it is translucent, then drain well. Pack it in measured amounts into heavy-duty resealable bags or freezer containers, leaving ½ inch of space at the top. Allow the steamed zucchini to cool, then seal the bags or containers and freeze. If the zucchini is watery when thawed, drain it before using it in your recipe.

Corn & Pepper Orzo

PREP/TOTAL TIME: 30 MINUTES
MAKES: 6 SERVINGS

- ¾ cup uncooked orzo pasta
- 1 large sweet red pepper, chopped
- 1 medium onion, chopped
- 1 tablespoon olive oil
- 2 cups frozen corn, thawed
- 2 teaspoons Italian seasoning
- ⅛ teaspoon salt
- ⅛ teaspoon pepper

1. Cook pasta according to package directions.

2. Meanwhile, in a large nonstick skillet coated with cooking spray, saute red pepper and onion in oil for 2 minutes. Add the corn, Italian seasoning, salt and pepper; cook and stir until vegetables are tender. Drain pasta; stir into the pan.

Nutrition Facts: ¾ cup equals 178 calories, 3 g fat (trace saturated fat), 0 cholesterol, 55 mg sodium, 34 g carbohydrate, 3 g fiber, 6 g protein. **Diabetic Exchanges:** 2 starch, ½ fat.

Savor a fragrant side dish that packs in flavor but keeps out extra fat, calories and sodium. Italian seasoning lends zip to the mix of corn, red pepper, orzo pasta and onion.
—**ANGELA HANKS** ST. ALBANS, WEST VIRGINIA

❓ Did you know?

Because orzo pasta has a mild flavor and a shape that's similar to rice, it can be used as a substitute for rice in many recipes. Ounce for ounce, rice and orzo also contain similar amounts of fat, sugar, carbohydrates and even sodium.

Seafood & Shells Salad

My family often asks for this refreshing, creamy salad during the summer months. It's become a real favorite.

—ROSALEE RAY LANSING, MICHIGAN

PREP/TOTAL TIME: 30 MINUTES **MAKES:** 13 SERVINGS

- 2 cups uncooked small pasta shells
- 3 packages (8 ounces each) imitation crabmeat
- 1 pound cooked small shrimp, peeled and deveined
- ¼ cup finely chopped sweet onion
- ¼ cup finely chopped celery
- 3 tablespoons each finely chopped green, sweet red and yellow pepper
- 3 tablespoons minced fresh parsley
- 2 tablespoons snipped fresh dill or 2 teaspoons dill weed
- 1½ cups fat-free mayonnaise
- 2 tablespoons lemon juice
- ¼ teaspoon salt
- ¼ teaspoon pepper

1. Cook pasta according to the package directions; drain and rinse in cold water.

2. In a large bowl, combine the crab, shrimp, onion, celery, peppers, parsley and dill. Stir in pasta. In a small bowl, combine the mayonnaise, lemon juice, salt and pepper. Pour over salad and toss to coat. Chill until serving.

Nutrition Facts: ¾ cup equals 164 calories, 2 g fat (trace saturated fat), 62 mg cholesterol, 612 mg sodium, 22 g carbohydrate, 1 g fiber, 14 g protein. **Diabetic Exchanges:** 2 lean meat, 1½ starch.

Grilled Portobellos with Mozzarella Salad

Portobello mushroom caps stuffed with mozzarella cheese and grape tomatoes are so filling, they're almost a meal in themselves. Try them the next time you fire up the grill.

—SARAH VASQUES MILFORD, NEW HAMPSHIRE

PREP/TOTAL TIME: 30 MINUTES **MAKES:** 4 SERVINGS

- 2 cups grape tomatoes, halved
- 3 ounces fresh mozzarella cheese, cubed
- 3 fresh basil leaves, thinly sliced
- 2 teaspoons olive oil
- 2 garlic cloves, minced
- ¼ teaspoon salt
- ¼ teaspoon pepper
- 4 large portobello mushrooms (4 to 4½ inches), stems removed
  Cooking spray

1. In a small bowl, combine the first seven ingredients; cover and chill until serving.

2. Spritz portobello mushrooms with cooking spray. Using long-handled tongs, moisten a paper towel with cooking oil and lightly coat the grill rack. Grill mushrooms, covered, over medium heat or broil 4 in. from the heat for 6-8 minutes on each side or until tender. Spoon ½ cup tomato mixture into each mushroom cap.

Nutrition Facts: 1 each equals 133 calories, 8 g fat (3 g saturated fat), 17 mg cholesterol, 190 mg sodium, 9 g carbohydrate, 2 g fiber, 7 g protein. **Diabetic Exchanges:** 2 vegetable, 1 lean meat, 1 fat.

106

111

126

Everyday Entrees

"Crunchy cabbage is a nice change of pace from rice in this sweet and savory stir-fry. You'll love the mango chutney and nutty flavor from the sesame oil."

DIDI DESJARDINS DARTMOUTH, MASSACHUSETTS
about her recipe, Turkey Stir-Fry with Cabbage, on page 114

Calypso Burritos

Because my spiced-up burritos are loaded with beans, vegetables, cheese and salsa, my husband doesn't care that he's not getting any meat. I also set out popular toppings such as reduced-fat or fat-free sour cream, chopped tomatoes and avocado.
—**DARLENE DEEG** VERNON, BRITISH COLUMBIA

PREP/TOTAL TIME: 30 MINUTES **MAKES:** 8 SERVINGS

- 2 small zucchini, shredded
- 2 medium carrots, shredded
- 1 medium onion, finely chopped
- 1 tablespoon canola oil
- 1 can (16 ounces) kidney beans, rinsed and drained
- 1 can (15 ounces) black beans, rinsed and drained
- 1½ cups frozen corn, thawed
- ¾ cup salsa
- 2 tablespoons reduced-sodium taco seasoning
- 2 teaspoons ground cumin
- 1 cup (4 ounces) shredded part-skim mozzarella cheese
- ¼ cup minced fresh cilantro
- 8 flour tortillas (8 inches), warmed

1. In a large skillet over medium heat, cook and stir the zucchini, carrots and onion in oil for 3-5 minutes or until tender. Stir in the beans, corn, salsa, taco seasoning and cumin. Cook and stir for 5-7 minutes or until the vegetables are tender.

2. Remove from the heat. Stir in cheese and cilantro. Spoon about ⅔ cupful filling off center on each tortilla. Fold sides and ends over filling and roll up.

Nutrition Facts: *1 burrito equals 349 calories, 7 g fat (2 g saturated fat), 8 mg cholesterol, 744 mg sodium, 55 g carbohydrate, 8 g fiber, 16 g protein.*

Linguine with Edamame and Tomatoes

Haven't tried edamame? You'll love it in this unusual entree. With fresh basil and cherry tomatoes, it's a wonderful meatless choice.
—**DIANA RIOS** LYTLE, TEXAS

PREP/TOTAL TIME: 25 MINUTES **MAKES:** 4 SERVINGS

- 8 ounces uncooked multigrain linguine
- 1½ cups frozen shelled edamame
- 4 green onions, thinly sliced
- 1 tablespoon olive oil
- 2 cups cherry tomatoes, halved
- 3 garlic cloves, minced
- 1 teaspoon dried oregano
- ½ teaspoon salt
- ¼ cup white wine or reduced-sodium chicken broth
- ¾ cup crumbled feta cheese
- 2 tablespoons minced fresh basil

1. Cook linguine according to package directions, adding edamame during the last 5 minutes; drain, reserving ½ cup cooking liquid.

2. In a large nonstick skillet, saute onions in oil until tender. Add the tomatoes, garlic, oregano and salt. Add the wine and reserved cooking liquid; cook and stir for 2 minutes.

3. Add the linguine and edamame; cook and stir 2-3 minutes longer. Remove from the heat. Sprinkle with cheese and basil; toss to coat.

Nutrition Facts: *1½ cups equals 370 calories, 11 g fat (3 g saturated fat), 11 mg cholesterol, 514 mg sodium, 54 g carbohydrate, 10 g fiber, 17 g protein.*

Turkey Divan

Here's a classic turkey favorite that seems like a splurge but has just 291 calories per serving. Pair it with a green salad and whole grain bread on the side for a complete dinner.

—**TASTE OF HOME TEST KITCHEN**

PREP/TOTAL TIME: 30 MINUTES **MAKES:** 8 SERVINGS

- 1½ cups water
- 16 fresh asparagus spears, trimmed
- 2 egg whites
- 1 egg
- 2 tablespoons fat-free milk
- 1¼ cups seasoned bread crumbs
- 1 package (17.6 ounces) turkey breast cutlets
- ¼ cup butter, cubed
- 8 slices deli ham
- 8 slices reduced-fat Swiss cheese

1. In a large skillet, bring water to a boil. Add asparagus; cover and boil for 3 minutes. Drain and pat dry.

2. In a shallow bowl, beat the egg whites, egg and milk. Place the bread crumbs in another shallow bowl. Dip turkey in egg mixture, then coat with crumbs.

3. In a large skillet, cook turkey in butter in batches for 2-3 minutes on each side or until meat is no longer pink. Layer with a ham slice, two asparagus spears and cheese. Cover and cook for 1 minute or until the cheese is melted. Transfer to a platter; keep warm.

Nutrition Facts: *1 serving equals 291 calories, 12 g fat (6 g saturated fat), 100 mg cholesterol, 595 mg sodium, 16 g carbohydrate, 1 g fiber, 31 g protein.* **Diabetic Exchanges:** *3 lean meat, 2 fat, 1 starch.*

Chicken Nuggets

I often fix these golden chicken nuggets because my whole family likes them and they're so quick and easy. The seasoning can also be used on chicken breast halves to make sandwiches.

—**ANNETTE ELLYSON** CAROLINA, WEST VIRGINIA

PREP/TOTAL TIME: 30 MINUTES **MAKES:** 8 SERVINGS

- 1 cup all-purpose flour
- 4 teaspoons seasoned salt
- 1 teaspoon poultry seasoning
- 1 teaspoon ground mustard
- 1 teaspoon paprika
- ½ teaspoon pepper
- 2 pounds boneless skinless chicken breasts
- ¼ cup canola oil

1. In a large resealable bag, combine the first six ingredients. Flatten the chicken to ½-in. thickness, then cut into 1½-in. pieces. Add the chicken, a few pieces at a time, to the bag and shake to coat.

2. In a large skillet, cook the chicken in oil in batches for 6-8 minutes or until the meat is no longer pink.

Nutrition Facts: *3 ounces cooked chicken equals 212 calories, 10 g fat (2 g saturated fat), 63 mg cholesterol, 435 mg sodium, 6 g carbohydrate, trace fiber, 24 g protein.* **Diabetic Exchanges:** *3 lean meat, 1½ fat, ½ starch.*

Loaded Mexican Pizza

My husband tends to be a picky eater, but he always looks forward to slices of my south-of-the-border pizza smothered with cheese, peppers, beans and more. Leftovers are never a problem because it tastes even better the next day.

—MARY BARKER KNOXVILLE, TENNESSEE

PREP/TOTAL TIME: 30 MINUTES
MAKES: 6 SLICES

- 1 can (15 ounces) black beans, rinsed and drained
- 1 medium red onion, chopped
- 1 small sweet yellow pepper, chopped
- 3 teaspoons chili powder
- ¾ teaspoon ground cumin
- 3 medium tomatoes, chopped
- 1 jalapeno pepper, seeded and finely chopped
- 1 garlic clove, minced
- 1 prebaked 12-inch thin pizza crust
- 2 cups chopped fresh spinach
- 2 tablespoons minced fresh cilantro
  Hot pepper sauce to taste
- ½ cup shredded reduced-fat cheddar cheese
- ½ cup shredded pepper jack cheese

1. In a small bowl, mash black beans. Stir in the onion, yellow pepper, chili powder and cumin. In another bowl, combine the tomatoes, jalapeno pepper and garlic.

2. Place the pizza crust on an ungreased 12-in. pizza pan; spread with the bean mixture. Top with tomato mixture and spinach. Sprinkle with cilantro, pepper sauce and cheeses.

3. Bake at 400° for 12-15 minutes or until the cheese is melted.

Editor's Note: *Wear disposable gloves when cutting hot peppers; the oils can burn skin. Avoid touching your face.*

Nutrition Facts: *1 slice equals 297 calories, 9 g fat (4 g saturated fat), 17 mg cholesterol, 566 mg sodium, 41 g carbohydrate, 6 g fiber, 15 g protein.* **Diabetic Exchanges:** *2½ starch, 1 lean meat, 1 vegetable.*

Homemade Fish Sticks

I'm a nutritionist and needed a healthy fish fix. Crunchy outside and moist inside, these cod strips are great with low-fat homemade tartar sauce and oven fries.

—JENNIFER ROWLAND ELIZABETHTOWN, KENTUCKY

PREP/TOTAL TIME: 25 MINUTES   **MAKES:** 2 SERVINGS

- ½ cup all-purpose flour
- 1 egg, beaten
- ½ cup dry bread crumbs
- ½ teaspoon salt
- ½ teaspoon paprika
- ½ teaspoon lemon-pepper seasoning
- ¾ pound cod fillets, cut into 1-inch strips
  Butter-flavored cooking spray

1. Place the flour and egg in separate shallow bowls. In another shallow bowl, combine the bread crumbs and seasonings. Dip the fish in the flour, then the egg, then roll in the crumb mixture.

2. Place on a baking sheet coated with cooking spray. Spritz the fish sticks with butter-flavored spray. Bake at 400° for 10-12 minutes or until the fish flakes easily with a fork, turning once.

Nutrition Facts: *1 serving equals 278 calories, 4 g fat (1 g saturated fat), 129 mg cholesterol, 718 mg sodium, 25 g carbohydrate, 1 g fiber, 33 g protein.* **Diabetic Exchanges:** *4 lean meat, 1½ starch.*

Special Scallops Salads

PREP/TOTAL TIME: 20 MINUTES
MAKES: 4 SERVINGS

- 1½ pounds sea scallops
- ¼ teaspoon salt
- ⅛ teaspoon pepper
- 3 tablespoons olive oil, divided
- 1 tablespoon fresh minced chives
- 1 tablespoon balsamic vinegar
- 2 garlic cloves, minced
- 2 teaspoons minced fresh tarragon
- 2 teaspoons honey
- 1 teaspoon Dijon mustard
- 1 package (5 ounces) spring mix salad greens
- 1 cup shredded carrots
- ½ cup chopped tomato

1. Sprinkle the scallops with salt and pepper. In a large skillet, saute scallops in 2 tablespoons oil until firm and opaque. Remove and keep warm. In the same skillet, combine the chives, balsamic vinegar, garlic, tarragon, honey, mustard and remaining oil. Bring to a boil; cook and stir for 30 seconds or until slightly thickened.

2. Divide the salad greens among four plates; top with the carrots, tomato and scallops. Drizzle with dressing.

Nutrition Facts: *1 serving equals 278 calories, 12 g fat (2 g saturated fat), 56 mg cholesterol, 482 mg sodium, 13 g carbohydrate, 2 g fiber, 30 g protein.*
Diabetic Exchanges: *4 lean meat, 2 fat, 1 vegetable, ½ starch.*

"What an easy way to fix a delicious seafood entree! The vinegar, fresh tarragon and honey blend beautifully."

—MARY RELYEA CANASTOTA, NEW YORK

? Did you know?

A member of the bivalve mollusk family, scallops are commonly found in two groups— the sea scallop, which yields 10-20 per pound, or the much smaller bay scallop, which yields 60-90 per pound. Scallops are usually available shucked, sold fresh or frozen and range in color from pale beige to creamy pink.

Chili Steak & Peppers

Savor a tender, juicy steak without the guilt. This recipe gets loads of flavor from chili sauce, peppers, horseradish and more.

—TASTE OF HOME TEST KITCHEN

PREP/TOTAL TIME: 30 MINUTES
MAKES: 4 SERVINGS

- 2 tablespoons chili sauce
- 1 tablespoon lime juice
- 1 teaspoon brown sugar
- ½ teaspoon crushed red pepper flakes
- ½ teaspoon salt, divided
- 1 beef top sirloin steak (1¼ pounds), cut into four steaks
- 1 medium onion, halved and sliced
- 1 medium green pepper, cut into strips
- 1 medium sweet yellow pepper, cut into strips
- 2 teaspoons olive oil
- 1 small garlic clove, minced
- ⅛ teaspoon pepper
- ¼ cup reduced-fat sour cream
- 1 teaspoon prepared horseradish

1. Combine the chili sauce, lime juice, brown sugar, red pepper flakes and ¼ teaspoon salt; brush over the steaks. Broil steaks 4-6 in. from the heat for 5-7 minutes on each side or until the meat reaches desired doneness (for medium-rare, a thermometer should read 145°; medium, 160°; well-done, 170°).
2. Meanwhile, in a large skillet, saute onion and green and yellow peppers in oil until tender. Add the garlic, pepper and remaining salt; cook 1 minute longer. In a small bowl, combine sour cream and horseradish. Serve steaks with pepper mixture and sauce.

Nutrition Facts: *1 steak with ⅓ cup pepper mixture and 1 tablespoon sauce equals 265 calories, 9 g fat (3 g saturated fat), 62 mg cholesterol, 491 mg sodium, 12 g carbohydrate, 2 g fiber, 32 g protein.*
Diabetic Exchanges: *4 lean meat, 1 vegetable, 1 fat.*

Pistachio-Crusted Fish Fillets

Here's a fresh, fun, delicious treatment for orange roughy fillets. With a nutty crunch from the pistachio-parsley coating, it's a family-pleasing way to bring more fish into your diet.

—MARIE STUPIN ROANOKE, VIRGINIA

PREP/TOTAL TIME: 25 MINUTES   **MAKES:** 4 SERVINGS

- 1 **egg white, beaten**
- ½ **cup pistachios, finely chopped**
- ⅓ **cup dry bread crumbs**
- ¼ **cup minced fresh parsley**
- ½ **teaspoon pepper**
- ¼ **teaspoon salt**
- 4 **orange roughy fillets (6 ounces each)**
- 4 **teaspoons butter, melted**

1. Place egg white in a shallow bowl. Combine the pistachios, bread crumbs, parsley, pepper and salt in another shallow bowl. Dip the orange roughy fillets in the egg white, then the pistachio mixture.

2. Place the fish on a baking sheet coated with cooking spray. Drizzle with butter. Bake at 450° for 8-10 minutes or until fish flakes easily with a fork.

Nutrition Facts: *1 fillet equals 295 calories, 13 g fat (3 g saturated fat), 112 mg cholesterol, 444 mg sodium, 11 g carbohydrate, 2 g fiber, 34 g protein.*

Makeover Beef Stroganoff

Slim down a classic dish using reduced-sodium beef broth and reduced-fat sour cream. You'll cut calories, saturated fat, sodium and cholesterol but keep all the satisfying taste.

—CANDACE CLARK CONNELL, WASHINGTON

PREP/TOTAL TIME: 30 MINUTES   **MAKES:** 6 SERVINGS

- ½ **cup plus 1 tablespoon all-purpose flour, divided**
- ½ **teaspoon pepper, divided**
- 1 **beef top round steak (1½ pounds), cut into thin strips**
- 2 **tablespoons canola oil**
- 1 **cup sliced fresh mushrooms**
- 1 **small onion, chopped**
- 1 **garlic clove, minced**
- 1 **can (14½ ounces) reduced-sodium beef broth**
- ½ **teaspoon salt**
- 1 **cup (8 ounces) reduced-fat sour cream**
- 3 **cups cooked yolk-free noodles**

1. Combine ½ cup flour and ¼ teaspoon pepper in a large resealable plastic bag. Add the beef, a few pieces at a time, and shake to coat.

2. In a large nonstick skillet over medium-high heat, cook beef in oil in batches until no longer pink. Remove and keep warm. In the same skillet, saute mushrooms and onion in drippings until tender. Add garlic; cook 1 minute longer.

3. Whisk the remaining flour and broth until smooth; stir into the skillet. Bring to a boil; cook and stir for 2 minutes or until thickened. Add the beef, salt and remaining pepper; heat through. Add the sour cream; heat through (do not boil). Serve with noodles.

Nutrition Facts: *1 cup beef Stroganoff with ½ cup noodles equals 351 calories, 12 g fat (4 g saturated fat), 78 mg cholesterol, 393 mg sodium, 25 g carbohydrate, 2 g fiber, 33 g protein.* **Diabetic Exchanges:** *3 lean meat, 2 fat, 1½ starch.*

Kid-Pleasing Taco Pizza

PREP/TOTAL TIME: 30 MINUTES **MAKES:** 10 PIECES

1 tube (13.8 ounces) refrigerated pizza crust
1 pound lean ground turkey
¾ cup water
1 envelope reduced-sodium taco seasoning
1 can (16 ounces) fat-free refried beans
1½ cups (6 ounces) shredded pizza cheese blend
3 medium tomatoes, chopped
7 cups shredded lettuce
2 cups crushed baked tortilla chip scoops

1. Unroll crust into a 15-in. x 10-in. x 1-in. baking pan coated with cooking spray; flatten dough and build up edges slightly. Bake at 425° for 8-10 minutes or until edges are lightly browned.
2. Meanwhile, in a large nonstick skillet, cook turkey over medium heat until no longer pink; drain. Stir in water and taco seasoning. Bring to a boil. Reduce heat; simmer, uncovered, for 5 minutes. Stir in refried beans until blended.
3. Spread turkey mixture over crust; sprinkle with cheese. Bake at 425° for 5-7 minutes or until cheese is melted. Top with tomatoes, lettuce and chips. Serve immediately.

Nutrition Facts: *1 piece equals 345 calories, 11 g fat (4 g saturated fat), 48 mg cholesterol, 873 mg sodium, 42 g carbohydrate, 5 g fiber, 20 g protein.*

❝Kids will love this easy recipe that combines two of their favorite foods—pizza and tacos. And you'll love the fact that it's a healthier choice for dinner.❞

—KIMBERLY THEOBALD GALESBURG, ILLINOIS

Bow Ties with Walnut-Herb Pesto

I'm a big fan of pasta and enjoy it at least once a week. To create a lighter option, I tossed together whole wheat bow ties, tomato and a homemade pesto. Now I can have second helpings!

—DIANE NEMITZ LUDINGTON, MICHIGAN

PREP/TOTAL TIME: 20 MINUTES **MAKES:** 6 SERVINGS

4 cups uncooked whole wheat bow tie pasta
1 cup fresh arugula
½ cup packed fresh parsley sprigs
½ cup loosely packed basil leaves
¼ cup grated Parmesan cheese
½ teaspoon salt
⅛ teaspoon crushed red pepper flakes
¼ cup chopped walnuts
⅓ cup olive oil
1 plum tomato, seeded and chopped

1. Cook the pasta according to the package directions.
2. Meanwhile, place the arugula, parsley, basil, cheese, salt and pepper flakes in a food processor; cover and pulse until chopped. Add walnuts; cover and process until blended. While processing, gradually add oil in a steady stream.
3. Drain pasta, reserving 3 tablespoons cooking water. In a large bowl, toss pasta with pesto, tomato and reserved water.

Nutrition Facts: *1 cup equals 323 calories, 17 g fat (3 g saturated fat), 3 mg cholesterol, 252 mg sodium, 34 g carbohydrate, 6 g fiber, 10 g protein.* **Diabetic Exchanges:** *2½ fat, 2 starch.*

Weeknight Chicken and Pasta

I tossed together leftover cooked chicken and bow tie pasta one night when I needed a main dish for surprise guests. It was such a success that I make a variation of it almost weekly.

—NANCY BROWN DAHINDA, ILLINOIS

PREP/TOTAL TIME: 25 MINUTES **MAKES:** 4 SERVINGS

- 2 cups uncooked whole wheat bow tie pasta
- 1 small onion, chopped
- 1 small sweet red pepper, chopped
- 1 tablespoon olive oil
- 1 garlic clove, minced
- 1½ cups cubed cooked chicken breast
- ½ cup reduced-fat sour cream
- ¼ cup fat-free milk
- ½ teaspoon salt
- ½ teaspoon pepper
- ½ teaspoon dried tarragon
- ½ teaspoon dried thyme
- 2 tablespoons shredded Parmesan cheese
- 2 teaspoons minced chives

1. Cook the pasta according to the package directions.
2. Meanwhile, in a large nonstick skillet, saute the onion and red pepper in oil until tender. Add the garlic; cook 1 minute longer. Stir in the chicken, sour cream, milk and seasonings; heat through. Drain the pasta; stir into skillet. Sprinkle with Parmesan cheese and chives.

Nutrition Facts: 1¼ cups equals 394 calories, 9 g fat (3 g saturated fat), 53 mg cholesterol, 399 mg sodium, 48 g carbohydrate, 7 g fiber, 28 g protein.

Turkey Stir-Fry with Cabbage

PREP/TOTAL TIME: 30 MINUTES
MAKES: 4 SERVINGS

- 1 tablespoon cornstarch
- 1¼ cups reduced-sodium chicken broth
- ⅓ cup plus 2 tablespoons mango chutney
- 4¼ teaspoons reduced-sodium soy sauce
- 1 teaspoon Chinese five-spice powder
- 1 garlic clove, minced
- 1 package (20 ounces) turkey breast tenderloins, cut into thin strips
- 7 teaspoons sesame oil, divided
- 1 large sweet red pepper, julienned
- 1½ cups fresh snow peas
- 6 cups shredded cabbage

1. In a small bowl, combine cornstarch and broth until smooth; stir in the chutney, soy sauce, five-spice powder and garlic.
2. In a large skillet, saute the turkey in 3 teaspoons oil for 6-8 minutes or until no longer pink; set aside. In the same skillet, saute red pepper and snow peas in 2 teaspoons oil for 2-3 minutes or until crisp-tender. Stir soy sauce mixture and add to skillet. Bring to a boil; cook and stir for 2 minutes or until thickened. Add turkey; heat through.
3. Meanwhile, in a large nonstick skillet coated with cooking spray, saute cabbage in remaining oil for 5 minutes or until crisp-tender. Serve with turkey mixture.

Nutrition Facts: 1¼ cups stir-fry with 1 cup cabbage equals 410 calories, 10 g fat (2 g saturated fat), 69 mg cholesterol, 803 mg sodium, 42 g carbohydrate, 5 g fiber, 38 g protein.

Did you know?

Snow peas and sugar snap peas are sweet, tender peas in an edible pod and are eaten whole. Snow peas have smaller peas and more translucent pods than sugar snap peas. Snow peas are available year-round, while sugar snap peas are generally available during spring and fall.

“Crunchy cabbage is a nice change of pace from rice in this sweet and savory stir-fry. You'll love the mango chutney and nutty flavor from the sesame oil.”

—DIDI DESJARDINS DARTMOUTH, MASSACHUSETTS

Breaded Curry Shrimp

A fruity dipping sauce adds to the fun and balances out the flavor of zippy breaded shrimp. Just try it and see!

—ANN NACE PERKASIE, PENNSYLVANIA

PREP/TOTAL TIME: 30 MINUTES
MAKES: 4 SERVINGS (½ CUP SAUCE)

- 1 egg
- 2 tablespoons water
- ¾ cup dry bread crumbs
- 1½ teaspoons curry powder
- ¼ teaspoon salt
  Dash pepper
- 1 pound uncooked medium shrimp, peeled and deveined
- 2 tablespoons butter, melted

MARMALADE DIPPING SAUCE
- 2 garlic cloves, minced
- ½ cup orange marmalade spreadable fruit
- 2 tablespoons reduced-sodium soy sauce
- ⅛ teaspoon ground ginger
- 1 teaspoon cornstarch
- 2 tablespoons lemon juice

1. In a shallow bowl, beat egg and water. In another bowl, combine the bread crumbs, curry, salt and pepper. Dip shrimp in egg mixture, then roll in crumb mixture.

2. Place in a 15-in. x 10-in. x 1-in. baking pan coated with cooking spray. Drizzle with butter. Bake at 400° for 7-9 minutes on each side or until golden brown.

3. In a small saucepan coated with cooking spray, cook garlic over medium heat for 1 minute. Add spreadable fruit, soy sauce and ginger. Bring to a boil. Combine cornstarch and lemon juice until smooth; stir into pan. Return to a boil; cook and stir for 1-2 minutes or until thickened. Serve with shrimp.

Nutrition Facts: *About 9 shrimp with 2 tablespoons sauce equals 327 calories, 9 g fat (4 g saturated fat), 237 mg cholesterol, 892 mg sodium, 37 g carbohydrate, 1 g fiber, 23 g protein.* **Diabetic Exchanges:** *3 lean meat, 2 starch, 1 fat.*

Santa Fe Chicken Pita Pizzas

These yummy chicken pizzas use convenient pita breads as the crust. Because you're making individual pies, each one can be tailored to suit the person's taste.
—**ATHENA RUSSELL** FLORENCE, SOUTH CAROLINA

PREP/TOTAL TIME: 30 MINUTES **MAKES:** 4 SERVINGS

- 4 pita breads (6 inches)
- ½ cup refried black beans
- ½ cup salsa
- 1 cup cubed cooked chicken breast
- 2 tablespoons chopped green chilies
- 2 tablespoons sliced ripe olives
- ¾ cup shredded Colby-Monterey Jack cheese
- ½ cup reduced-fat sour cream
- 1 green onion, chopped

1. Place the pita breads on an ungreased baking sheet; spread with the beans. Top with the salsa, chicken, green chilies, ripe olives and cheese.
2. Bake at 350° for 8-10 minutes or until the cheese is melted. Serve with sour cream; sprinkle with onion.
Nutrition Facts: *1 pita pizza with 2 tablespoons sour cream equals 380 calories, 11 g fat (7 g saturated fat), 56 mg cholesterol, 796 mg sodium, 43 g carbohydrate, 4 g fiber, 24 g protein.* **Diabetic Exchanges:** *3 starch, 2 lean meat, 1 fat.*

Dilly Salmon Patties

Here's a quick and easy way to serve healthy salmon. I like to pair the tender skillet patties with a crisp side salad.
—**AERIAL RYAN** ACRA, NEW YORK

PREP/TOTAL TIME: 25 MINUTES **MAKES:** 4 SERVINGS

- 2 eggs, lightly beaten
- 1 medium onion, finely chopped
- ¼ cup mashed potato flakes
- ¼ cup seasoned bread crumbs
- 1 garlic clove, minced
- ¼ teaspoon dill weed
- ¼ teaspoon pepper
- ⅛ teaspoon celery salt
- 1 can (14¾ ounces) salmon, drained, bones and skin removed
- 1 teaspoon olive oil

1. In a small bowl, combine the first eight ingredients. Crumble the salmon over the mixture and mix well. Shape mixture into four patties.
2. In a large nonstick skillet coated with cooking spray, cook patties in oil over medium heat for 5 minutes on each side or until browned.
Nutrition Facts: *1 patty equals 265 calories, 12 g fat (3 g saturated fat), 152 mg cholesterol, 761 mg sodium, 12 g carbohydrate, 1 g fiber, 27 g protein.*

Soft Fish Tacos

My husband and I experimented in the kitchen to come up with our own version of fish tacos. The combination of tilapia and cabbage may seem unusual, but after one bite, we were hooked!

—CARRIE BILLUPS FLORENCE, OREGON

PREP/TOTAL TIME: 25 MINUTES **MAKES:** 5 SERVINGS

- 4 cups coleslaw mix
- ½ cup fat-free tartar sauce
- ½ teaspoon salt
- ½ teaspoon ground cumin
- ¼ teaspoon pepper
- 1½ pounds tilapia fillets
- 2 tablespoons olive oil
- 1 tablespoon lemon juice
- 10 corn tortillas (6 inches), warmed
    Shredded cheddar cheese, chopped tomato and sliced avocado, optional

1. In a large bowl, toss the coleslaw mix, tartar sauce, salt, cumin and pepper; set aside. In a large nonstick skillet coated with cooking spray, cook the tilapia in oil and lemon juice over medium heat for 4-5 minutes on each side or until fish flakes easily with a fork.

2. Place tilapia on tortillas; top with coleslaw mixture. Serve with cheese, tomato and avocado if desired.

Nutrition Facts: *2 tacos (calculated without optional toppings) equals 310 calories, 8 g fat (2 g saturated fat), 66 mg cholesterol, 542 mg sodium, 31 g carbohydrate, 4 g fiber, 29 g protein.* **Diabetic Exchanges:** *4 lean meat, 2 starch, 1 fat.*

Light Linguine Carbonara

PREP/TOTAL TIME: 20 MINUTES **MAKES:** 4 SERVINGS

- 8 ounces uncooked linguine
- 1 egg, lightly beaten
- 1 cup fat-free evaporated milk
- ¼ cup finely chopped sweet red pepper
- ⅛ teaspoon crushed red pepper flakes
- ⅛ teaspoon pepper
- ½ cup grated Parmesan cheese, divided
- ½ cup frozen peas, thawed
- 2 bacon strips, cooked and crumbled

1. Cook linguine according to package directions. Meanwhile, in a small saucepan, combine the next five ingredients. Cook and stir over medium-low heat until mixture reaches 160° and coats the back of a metal spoon. Stir in ¼ cup Parmesan cheese, peas and bacon; heat through. Drain linguine; toss with sauce. Sprinkle with the remaining Parmesan cheese.

Nutrition Facts: *One serving (1 cup) equals 352 calories, 7 g fat (3 g saturated fat), 66 mg cholesterol, 349 mg sodium, 52 g carbohydrate, 3 g fiber, 20 g protein.* **Diabetic Exchanges:** *3 starch, 1 lean meat, 1 fat, ½ fat-free milk.*

"Our family is always on the go. When we need to rush off to an evening sporting event or meeting, I prepare my linguine carbonara with breadsticks or garlic toast for a quick yet light dinner."

—MARY JO MILLER MANSFIELD, OHIO

Mediterranean Tuna Salad

Enjoy healthy tuna in this refreshing main-dish medley. Featuring a homemade dressing, the cold salad is perfect for summer meals.

—**RENEE NASH** SNOQUALMIE, WASHINGTON

PREP/TOTAL TIME: 25 MINUTES **MAKES:** 4 SERVINGS

- 1 **can (15 ounces) garbanzo beans or chickpeas, rinsed and drained**
- 3 **celery ribs, chopped**
- 1 **small sweet red pepper, chopped**
- 4 **green onions, chopped**
- 2 **tablespoons olive oil**
- 2 **tablespoons balsamic vinegar**
- 2 **tablespoons spicy brown mustard**
- ½ **teaspoon dried basil**
- ¼ **teaspoon salt**
- ¼ **teaspoon pepper**
- 2 **cans (5 ounces each) albacore white tuna in water**
- 4 **cups shredded lettuce**
- ½ **cup crumbled feta or blue cheese, optional**

1. In a large bowl, combine the beans, celery, red pepper and onions. In a small bowl, whisk the oil, vinegar, mustard, basil, salt and pepper. Pour over bean mixture; toss to coat. Gently stir in tuna. Serve over lettuce. Sprinkle with cheese if desired.

Nutrition Facts: *1½ cups tuna salad with 1 cup shredded lettuce (calculated without cheese) equals 282 calories, 11 g fat (2 g saturated fat), 30 mg cholesterol, 682 mg sodium, 23 g carbohydrate, 6 g fiber, 23 g protein.* **Diabetic Exchanges:** *3 lean meat, 1 starch, 1 vegetable, 1 fat.*

Vegetarian Spaghetti

Who says spaghetti needs meat to be satisfying? I streamlined my original recipe to reduce its 2-hour simmer time to just 10 minutes. Sprinkle each serving with a little Parmesan cheese.

—**MARGARET WILSON** SUN CITY, CALIFORNIA

PREP/TOTAL TIME: 25 MINUTES **MAKES:** 6 SERVINGS

- 1 **package (16 ounces) spaghetti**
- 1 **cup chopped onion**
- ½ **cup chopped celery**
- 1 **teaspoon garlic powder**
- 3 **tablespoons canola oil**
- 1 **jar (26 ounces) meatless spaghetti sauce**
- 1 **can (15 ounces) garbanzo beans or chickpeas, rinsed and drained**
- 1 **can (14½ ounces) diced tomatoes with garlic and onion, undrained**
- 1 **teaspoon sugar**
- ½ **teaspoon salt**
- ½ **teaspoon dried oregano**
- 1 **bay leaf**
- ¼ **cup grated Parmesan cheese**

1. Cook the spaghetti according to the package directions. Meanwhile, in a large skillet, saute the onion, celery and garlic powder in oil until tender. Add spaghetti sauce, beans, tomatoes, sugar, salt, oregano and bay leaf.

2. Bring to a boil; cover and simmer for 10 minutes. Discard bay leaf. Drain spaghetti; top with sauce and cheese.

Nutrition Facts: *1 cup equals 511 calories, 11 g fat (1 g saturated fat), 3 mg cholesterol, 1,225 mg sodium, 87 g carbohydrate, 8 g fiber, 17 g protein.*

My hearty salad combines peppers, beans, tomato and strips of beef. The meat marinates for just 10 minutes but gets plenty of flavor from the chili powder, cilantro and lime juice. —**ARDEENA HARRIS** ROANOKE, ALABAMA

Beef Fajita Salad

PREP/TOTAL TIME: 30 MINUTES
MAKES: 4 SERVINGS

- ¼ cup lime juice
- 2 tablespoons minced fresh cilantro
- 1 garlic clove, minced
- 1 teaspoon chili powder
- ¾ pound beef top sirloin steak, cut into thin strips
- 1 medium green pepper, julienned
- 1 medium sweet red pepper, julienned
- 1 medium onion, sliced and halved
- 1 teaspoon olive oil
- 1 can (16 ounces) kidney beans, rinsed and drained
- 4 cups torn mixed salad greens
- 1 medium tomato, chopped
- 4 tablespoons fat-free sour cream
- 2 tablespoons salsa

1. In a large resealable plastic bag, combine the lime juice, cilantro, garlic and chili powder; add beef. Seal bag and turn to coat; refrigerate for 10 minutes, turning once.

2. Meanwhile, in a nonstick skillet, cook the peppers and onion in oil over medium-high heat for 5 minutes or until tender. Remove and keep warm. Add the beef with the marinade to the skillet; cook and stir for 4-5 minutes or until the meat is tender and the mixture comes to a boil. Add beans and pepper mixture; heat through.

3. Divide the salad greens and tomato among four bowls; top each salad with 1¼ cups beef mixture, 1 tablespoon sour cream and 1½ teaspoons salsa.

Nutrition Facts: *1 serving equals 291 calories, 6 g fat (2 g saturated fat), 50 mg cholesterol, 291 mg sodium, 34 g carbohydrate, 9 g fiber, 27 g protein.*
Diabetic Exchanges: *2 lean meat, 2 vegetable, 1½ starch.*

Skewerless Stovetop Kabobs

We never have leftovers when I serve this quick-and-easy skillet entree of sauteed pork and garden-fresh vegetables. It's delicious made on the grill, too.
—**JENNIFER MITCHELL** ALTOONA, PENNSYLVANIA

PREP/TOTAL TIME: 30 MINUTES   **MAKES:** 4 SERVINGS

- 1 pork tenderloin (1 pound), cut into ¾-inch cubes
- ¾ cup fat-free Italian salad dressing, divided
- 2 large green peppers, cut into ¾-inch pieces
- 2 small zucchini, cut into ½-inch slices
- ½ pound medium fresh mushrooms, halved
- 1 large sweet onion, cut into wedges
- 1 cup cherry tomatoes
- ¼ teaspoon pepper
- ⅛ teaspoon seasoned salt

1. In a large nonstick skillet, saute pork in ¼ cup salad dressing until no longer pink. Remove and keep warm.

2. In the same pan, cook the peppers, zucchini, mushrooms, onion, tomatoes, pepper and seasoned salt in remaining salad dressing until vegetables are tender. Return pork to skillet; heat through.

Nutrition Facts: *2 cups equals 236 calories, 5 g fat (2 g saturated fat), 65 mg cholesterol, 757 mg sodium, 22 g carbohydrate, 4 g fiber, 27 g protein.* **Diabetic Exchanges:** *3 lean meat, 2 starch.*

Shrimp Tostadas with Avocado Salsa

PREP/TOTAL TIME: 30 MINUTES
MAKES: 6 SERVINGS

- 1 medium ripe avocado, peeled and chopped, divided
- 1 tablespoon water
- 3 teaspoons lime juice, divided
- 2 teaspoons blackened seasoning, divided
- 1 teaspoon ground cumin
- 1 can (15 ounces) black beans, rinsed and drained, divided
- 1 small navel orange, peeled and chopped
- ¼ cup chopped red onion
- 1 jalapeno pepper, seeded and chopped
- 1 tablespoon minced fresh cilantro
- 6 tostada shells
- 1 cup (4 ounces) shredded reduced-fat Mexican cheese blend
- 1 pound uncooked large shrimp, peeled and deveined

1. In a small bowl, combine 2 tablespoons avocado, water, 1 teaspoon lime juice, 1 teaspoon blackened seasoning and cumin. Set aside ¼ cup beans; add the remaining beans to avocado mixture and mash with a fork. Stir in reserved beans. Set aside.

2. For salsa, in a small bowl, combine the orange, onion, jalapeno, cilantro and remaining avocado and lime juice. Cover and refrigerate until serving.

3. Place tostada shells on ungreased baking sheets; spread with the bean mixture. Sprinkle with cheese. Bake at 350° for 4-6 minutes or until the cheese is melted.

4. Meanwhile, in a large nonstick skillet coated with cooking spray, cook shrimp and remaining blackened seasoning over medium-high heat for 4-6 minutes or until shrimp turn pink. Arrange over tostada shells; serve with salsa.

Editor's Note: *Wear disposable gloves when cutting hot peppers; the oils can burn skin. Avoid touching your face.*

Nutrition Facts: *1 tostada with 2 tablespoons salsa equals 285 calories, 12 g fat (3 g saturated fat), 125 mg cholesterol, 517 mg sodium, 23 g carbohydrate, 6 g fiber, 22 g protein.* **Diabetic Exchanges:** *3 lean meat, 2 fat, 1½ starch.*

Try this 30-minute entree for a different yet fun take on Southwestern fare. A splash of lime in the black beans balances the rich avocado salsa and seasoned shrimp.
—**KAREN GULKIN** GREELEY, COLORADO

Easy Crab Cakes

Canned crabmeat makes delicate cakes that are simple enough for busy weekdays. If you prefer, form the crab mixture into four thick patties instead of eight cakes.

—CHARLENE SPELOCK
APOLLO, PENNSYLVANIA

PREP/TOTAL TIME: 25 MINUTES
MAKES: 4 SERVINGS

> 2 cans (6 ounces each) crabmeat, drained, flaked and cartilage removed
> 1 cup seasoned bread crumbs, divided
> 1 egg, lightly beaten
> ¼ cup finely chopped green onions
> ¼ cup finely chopped sweet red pepper
> ¼ cup reduced-fat mayonnaise
> 1 tablespoon lemon juice
> ½ teaspoon garlic powder
> ⅛ teaspoon cayenne pepper
> 1 tablespoon butter

1. In a large bowl, combine the crab, ⅓ cup bread crumbs, egg, onions, red pepper, mayonnaise, lemon juice, garlic powder and cayenne.
2. Divide mixture into eight portions; shape into 2-in. balls. Roll in remaining bread crumbs. Flatten to ½-in. thickness.
3. In a large nonstick skillet, cook crab cakes in butter for 3-4 minutes on each side or until golden brown.

Nutrition Facts: *2 crab cakes equals 295 calories, 12 g fat (3 g saturated fat), 142 mg cholesterol, 879 mg sodium, 23 g carbohydrate, 1 g fiber, 23 g protein.* **Diabetic Exchanges:** *3 lean meat, 1½ starch, 1½ fat.*

Homemade Crumbs

Unless a recipe specifically calls for soft bread crumbs, use dry crumbs. To make your own seasoned bread crumbs, break dried bread into pieces and process them in a blender or food processor until you have fine crumbs. (One slice of dried bread will yield about ¼ cup of fine crumbs.) Season them as desired—for example, try dried basil and oregano, garlic and onion powder, grated Parmesan cheese, paprika and salt. Start with small amounts of seasonings and add more as needed.

Pork Parmigiana

Bring home the cuisine of Italy with a tempting Parmigiana. Baked in just 5 minutes, the crispy yet moist pork tenderloin combines with pasta for a special dinner any night of the week.
—**JULEE WALLBERG** SALT LAKE CITY, UTAH

PREP/TOTAL TIME: 30 MINUTES **MAKES:** 4 SERVINGS

- 1⅓ cups uncooked spiral pasta
- 2 cups meatless spaghetti sauce
- 1 pork tenderloin (1 pound)
- ¼ cup egg substitute
- ⅓ cup seasoned bread crumbs
- 3 tablespoons grated Parmesan cheese, divided
- ¼ cup shredded part-skim mozzarella cheese

1. Cook the pasta according to the package directions. Place spaghetti sauce in a small saucepan; cook over low heat until heated through, stirring occasionally.
2. Meanwhile, cut the tenderloin into eight slices; flatten to ¼-in. thickness. Place the egg substitute in a shallow bowl. In another shallow bowl, combine bread crumbs and 1 tablespoon Parmesan cheese. Dip pork slices in egg substitute, then roll in crumb mixture.
3. Place on a baking sheet coated with cooking spray. Bake at 425° for 5-6 minutes on each side or until meat is tender. Drain pasta; serve with the spaghetti sauce and pork. Sprinkle with mozzarella cheese and remaining Parmesan cheese.

Nutrition Facts: *2 slices of pork with ½ cup pasta and ½ cup sauce equals 365 calories, 7 g fat (3 g saturated fat), 70 mg cholesterol, 878 mg sodium, 39 g carbohydrate, 3 g fiber, 34 g protein.* **Diabetic Exchanges:** *4 lean meat, 2 starch, 2 vegetable.*

Shrimp 'n' Veggie Pizza

Why settle for delivery when you can easily make your own pizza? Half an hour is all you'll need to assemble a yummy shrimp-topped pie. It's a great way to use up excess vegetables, too.
—**TERRI WEBBER** MIAMI, FLORIDA

PREP/TOTAL TIME: 30 MINUTES **MAKES:** 6 SLICES

- ½ cup sliced onion
- ½ cup sliced fresh mushrooms
- 3 asparagus spears, trimmed and cut into 1-inch pieces
- 1 garlic clove, minced
- 2 teaspoons olive oil
- 4 ounces uncooked medium shrimp, peeled, deveined and halved lengthwise
- 1 prebaked 12-inch thin pizza crust
- ½ cup pizza sauce
- 1 cup (4 ounces) shredded part-skim mozzarella cheese

1. In a nonstick skillet, saute onion, mushrooms, asparagus and garlic in oil until almost tender. Add shrimp; cook until shrimp turn pink. Remove from the heat.
2. Place the crust on a pizza pan or baking sheet. Spread with pizza sauce. Top with shrimp mixture. Sprinkle with cheese. Bake at 450° for 8-10 minutes or until cheese is melted.

Nutrition Facts: *1 slice equals 215 calories, 7 g fat (2 g saturated fat), 38 mg cholesterol, 426 mg sodium, 24 g carbohydrate, 1 g fiber, 13 g protein.* **Diabetic Exchanges:** *1½ starch, 1 lean meat, 1 fat.*

Hearty Beef Ravioli

You're only 30 minutes away from a terrific new entree. Slices of crusty bread go perfectly with this beef ravioli.
—TASTE OF HOME TEST KITCHEN

PREP/TOTAL TIME: 30 MINUTES **MAKES:** 6 SERVINGS

- 1 package (25 ounces) frozen beef ravioli
- ½ pound extra-lean ground beef (95% lean)
- 1 medium green pepper, chopped
- 1 can (14½ ounces) no-salt-added diced tomatoes
- 1 can (8 ounces) no-salt-added tomato sauce
- 2 tablespoons reduced-sodium taco seasoning
- ¾ cup shredded reduced-fat cheddar cheese
- 1 can (2¼ ounces) sliced ripe olives, drained

1. Cook the ravioli according to the package directions.
2. Meanwhile, in a large nonstick skillet, cook the beef and green pepper over medium heat until meat is no longer pink. Stir in the tomatoes, tomato sauce and taco seasoning. Bring to a boil. Reduce heat; simmer, uncovered, for 5-7 minutes or until slightly thickened.
3. Drain pasta. Serve with sauce. Sprinkle each serving with 2 tablespoons cheese and about 1 tablespoon olives.
Nutrition Facts: *1 serving equals 375 calories, 10 g fat (5 g saturated fat), 44 mg cholesterol, 695 mg sodium, 49 g carbohydrate, 4 g fiber, 21 g protein.*

Blackened Chicken and Beans

My husband is a fan of spicy food, and this is a healthier recipe we both can enjoy. While the chicken cooks, put together individual salads of packaged shredded lettuce, chopped tomatoes, avocado and cheddar cheese to round out the meal.
—CHRISTINE ZONGKER SPRING HILL, KANSAS

PREP/TOTAL TIME: 15 MINUTES **MAKES:** 4 SERVINGS

- 2 teaspoons chili powder
- ¼ teaspoon salt
- ¼ teaspoon pepper
- 4 boneless skinless chicken breast halves (4 ounces each)
- 1 tablespoon canola oil
- 1 can (15 ounces) black beans, rinsed and drained
- 1 cup frozen corn
- 1 cup chunky salsa

1. Combine the chili powder, salt and pepper; rub over both sides of chicken. In a large nonstick skillet, cook chicken in oil over medium heat for 4-5 minutes on each side or until a thermometer reads 170°. Remove and keep warm.
2. Add the beans, corn and salsa to the pan; heat through. Serve with chicken.
Nutrition Facts: *1 chicken breast half with ¾ cup bean mixture equals 297 calories, 7 g fat (1 g saturated fat), 63 mg cholesterol, 697 mg sodium, 30 g carbohydrate, 10 g fiber, 33 g protein.* **Diabetic Exchanges:** *3 lean meat, 2 starch, 1 fat.*

Crispy Asian Chicken Salad

Craving a taste of the Far East? Try this main dish boasting crispy breaded chicken, almonds and sesame-ginger dressing.

—**BETH DAUENHAUER** PUEBLO, COLORADO

PREP/TOTAL TIME: 30 MINUTES
MAKES: 2 SERVINGS

- 2 **boneless skinless chicken breast halves (4 ounces each)**
- 2 **teaspoons hoisin sauce**
- 1 **teaspoon sesame oil**
- ½ **cup panko (Japanese) bread crumbs**
- 4 **teaspoons sesame seeds**
- 2 **teaspoons canola oil**
- 4 **cups spring mix salad greens**
- 1 **small green pepper, julienned**
- 1 **small sweet red pepper, julienned**
- 1 **medium carrot, julienned**
- ½ **cup sliced fresh mushrooms**
- 2 **tablespoons thinly sliced onion**
- 2 **tablespoons sliced almonds, toasted**
- ¼ **cup reduced-fat sesame ginger salad dressing**

1. Flatten chicken breasts to ½-in. thickness. Combine hoisin sauce and sesame oil; brush over chicken. In a shallow bowl, combine panko and sesame seeds; dip chicken in mixture.
2. In a large nonstick skillet coated with cooking spray, cook chicken in oil for 4-5 minutes on each side or until a thermometer reads 170°.
3. Meanwhile, divide the salad greens between two plates. Top with peppers, carrot, mushrooms and onion. Slice chicken; place on top. Sprinkle with almonds and drizzle with dressing.

Nutrition Facts: *1 salad equals 386 calories, 17 g fat (2 g saturated fat), 63 mg cholesterol, 620 mg sodium, 29 g carbohydrate, 6 g fiber, 30 g protein.* **Diabetic Exchanges:** *3 lean meat, 2 vegetable, 2 fat, 1 starch.*

Chicken Breast Basics

Buying skinned and boned chicken breasts can cut up to 15 minutes from your cooking time. Save money by purchasing larger-size packages, then rewrap the chicken in the smaller-size portions you'll need and freeze.

Asian Salmon Fillets

Inspired by a visit to Hawaii, I experimented in the kitchen and came up with a new salmon recipe. I like it for both busy weeknights and special occasions.

—**SUSAN CORYELL** HUDDLESTON, VIRGINIA

PREP/TOTAL TIME: 25 MINUTES **MAKES:** 4 SERVINGS

- 4 **green onions, thinly sliced**
- 1 **garlic clove, minced**
- 1 **teaspoon olive oil**
- 1 **teaspoon minced fresh gingerroot**
- 4 **salmon fillets (5 ounces each)**
- ¼ **cup white wine or reduced-sodium chicken broth**
- 2 **tablespoons reduced-sodium soy sauce**
- 2 **tablespoons oyster sauce**

1. In a large nonstick skillet over medium heat, cook the onions and garlic in oil for 1 minute. Add ginger; cook 1 minute longer. Transfer to a small bowl; set aside.
2. Spritz fillets with cooking spray; add to skillet. Cook for 4-6 minutes on each side or until lightly browned.
3. Combine the wine, soy sauce, oyster sauce and reserved onion mixture; pour over salmon. Cook for 2-3 minutes or until fish flakes easily with a fork. Remove fillets. Cook sauce 1-2 minutes longer or until thickened; serve over salmon.

Nutrition Facts: *1 fillet with 1 tablespoon sauce equals 300 calories, 17 g fat (3 g saturated fat), 84 mg cholesterol, 725 mg sodium, 3 g carbohydrate, trace fiber, 30 g protein.* **Diabetic Exchanges:** *4 lean meat, 1 fat.*

Pork Medallions with Asian Flair

PREP/TOTAL TIME: 25 MINUTES
MAKES: 4 SERVINGS

- 1 pork tenderloin (1 pound), halved and thinly sliced
- 1 tablespoon sesame oil
- ¼ cup sherry or reduced-sodium chicken broth
- 3 tablespoons reduced-sodium soy sauce
- 1 tablespoon brown sugar
- 1 tablespoon hoisin saauce
- 1 garlic clove, minced
- ⅛ teaspoon cayenne pepper
  Hot cooked brown rice, optional

1. In a large nonstick skillet, saute pork in oil in batches until tender. Remove and keep warm. Add the remaining ingredients to the pan; cook and stir over medium heat for 3-4 minutes or until thickened. Return pork to the pan; heat through. Serve with rice if desired.

Nutrition Facts: *3 ounces cooked pork (calculated without rice) equals 202 calories, 7 g fat (2 g saturated fat), 63 mg cholesterol, 566 mg sodium, 6 g carbohydrate, trace fiber, 23 g protein.* **Diabetic Exchanges:** *3 lean meat, ½ starch, ½ fat.*

When I became serious about losing weight and eating healthier, my kids missed the Chinese delivery I used to order so frequently. I combined a few recipes to create a lighter dish they love. —**DIANNE LUEHRING** EDMOND, OKLAHOMA

Thai Chicken Pasta

When you have leftover cooked chicken, put it to delicious use in this Thai specialty. It tastes like it's from a restaurant but comes together easily in your own kitchen.

—JENI PITTARD COMMERCE, GEORGIA

PREP/TOTAL TIME: 25 MINUTES
MAKES: 2 SERVINGS

- 3 **ounces uncooked multigrain linguine**
- ½ **cup salsa**
- 2 **tablespoons reduced-fat creamy peanut butter**
- 1 **tablespoon orange juice**
- 1½ **teaspoons honey**
- 1 **teaspoon reduced-sodium soy sauce**
- 1 **cup cubed cooked chicken breast**
- 1 **tablespoon chopped unsalted peanuts**
- 1 **tablespoon minced fresh cilantro**

1. Cook the linguine according to the package directions.

2. Meanwhile, in a microwave-safe dish, combine the salsa, peanut butter, orange juice, honey and soy sauce. Cover and microwave on high for 1 minute; stir. Add the chicken; heat through.

3. Drain the linguine. Serve with the chicken mixture. Garnish with peanuts and cilantro.

Editor's Note: *This recipe was tested in a 1,100-watt microwave.*

Nutrition Facts: *1 serving equals 409 calories, 10 g fat (2 g saturated fat), 54 mg cholesterol, 474 mg sodium, 46 g carbohydrate, 6 g fiber, 33 g protein.*

Did you know?

With its slightly sharp flavor, cilantro—also known as Chinese parsley—gives a distinctive taste to Mexican, Latin American and Asian dishes. (The spice coriander comes from the seed of the cilantro plant.) Fresh cilantro should be used as soon as possible. For short-term storage, immerse the freshly cut stems in water about 2 inches deep. Cover leaves loosely with a plastic bag and refrigerate for several days. Wash cilantro just before using.

Turkey Alfredo Pizza

With creamy Alfredo sauce and Parmesan cheese, my thin-crust pizza is a long-time family favorite. It's also an excellent way to use up leftover cooked turkey after a big holiday feast.

—**EDIE DESPAIN** LOGAN, UTAH

PREP/TOTAL TIME: 25 MINUTES **MAKES:** 6 SERVINGS

- 1 **prebaked 12-inch thin pizza crust**
- 1 **garlic clove, peeled and halved**
- ¾ **cup reduced-fat Alfredo sauce, divided**
- 1 **package (10 ounces) frozen chopped spinach, thawed and squeezed dry**
- 2 **teaspoons lemon juice**
- ¼ **teaspoon salt**
- ⅛ **teaspoon pepper**
- 2 **cups shredded cooked turkey breast**
- ¾ **cup shredded Parmesan cheese**
- ½ **teaspoon crushed red pepper flakes**

1. Place the pizza crust on a baking sheet; rub with the cut sides of the garlic. Discard the garlic. Spread ½ cup Alfredo sauce over the crust.

2. In a small bowl, combine the spinach, lemon juice, salt and pepper; spoon evenly over sauce. Top with turkey; drizzle with remaining Alfredo sauce. Sprinkle with Parmesan cheese and pepper flakes.

3. Bake at 425° for 11-13 minutes or until heated through and cheese is melted.

Nutrition Facts: *1 slice equals 300 calories, 9 g fat (4 g saturated fat), 60 mg cholesterol, 823 mg sodium, 27 g carbohydrate, 2 g fiber, 25 g protein.* **Diabetic Exchanges:** *3 lean meat, 2 starch.*

Greek Pita Pizzas

Crunchy and packed with fresh vegetables such as mushrooms and spinach, these individual-size pies taste just like a Greek salad. Whole wheat pitas have never been more delicious!

—**TRISHA KRUSE** EAGLE, IDAHO

PREP/TOTAL TIME: 25 MINUTES **MAKES:** 6 SERVINGS

- 6 **whole wheat pita breads (6 inches)**
- 1½ **cups meatless spaghetti sauce**
- 1 **can (14 ounces) water-packed artichoke hearts, rinsed, drained and quartered**
- 2 **cups fresh baby spinach, chopped**
- 1½ **cups sliced fresh mushrooms**
- ½ **cup crumbled feta cheese**
- 1 **small green pepper, thinly sliced**
- ¼ **cup thinly sliced red onion**
- ¼ **cup sliced ripe olives**
- 3 **tablespoons grated Parmesan cheese**
- ¼ **teaspoon pepper**

1. Place pita breads on an ungreased baking sheet; spread with spaghetti sauce. Top with remaining ingredients.

2. Bake at 350° for 8-12 minutes or until cheese is melted. Serve immediately.

Nutrition Facts: *1 pizza equals 273 calories, 5 g fat (2 g saturated fat), 7 mg cholesterol, 969 mg sodium, 48 g carbohydrate, 7 g fiber, 13 g protein.* **Diabetic Exchanges:** *2 starch, 1 medium-fat meat, 1 vegetable.*

Ranch Ham 'n' Cheese Pasta

Craving comfort food? Indulge in a cheesy ham-and-pasta dish without worrying about your waistline. Using lighter ingredients cuts about two-thirds of the calories and more than half the fat, cholesterol and sodium found in similar recipes.

—TASTE OF HOME TEST KITCHEN

PREP/TOTAL TIME: 25 MINUTES **MAKES:** 10 SERVINGS

- 1 package (16 ounces) penne pasta
- 1 tablespoon butter
- 1 tablespoon all-purpose flour
- 1 cup fat-free milk
- 2 teaspoons dried parsley flakes
- 1 teaspoon garlic salt
- 1 teaspoon salt-free lemon-pepper seasoning
- ½ teaspoon garlic powder
- ½ teaspoon dried minced onion
- ½ teaspoon dill weed
- ¼ teaspoon onion powder
- ⅛ teaspoon pepper
- 1 cup (8 ounces) reduced-fat sour cream
- 2 cups cubed fully cooked lean ham
- 1½ cups (6 ounces) shredded reduced-fat Mexican cheese blend
- ¼ cup shredded Parmesan cheese

1. Cook pasta according to package directions; drain. In a Dutch oven, melt butter; whisk in flour until smooth. Gradually add milk and seasonings. Bring to a boil; cook and stir for 2 minutes or until thickened.

2. Reduce heat; fold in sour cream until blended. Add ham and pasta; cook and stir until heated through. Remove from the heat; stir in Mexican cheese blend until melted. Sprinkle with Parmesan cheese.

Nutrition Facts: *1 cup equals 306 calories, 9 g fat (5 g saturated fat), 27 mg cholesterol, 612 mg sodium, 38 g carbohydrate, 2 g fiber, 20 g protein.* **Diabetic Exchanges:** *2½ starch, 2 lean meat.*

French-Style Chicken

When I have friends over for dinner, I make this elegant light entree and serve it with a tossed salad and crisp French bread. If you like, sprinkle toasted almonds on top for an extra-special touch.

—CATHERINE JOHNSTON STAFFORD, NEW YORK

PREP/TOTAL TIME: 25 MINUTES **MAKES:** 6 SERVINGS

- 6 boneless skinless chicken breast halves (4 ounces each)
- ¾ teaspoon salt-free lemon-pepper seasoning
- 1⅓ cups reduced-sodium chicken broth
- 3 medium unpeeled apples, cut into wedges
- 1 medium onion, thinly sliced
- 4 tablespoons apple cider or juice, divided
- ¼ teaspoon ground cinnamon
- ⅛ teaspoon ground nutmeg
- 1 tablespoon cornstarch
  Minced fresh parsley

1. Sprinkle chicken with lemon-pepper. In a large nonstick skillet coated with cooking spray, cook chicken for 5-6 minutes on each side or until a thermometer reads 170°. Remove and keep warm.

2. In the same skillet, combine the chicken broth, apples, onion, 3 tablespoons cider, cinnamon and nutmeg. Bring to a boil. Combine the cornstarch and remaining cider until smooth; stir into apple mixture. Bring to a boil; cook and stir for 1-2 minutes or until thickened. Top with chicken; sprinkle with parsley.

Nutrition Facts: *1 serving equals 186 calories, 3 g fat (1 g saturated fat), 63 mg cholesterol, 194 mg sodium, 16 g carbohydrate, 2 g fiber, 24 g protein.* **Diabetic Exchanges:** *3 lean meat, 1 fruit.*

Spinach and Mushroom Smothered Chicken

PREP/TOTAL TIME: 30 MINUTES
MAKES: 4 SERVINGS

- 3 cups fresh baby spinach
- 1¾ cups sliced fresh mushrooms
- 3 green onions, sliced
- 2 tablespoons chopped pecans
- 1½ teaspoons olive oil
- 4 boneless skinless chicken breast halves (4 ounces each)
- ½ teaspoon rotisserie chicken seasoning
- 2 slices reduced-fat provolone cheese, halved

1. In a large skillet, saute the spinach, mushrooms, onions and pecans in oil until mushrooms are tender. Set aside and keep warm.
2. Sprinkle the chicken with seasoning. Using long-handled tongs, moisten a paper towel with cooking oil and lightly coat the grill rack.
3. Grill the chicken, covered, over medium heat or broil 4 in. from the heat for 4-5 minutes on each side or until a thermometer reads 170°.
4. Top with cheese. Cover and grill 2-3 minutes longer or until cheese is melted. To serve, top each chicken breast with reserved spinach mixture.

Nutrition Facts: *1 chicken breast half equals 203 calories, 9 g fat (2 g saturated fat), 68 mg cholesterol, 210 mg sodium, 3 g carbohydrate, 2 g fiber, 27 g protein.*
Diabetic Exchanges: *3 lean meat, 1 vegetable, 1 fat.*

Sweet Onion 'n' Sausage Spaghetti

Sweet onion seasons turkey sausage, adding rich flavor to this pasta dish. I toss it together with half-and-half cream, basil and tomatoes for a satisfying meal in minutes.
—MARY RELYEA CANASTOTA, NEW YORK

PREP/TOTAL TIME: 30 MINUTES **MAKES:** 5 SERVINGS

- 6 ounces uncooked whole wheat spaghetti
- ¾ pound Italian turkey sausage links, casings removed
- 2 teaspoons olive oil
- 1 sweet onion, thinly sliced
- 1 pint cherry tomatoes, halved
- ½ cup loosely packed fresh basil leaves, thinly sliced
- ½ cup half-and-half cream
  Shaved Parmesan cheese, optional

1. Cook the spaghetti according to package directions. Meanwhile, in a large nonstick skillet over medium heat, cook the sausage in oil for 5 minutes. Add onion; cook 8-10 minutes longer or until meat is no longer pink and onion is tender.
2. Stir in the tomatoes and basil; heat through. Add the cream; bring to a boil. Drain spaghetti; toss with sausage mixture. Garnish with cheese if desired.
Nutrition Facts: *1¼ cups (calculated without Parmesan cheese) equals 305 calories, 11 g fat (4 g saturated fat), 48 mg cholesterol, 442 mg sodium, 33 g carbohydrate, 6 g fiber, 18 g protein.*
Diabetic Exchanges: *2 lean meat, 1½ starch, 1 vegetable, 1 fat.*

Did you know?

Vidalia and other sweet onions are mild-flavored onions that are high in sugar and water content and low in tear-inducing sulfur compounds. Because of these properties, they are not suited for long-term storage, so you should use them within several weeks of purchase.

Here's an extra-special yet surprisingly fuss-free entree. The chicken stays nice and moist under a mushroom and spinach topping and a blanket of melted cheese.
—**KATRINA WAGNER** GRAIN VALLEY, MISSOURI

150

144

153

Mealtime Menus

"I received the recipe for these moist, tender pork chops years ago from my best friend. I love the fact that I can get them on the table in less than half an hour. They make a terrific choice for busy weekdays when I need a 30-minute dinner."

GINA YOUNG LAMAR, COLORADO
about her recipe, Sweet 'n' Sour Pork Chops, on page 151

A WINNING CHICKEN DINNER

Sit down to a good, old-fashioned chicken supper—made lighter and easier to prepare for busy yet health-conscious cooks. You won't miss out on a bit of comforting, home-style flavor.

Country Chicken with Gravy

PREP/TOTAL TIME: 30 MINUTES
MAKES: 4 SERVINGS

- ¾ cup crushed cornflakes
- ½ teaspoon poultry seasoning
- ½ teaspoon paprika
- ¼ teaspoon salt
- ¼ teaspoon dried thyme
- ¼ teaspoon pepper
- 2 tablespoons fat-free evaporated milk
- 4 boneless skinless chicken breast halves (4 ounces each)
- 2 teaspoons canola oil

GRAVY

- 1 tablespoon butter
- 1 tablespoon all-purpose flour
- ¼ teaspoon pepper
- ⅛ teaspoon salt
- ½ cup fat-free evaporated milk
- ¼ cup condensed chicken broth, undiluted
- 1 teaspoon sherry or additional condensed chicken broth
- 2 tablespoons minced chives

1. In a shallow bowl, combine the first six ingredients. Place milk in another shallow bowl. Dip chicken in milk, then roll in cornflake mixture.

2. In a large nonstick skillet coated with cooking spray, cook chicken in oil over medium heat for 6-8 minutes on each side or until a thermometer reads 170°.

3. Meanwhile, in a small saucepan, melt the butter. Stir in the flour, pepper and salt until smooth. Gradually stir in the milk, chicken broth and sherry. Bring to a boil; cook and stir for 1-2 minutes or until thickened. Stir in chives. Serve with chicken.

Nutrition Facts: *1 chicken breast half with 2 tablespoons gravy equals 274 calories, 8 g fat (3 g saturated fat), 72 mg cholesterol, 569 mg sodium, 20 g carbohydrate, trace fiber, 28 g protein.* **Diabetic Exchanges:** *3 lean meat, 1 starch, ½ fat.*

Complete with homemade gravy, this lightened-up classic comes together in just half an hour. It always gets raves.
—RUTH HELMUTH ABBEVILLE, SOUTH CAROLINA

Bananas Foster Sundaes

I have wonderful memories of eating Bananas Foster while in New Orleans. As a dietitian, I wanted to find a healthier version I could make myself. So I combined the best elements of two different recipes and added a few of my own tweaks.

—**LISA VARNER** EL PASO, TEXAS

PREP/TOTAL TIME: 15 MINUTES **MAKES:** 6 SERVINGS

- 1 **tablespoon butter**
- 3 **tablespoons brown sugar**
- 1 **tablespoon orange juice**
- ¼ **teaspoon ground cinnamon**
- ¼ **teaspoon ground nutmeg**
- 3 **large firm bananas, sliced**
- 2 **tablespoons chopped pecans, toasted**
- ½ **teaspoon rum extract**
- 3 **cups reduced-fat vanilla ice cream**

1. In a large nonstick skillet, melt butter over medium-low heat. Stir in the brown sugar, orange juice, cinnamon and nutmeg until blended. Add the bananas and pecans; cook, stirring gently, for 2-3 minutes or until bananas are glazed and slightly softened. Remove from the heat; stir in extract. Serve with ice cream.

Nutrition Facts: *⅓ cup banana mixture with ½ cup ice cream equals 233 calories, 7 g fat (3 g saturated fat), 23 mg cholesterol, 66 mg sodium, 40 g carbohydrate, 2 g fiber, 4 g protein.*

Garlic Mashed Cauliflower

PREP/TOTAL TIME: 20 MINUTES **MAKES:** 4 SERVINGS

- 5 **cups fresh cauliflowerets**
- 1 **garlic clove, minced**
- 3 **tablespoons fat-free milk**
- 3 **tablespoons reduced-fat mayonnaise**
- ½ **teaspoon salt**
- ⅛ **teaspoon white pepper**

1. Place 1 in. of water in a large saucepan; add cauliflower and garlic. Bring to a boil. Reduce heat; cover and simmer for 10-15 minutes or until tender.

2. Drain; transfer to a small bowl. Add the milk, mayonnaise, salt and pepper; beat until blended. If desired, shape mixture into individual molds by packing ½ cup at a time into a 2-in. biscuit cutter.

Nutrition Facts: *½ cup equals 74 calories, 4 g fat (1 g saturated fat), 4 mg cholesterol, 428 mg sodium, 8 g carbohydrate, 3 g fiber, 3 g protein.*

❝ One of our favorite restaurants serves delicious mashed cauliflower. When I tried duplicating it at home, the result was this dish. It's a great low-carb alternative to mashed potatoes.❞

—**JEAN KEISER** WEST CHESTER, PENNSYLVANIA

HOME-STYLE PORK SUPPER

Lightly coated pork, well-seasoned corn and luscious peach desserts all add up to a satisfying meal. And because each dish comes together in less than 30 minutes, you'll be eating in a flash!

Honey Lemon Schnitzel

PREP/TOTAL TIME: 25 MINUTES
MAKES: 4 SERVINGS

- 2 **tablespoons all-purpose flour**
- ½ **teaspoon salt**
- ½ **teaspoon pepper**
- 4 **pork sirloin cutlets (4 ounces each)**
- 2 **tablespoons butter**
- ¼ **cup lemon juice**
- ¼ **cup honey**

1. In a large resealable plastic bag, combine the flour, salt and pepper. Add pork, two pieces at a time, and shake to coat. In a large skillet, cook pork in butter over medium heat for 3-4 minutes on each side or until the juices run clear. Remove and keep warm.
2. Add the lemon juice and honey to the skillet; cook and stir for 3 minutes or until thickened. Return the pork to the pan; cook 2-3 minutes longer or until heated through.

Nutrition Facts: *1 cutlet equals 298 calories, 13 g fat (6 g saturated fat), 88 mg cholesterol, 393 mg sodium, 22 g carbohydrate, trace fiber, 24 g protein.*

Chive 'n' Garlic Corn

Here's a delicious way to dress up frozen corn. Simply toss in some onion, chives, garlic and a few other pantry staples.
—TASTE OF HOME TEST KITCHEN

PREP/TOTAL TIME: 15 MINUTES
MAKES: 4 SERVINGS

- 1 **package (16 ounces) frozen corn, thawed**
- ½ **cup finely chopped onion**
- 2 **tablespoons butter**
- ¼ **cup minced chives**
- ½ **teaspoon minced garlic**
- ⅛ **teaspoon salt**
   Pepper to taste

1. In a large skillet, saute corn and onion in butter for 5-7 minutes or until tender. Stir in the chives, garlic, salt and pepper.

Nutrition Facts: *½ cup equals 159 calories, 7 g fat (4 g saturated fat), 15 mg cholesterol, 136 mg sodium, 26 g carbohydrate, 3 g fiber, 4 g protein.* **Diabetic Exchanges:** *1½ starch, 1½ fat.*

Creamy Peaches

Smooth and refreshing, this pretty treat featuring peaches is high in protein and virtually fat-free. Enjoy it not only as a dessert, but also for breakfast.
—DON PROKIDANSKY NEW PORT RICHEY, FLORIDA

PREP/TOTAL TIME: 10 MINUTES   **MAKES:** 4 SERVINGS

- 1 **can (15 ounces) sliced peaches in extra-light syrup, drained**
- 1½ **cups (12 ounces) fat-free cottage cheese**
- 4 **ounces fat-free cream cheese, cubed**
   Sugar substitute equivalent to 1 tablespoon sugar

1. Thinly slice four peach slices; set aside for garnish. Place remaining peaches in a food processor; add cottage cheese. Cover and process until blended. Add cream cheese and sugar substitute; cover and process until blended.
2. Spoon into four serving dishes. Top with reserved peaches. Refrigerate until serving.
Editor's Note: *This recipe was tested with Splenda no-calorie sweetener.*

Nutrition Facts: *1 cup equals 127 calories, trace fat (trace saturated fat), 6 mg cholesterol, 443 mg sodium, 15 g carbohydrate, 1 g fiber, 15 g protein.* **Diabetic Exchanges:** *2 lean meat, ½ starch, ½ fruit.*

"These simple pork cutlets are coated in a sweet sauce of honey, lemon juice and butter. Quick to fix on the stovetop, they're perfect for busy weekdays. Very seldom are there leftovers!"

—CAROLE FRASER NORTH YORK, ONTARIO

A BREATH OF FRESH AIR

Whether you want to pack a picnic basket or dine inside, this menu is a refreshing change of pace. Enjoy a colorful chicken salad, cheese for dipping and sweetly stuffed fruit.

Honey-Balsamic Goat Cheese Dip

PREP/TOTAL TIME: 10 MINUTES
MAKES: 8 SERVINGS (¾ CUP DIP)

- 1 **cup crumbled goat cheese**
- ⅓ **cup fat-free mayonnaise**
- 2 **tablespoons honey**
- 1 **tablespoon balsamic vinegar**
- 1 **medium apple, sliced**
- 8 **slices French bread (¼ inch thick)**

1. In a small bowl, beat the goat cheese, mayonnaise, honey and balsamic vinegar until smooth. Serve with apple and bread slices.

Nutrition Facts: *1 each equals 101 calories, 5 g fat (3 g saturated fat), 12 mg cholesterol, 189 mg sodium, 12 g carbohydrate, 1 g fiber, 4 g protein.*

This easy but out-of-the-ordinary dip for apple slices and French bread is so delicious, you can't stop eating it! Look for both the honey and goat cheese at your local farmers market. —**JONI HILTON** ROCKLIN, CALIFORNIA

Did you know?
Goat cheese is a soft, easily spread cheese with a distinctively tangy flavor made from the milk of goats. Goat cheese is often found in Middle Eastern or Mediterranean cuisines. Common varieties include chevre, a very soft cheese, and feta, a semi-soft cheese.

Mediterranean Chicken Salad

I combined two of my all-time favorite salads into one main-dish creation. My family likes it as a light meal on warm days.
—AMY LEWIS CARMICHAEL, CALIFORNIA

PREP/TOTAL TIME: 25 MINUTES **MAKES:** 6 SERVINGS

- 3 cups cubed cooked chicken breast
- 1½ cups chopped tomatoes
- 1 cup water-packed artichoke hearts, rinsed, drained and quartered
- ½ cup crumbled feta cheese
- ½ cup pitted Greek olives
- ⅓ cup dried currants
- ¼ cup finely chopped red onion

DRESSING
- ¼ cup olive oil
- 2 tablespoons tarragon vinegar
- 1 tablespoon minced fresh tarragon or 1 teaspoon dried tarragon
- 1½ teaspoons lemon juice
- 1½ teaspoons Dijon mustard
- ¼ teaspoon salt
- ⅛ teaspoon pepper

1. In a large bowl, combine the first seven ingredients. In a small bowl, whisk the dressing ingredients. Pour over chicken mixture and toss to coat. Refrigerate until serving.

Nutrition Facts: *1 cup equals 291 calories, 16 g fat (3 g saturated fat), 59 mg cholesterol, 544 mg sodium, 12 g carbohydrate, 2 g fiber, 24 g protein.* **Diabetic Exchanges:** *3 lean meat, 2 fat, 1 vegetable, ½ fruit.*

Amaretto Cheese-Filled Apricots

I discovered these treats at a holiday party and thought they were excellent. You get loads of flavor in each sweet little bite.
—YVONNE STARLIN HERMITAGE, TENNESSEE

PREP/TOTAL TIME: 30 MINUTES **MAKES:** ABOUT 2 DOZEN

- 1 package (7 ounces) dried pitted Mediterranean apricots
- 4 ounces fat-free cream cheese
- ½ cup finely chopped almonds, toasted, divided
- ¼ cup dried cherries, finely chopped
- 2 tablespoons amaretto or ½ teaspoon almond extract plus 5 teaspoons orange juice

1. Gently loosen a long side of each apricot, splitting apricots to resemble clamshells. In a small bowl, beat the cream cheese, ¼ cup almonds, cherries and amaretto until blended. Spoon 1¼ teaspoons filling into each apricot.
2. Place the remaining almonds in a small shallow dish; roll exposed cheese portions of apricots in nuts.

Nutrition Facts: *1 filled apricot equals 42 calories, 1 g fat (trace saturated fat), trace cholesterol, 30 mg sodium, 7 g carbohydrate, 1 g fiber, 1 g protein.*

PERFECT PASTA—PRONTO!

You can't go wrong with a main course of Chicken Pasta Primavera. A batch of warm-from-the-oven biscuits and yummy Fruit-Filled Quesadillas round out this memorable meal.

Chicken Pasta Primavera

Canned soup, frozen veggies and other kitchen staples combine for this family-pleasing entree. It's a wonderful way to use up any leftover cooked chicken in the fridge.

—MARGARET WILSON SUN CITY, CALIFORNIA

PREP/TOTAL TIME: 20 MINUTES **MAKES:** 6 SERVINGS

- 6 **ounces uncooked spaghetti**
- 1 **can (10¾ ounces) reduced-fat reduced-sodium condensed cream of chicken soup, undiluted**
- ¾ **cup water**
- 1 **tablespoon lemon juice**
- 1½ **teaspoons dried basil**
- ¾ **teaspoon garlic powder**
- ½ **teaspoon salt**
- ¼ **teaspoon pepper**
- 1 **package (16 ounces) frozen California-blend vegetables, thawed**
- 4 **cups cubed cooked chicken breast**
- 3 **tablespoons grated Parmesan cheese**

1. Cook the spaghetti according to the package directions. Meanwhile, in a large saucepan, combine the soup, water, lemon juice, basil, garlic powder, salt and pepper. Stir in the vegetables; bring to a boil. Reduce heat; cover and simmer for 3-5 minutes or until vegetables are tender.
2. Stir in the chicken; heat through. Drain spaghetti; add to chicken mixture and toss to coat. Sprinkle with cheese.
Nutrition Facts: *1⅓ cups equals 342 calories, 5 g fat (2 g saturated fat), 78 mg cholesterol, 526 mg sodium, 36 g carbohydrate, 4 g fiber, 35 g protein.* **Diabetic Exchanges:** *4 lean meat, 2 starch, 1 vegetable.*

Fruit-Filled Quesadillas

Dessert doesn't get much easier than this stovetop treat loaded with fresh apricots and berries. Served with a scoop of frozen yogurt or low-fat ice cream, it seems anything but light.

—CATHY YATES CICERO, NEW YORK

PREP/TOTAL TIME: 15 MINUTES **MAKES:** 4 SERVINGS

- 5 **fresh apricots, halved**
- ¼ **cup apricot nectar**
- 2 **teaspoons sugar, divided**
- ½ **cup sliced fresh strawberries**
- ½ **teaspoon ground cinnamon**
- 2 **flour tortillas (8 inches)**
  Butter-flavored cooking spray
- 2 **cups reduced-fat vanilla ice cream**
- ¼ **cup fresh raspberries**

1. In a nonstick skillet, cook and stir the apricots, nectar and 1 teaspoon sugar over low heat until apricots are tender, about 5 minutes. Stir in the strawberries; cover and remove from the heat. Combine cinnamon and remaining sugar; set aside.
2. In another nonstick skillet, cook one tortilla over low heat for 1-2 minutes on each side or until golden and crisp. Spritz one side with butter-flavored spray and sprinkle with half of the cinnamon-sugar. Repeat with remaining tortilla.
3. Place a tortilla sugared side down; spread with the fruit mixture. Top with the remaining tortilla, sugared side up; cut into four wedges. Serve each wedge with ½ cup of ice cream and 1 tablespoon of raspberries.
Nutrition Facts: *1 piece equals 214 calories, 5 g fat (2 g saturated fat), 9 mg cholesterol, 182 mg sodium, 39 g carbohydrate, 2 g fiber, 6 g protein.*

> "Homemade buttermilk biscuits are surprisingly easy to make in just 30 minutes. Golden on the outside and tender on the inside, these flaky goodies boast mild onion flavor in every bite."

—TASTE OF HOME TEST KITCHEN

Onion Poppy Seed Biscuits

PREP/TOTAL TIME: 30 MINUTES **MAKES:** 1 DOZEN

- 1   medium onion, finely chopped
- 2   cups all-purpose flour
- 1   teaspoon baking powder
- 1   teaspoon brown sugar
- ¾   teaspoon poppy seeds
- ½   teaspoon salt
- ½   teaspoon baking soda
- ¼   cup cold butter, cubed
- 1   cup buttermilk

1. In a small nonstick skillet coated with cooking spray, saute the onion until tender; set aside. In a large bowl, combine the flour, baking powder, brown sugar, poppy seeds, salt and baking soda. Cut in the butter until the mixture resembles coarse crumbs. Stir in the onions. Stir in the buttermilk just until moistened.

2. Turn dough onto a lightly floured surface; knead 6-8 times. Pat to ½-in. thickness; cut with a floured 2½-in. biscuit cutter. Place 2 in. apart on baking sheets coated with cooking spray.

3. Bake at 450° for 9-12 minutes or until golden brown. Serve warm.

Nutrition Facts: *1 biscuit equals 125 calories, 4 g fat (3 g saturated fat), 11 mg cholesterol, 245 mg sodium, 18 g carbohydrate, 1 g fiber, 3 g protein.* **Diabetic Exchanges:** *1 starch, 1 fat.*

? Did you know?

There are a number of substitutes for buttermilk in baking. For each cup of buttermilk, you can substitute 1 tablespoon of white vinegar or lemon juice plus enough milk to measure 1 cup. Stir, then let it stand for 5 minutes. You can also use 1 cup of plain yogurt or 1¾ teaspoons cream of tartar plus 1 cup milk. Keeping powdered buttermilk blend in your pantry is a convenient way to always have buttermilk on hand. You can reconstitute the amount needed for your recipe in just seconds. Powdered buttermilk is found near the dry and canned milk in most grocery stores.

FAMILY-PLEASING PORK CHOPS

Weeknight dinner will be anything but ordinary when you prepare this tongue-tingling main course, side salad and dessert. Each delicious dish is light yet conveniently fast to fix.

Saucy Poached Pears

Here's an unexpected treat you're sure to enjoy. Covered with a smooth orange-strawberry sauce, the beautiful poached pears are dressed up enough for the fanciest meal. I like to sprinkle them with chopped pistachios for a bit of crunch.

—AUDREY THIBODEAU GILBERT, ARIZONA

PREP/TOTAL TIME: 30 MINUTES **MAKES:** 6 SERVINGS

- 6 medium pears
- ¼ cup minced fresh mint
- 1 can (11 ounces) mandarin oranges, drained
- 1 package (10 ounces) frozen unsweetened strawberries, thawed
- 2 teaspoons sugar
- 2 tablespoons finely chopped pistachios

1. Peel the pears, leaving the stem attached. Place in a Dutch oven and cover with water; add mint. Bring to a boil. Reduce heat; cover and simmer for 8-12 minutes or until pears are tender but firm. Remove with a slotted spoon. Refrigerate until serving.

2. For sauce, in a blender, combine the oranges, strawberries and sugar; cover and process until blended. Serve with the poached pears; sprinkle with pistachios.

Nutrition Facts: *1 pear with ⅓ cup sauce equals 159 calories, 2 g fat (trace saturated fat), 0 cholesterol, 12 mg sodium, 37 g carbohydrate, 5 g fiber, 2 g protein.* **Diabetic Exchanges:** *2½ fruit, ½ fat.*

❝This crisp, summery medley keeps very well in the refrigerator—if it lasts that long! The toasty flavor and tangy sweetness of the homemade sesame dressing are wonderful.❞

—TRISHA KRUSE EAGLE, IDAHO

Gingered Green Bean Salad

PREP/TOTAL TIME: 30 MINUTES **MAKES:** 8 SERVINGS

- 2 pounds fresh green beans, trimmed
- 1 cup thinly sliced red onion, separated into rings
- 1 cup canned bean sprouts, rinsed and drained

VINAIGRETTE
- ¼ cup rice vinegar
- 2 tablespoons sesame oil
- 1 tablespoon minced fresh gingerroot
- 1 tablespoon reduced-sodium soy sauce
- 2 teaspoons sesame seeds, toasted
- 1 teaspoon honey
- ½ teaspoon minced garlic

1. Place the green beans in a large saucepan and cover with water. Bring to a boil. Cook, uncovered, for 4-7 minutes or until crisp-tender. Drain and immediately place in ice water; drain and pat dry.

2. In a large salad bowl, combine the beans, onion and bean sprouts. In a small bowl, whisk the vinaigrette ingredients. Pour over bean mixture and toss to coat.

Nutrition Facts: *1 cup equals 88 calories, 4 g fat (1 g saturated fat), 0 cholesterol, 93 mg sodium, 12 g carbohydrate, 4 g fiber, 3 g protein.* **Diabetic Exchanges:** *2 vegetable, 1 fat.*

 top tip Toast sesame seeds in a dry skillet over medium heat for 3-5 minutes or until lightly browned, stirring occasionally. Or bake the sesame seeds on an ungreased baking sheet at 350° for 8-10 minutes or until lightly browned. Check them during baking to avoid scorching.

I received the recipe for these moist, tender pork chops years ago from my best friend. I love the fact that I can get them on the table in less than half an hour. They make a terrific choice for busy weekdays when I need a 30-minute dinner. —GINA YOUNG LAMAR, COLORADO

Sweet 'n' Sour Pork Chops

PREP/TOTAL TIME: 25 MINUTES
MAKES: 6 SERVINGS

- 6 boneless pork loin chops (4 ounces each)
- ¾ teaspoon pepper
- ½ cup water
- ⅓ cup cider vinegar
- ¼ cup packed brown sugar
- 2 tablespoons reduced-sodium soy sauce
- 1 tablespoon Worcestershire sauce
- 1 tablespoon cornstarch
- 2 tablespoons cold water

1. Sprinkle pork chops with pepper. In a large nonstick skillet coated with cooking spray, cook pork chops over medium heat for 4-6 minutes on each side or until lightly browned. Remove and keep warm.

2. Add the water, vinegar, brown sugar, soy sauce and Worcestershire sauce to the skillet; stir to loosen browned bits. Bring to a boil. Combine the cornstarch and cold water until smooth; stir into the skillet. Bring to a boil; cook and stir for 2 minutes or until thickened.

3. Return the chops to the pan. Reduce heat; cover and simmer for 4-5 minutes or until meat is tender.

Nutrition Facts: *1 pork chop with 3 tablespoons sauce equals 198 calories, 6 g fat (2 g saturated fat), 55 mg cholesterol, 265 mg sodium, 12 g carbohydrate, trace fiber, 22 g protein.* **Diabetic Exchanges:** *3 lean meat, 1 starch.*

ALL WRAPPED UP FOR YOU

Keep things casual! Avocado Turkey Wraps, Warm Spinach Dip and No-Bake Peanut Butter Treats combine for a fuss-free meal your family is bound to request time and again.

"These delicious sandwiches are perfect for brown-bag lunches or quick meals at home. Featuring deli turkey, avocado and cheese, the wraps are loaded with flavor. If you'd like a little extra zip, replace the tomato slices with a well-drained chunky salsa."

—TASTE OF HOME TEST KITCHEN

Avocado Turkey Wraps

PREP/TOTAL TIME: 15 MINUTES
MAKES: 2 SERVINGS

- 2 **whole wheat tortillas (8 inches), room temperature**
- 2 **tablespoons fat-free mayonnaise**
- ¼ **pound thinly sliced deli turkey**
- 8 **thin slices tomato**
- 2 **teaspoons finely chopped jalapeno pepper**
- ¼ **cup shredded reduced-fat cheddar cheese**
- 2 **teaspoons minced fresh cilantro**
- ½ **medium ripe avocado, peeled and thinly sliced**

1. Spread tortillas with mayonnaise. Top each with turkey, tomato, jalapeno, cheese, cilantro and avocado. Roll up and cut in half.

Editor's Note: *Wear disposable gloves when cutting hot peppers; the oils can burn skin. Avoid touching your face.*

Nutrition Facts: *1 wrap equals 342 calories, 15 g fat (4 g saturated fat), 37 mg cholesterol, 1,079 mg sodium, 34 g carbohydrate, 6 g fiber, 18 g protein.*

Warm Spinach Dip

I developed my version of hot spinach dip after my family enjoyed a similar dish at a restaurant. Just add tortilla chips, bagel chips or low-fat wheat crackers.

—DEBBIE MARRONE
WARNER ROBINS, GEORGIA

PREP/TOTAL TIME: 20 MINUTES
MAKES: 2 CUPS

- 1 **package (10 ounces) frozen chopped spinach, thawed and squeezed dry**
- 4 **ounces fat-free cream cheese**
- ½ **cup shredded reduced-fat cheddar cheese**
- ½ **cup reduced-fat sour cream**
- 1 **tablespoon spicy brown mustard**
- 1 **teaspoon minced garlic**
- ¾ **teaspoon hot pepper sauce**
- ¼ **teaspoon salt**
  Assorted fresh vegetables

1. In a large saucepan, combine the first eight ingredients. Bring to a boil over medium heat. Reduce heat; simmer, uncovered, for 7-8 minutes or until cheese is melted, stirring occasionally. Serve warm with vegetables.

Nutrition Facts: *¼ cup (calculated without vegetables) equals 64 calories, 3 g fat (2 g saturated fat), 11 mg cholesterol, 259 mg sodium, 4 g carbohydrate, 1 g fiber, 6 g protein.*

No-Bake Peanut Butter Treats

You'll need peanut butter and only five other ingredients to whip up these no-bake goodies. They won't stick to your hands, so you're sure to want more than one!

—SONIA ROHDA WAVERLY, NEBRASKA

PREP/TOTAL TIME: 10 MINUTES **MAKES:** 15 TREATS

- ⅓ **cup chunky peanut butter**
- ¼ **cup honey**
- ½ **teaspoon vanilla extract**
- ⅓ **cup nonfat dry milk powder**
- ⅓ **cup quick-cooking oats**
- 2 **tablespoons graham cracker crumbs**

1. In a small bowl, combine the peanut butter, honey and vanilla. Stir in the milk powder, oats and graham cracker crumbs. Shape into 1-in. balls. Cover and refrigerate until serving.

Nutrition Facts: *1 treat equals 70 calories, 3 g fat (1 g saturated fat), 1 mg cholesterol, 46 mg sodium, 9 g carbohydrate, 1 g fiber, 3 g protein.* **Diabetic Exchanges:** *½ starch, ½ fat.*

THE CATCH OF THE DAY

A plate filled with Sauteed Spiced Salmon and Squash Medley is sure to net compliments from your family. Don't forget bowls of luscious Cinnamon-Spiced Bananas for dessert!

Cinnamon-Spiced Bananas

This microwave treat is not only yummy, but it's also a great way to bring more fruit into your diet. A scoop of reduced-fat vanilla ice cream is my favorite finishing touch.
—**JANET HOMES** SURPRISE, ARIZONA

PREP/TOTAL TIME: 10 MINUTES   **MAKES:** 4 SERVINGS

- 3 **large bananas, sliced**
- 3 **tablespoons brown sugar**
- ¾ **teaspoon vanilla extract**
- ¼ **teaspoon ground cinnamon**
- 1 **tablespoon butter**
- 1 **cup reduced-fat vanilla ice cream**

1. Place bananas in a small microwave-safe bowl. Top with brown sugar, vanilla and cinnamon; dot with butter.
2. Cover and microwave on high for 1-2 minutes or until sugar is melted, stirring once. Spoon banana mixture into bowls; top with ice cream. Serve immediately.
Nutrition Facts: *½ cup banana mixture with ¼ cup reduced-fat vanilla ice cream equals 211 calories, 5 g fat (3 g saturated fat), 16 mg cholesterol, 50 mg sodium, 42 g carbohydrate, 3 g fiber, 3 g protein.*

Sauteed Spiced Salmon

PREP/TOTAL TIME: 15 MINUTES   **MAKES:** 4 SERVINGS

- 2 **teaspoons dill weed**
- 2 **teaspoons chili powder**
- 1 **teaspoon salt-free lemon-pepper seasoning**
- ½ **teaspoon ground cumin**

- 4 **salmon fillets (4 ounces each), skin removed**
- 1 **tablespoon canola oil**
   Lemon wedges, optional

1. Combine the dill, chili powder, lemon-pepper seasoning and cumin; rub over fillets.
2. In a large nonstick skillet coated with cooking spray, cook salmon in oil over medium-high heat for 5-6 minutes on each side or until fish flakes easily with a fork. Serve with lemon if desired.
Nutrition Facts: *1 fillet equals 246 calories, 16 g fat (3 g saturated fat), 67 mg cholesterol, 82 mg sodium, 2 g carbohydrate, 1 g fiber, 23 g protein.* **Diabetic Exchanges:** *3 lean meat, 1½ fat.*

Squash Medley

I'm trying to improve my health by eating better. I like to saute squash, onion and red pepper with seasonings, then mix in some tomato for an easy, fresh-tasting side dish.
—**MARLENE AGNELLY**
OCEAN SPRINGS, MISSISSIPPI

PREP/TOTAL TIME: 30 MINUTES
MAKES: 6 SERVINGS

- 1 **yellow summer squash, quartered and sliced**
- 1 **medium zucchini, quartered and sliced**
- 1 **medium onion, chopped**
- 1 **medium sweet red pepper, cut into 1-inch pieces**
- 1 **tablespoon olive oil**
- 2 **garlic cloves, minced**
- ½ **teaspoon salt-free spicy seasoning blend**
- ¼ **teaspoon salt**
- ⅛ **teaspoon pepper**
- 1 **medium tomato, chopped**

1. In a large skillet, saute the yellow squash, zucchini, onion and red pepper in oil for 5 minutes. Add garlic and seasonings; saute 2-3 minutes longer or until vegetables are crisp-tender. Stir in tomato; heat through.
Nutrition Facts: *⅔ cup equals 53 calories, 2 g fat (trace saturated fat), 0 cholesterol, 104 mg sodium, 8 g carbohydrate, 2 g fiber, 2 g protein.* **Diabetic Exchanges:** *1 vegetable, ½ fat.*

FISHING FOR COMPLIMENTS

Trying to fit more fish into your menus? Reel in a light but easy-to-fix meal anytime with this simple stovetop entree and side, plus some spiced treats that bake in a jiffy.

Crumb-Coated Red Snapper

PREP/TOTAL TIME: 30 MINUTES
MAKES: 4 SERVINGS

- ½ cup dry bread crumbs
- 2 tablespoons grated Parmesan cheese
- 1 teaspoon lemon-pepper seasoning
- ¼ teaspoon salt
- 4 red snapper fillets (6 ounces each)
- 2 tablespoons olive oil

1. In a shallow bowl, combine the bread crumbs, cheese, lemon-pepper seasoning and salt; add the fillets, one at a time, and turn to coat.

2. In a heavy skillet over medium heat, cook the fillets in oil in batches for 4-5 minutes on each side or until fish flakes easily with a fork.

Nutrition Facts: *1 fillet equals 288 calories, 10 g fat (2 g saturated fat), 62 mg cholesterol, 498 mg sodium, 10 g carbohydrate, trace fiber, 36 g protein.* **Diabetic Exchanges:** *5 lean meat, 1 fat, ½ starch.*

Parmesan cheese, bread crumbs, lemon-pepper and a bit of salt make a wonderful coating for fish. Try it—you'll love it!
—**CHARLOTTE ELLIOTT** NEENAH, WISCONSIN

Vegetable Curried Rice

I've served my vegetable rice dish to family and friends countless times. With its mild curry flavor and crunchy almonds, the colorful side complements a variety of main courses. Plus, the recipe is easy to double for picnics or other get-togethers.

—FRANCES EASTON WARRENTON, VIRGINIA

PREP/TOTAL TIME: 30 MINUTES **MAKES:** 4 SERVINGS

- ½ cup uncooked long grain rice
- ⅓ cup chopped onion
- 1 tablespoon olive oil
- 1 cup reduced-sodium chicken broth or vegetable broth
- ½ teaspoon curry powder
- ¼ teaspoon salt
- ⅛ teaspoon ground turmeric
- ⅓ cup frozen corn, thawed
- ⅓ cup frozen peas, thawed
- ¼ cup slivered almonds, toasted

1. In a small saucepan, cook rice and onion in oil until rice is lightly browned and onion is tender. Stir in the broth, curry powder, salt and turmeric. Bring to a boil. Reduce heat; cover and simmer for 12 minutes.

2. Stir in corn and peas. Cover and simmer 3-6 minutes longer or until rice and vegetables are tender. Sprinkle with almonds.

Nutrition Facts: ½ cup equals 184 calories, 7 g fat (1 g saturated fat), 0 cholesterol, 318 mg sodium, 26 g carbohydrate, 2 g fiber, 5 g protein. **Diabetic Exchanges:** 1½ starch, 1½ fat.

Cinnamon-Raisin Bites

These little scone-like treats are good not only warm from the oven, but also at room temperature. Grab a few when you're on your way out the door for work or school.

—HANNAH BARRINGER LOUDON, TENNESSEE

PREP/TOTAL TIME: 25 MINUTES **MAKES:** 2 DOZEN

- 2 cups all-purpose flour
- 3 teaspoons baking powder
- ½ teaspoon salt
- ½ teaspoon ground cinnamon
- ¼ teaspoon ground nutmeg
- 1 cup fat-free milk
- ¼ cup canola oil
- ¼ cup honey
- ½ cup raisins

1. In a large bowl, combine the flour, baking powder, salt, cinnamon and nutmeg.

2. In a small bowl, combine the milk, oil and honey; add to the dry ingredients and stir just until moistened. Stir in raisins.

3. Drop by tablespoonfuls onto baking sheets coated with cooking spray. Bake at 425° for 8-10 minutes or until lightly browned. Remove to wire racks.

Nutrition Facts: 1 piece equals 82 calories, 2 g fat (trace saturated fat), trace cholesterol, 104 mg sodium, 14 g carbohydrate, trace fiber, 2 g protein. **Diabetic Exchanges:** 1 starch, ½ fat.

Did you know?

Curry is a blend of many different ground spices used to replicate the individual spices combined in the cuisine of India. Curry powder imparts a distinctive flavor and rich golden color to recipes and can be found in both mild and hot versions. Most cooks season dishes lightly with curry powder and add more as desired to reach an acceptable spice level. Enjoy the unique flavor of curry in Vegetable Curried Rice (recipe above left).

ITALY

STEAK WITH A TASTE OF ITALY

A genuine Italian accent brings sensational flavor to this lighter meal. Saucy steaks, a colorful squash side dish and cappuccino-inspired treats for dessert are guaranteed to please.

Cappuccino Pudding

With the popular combination of chocolate, coffee and cinnamon, this smooth and creamy pudding is one of my very favorite desserts. Plus, it takes just 20 minutes to make! Finish each serving with a dollop of whipped topping and chocolate wafer crumbs.

—**CINDY BERTRAND** FLOYDADA, TEXAS

PREP/TOTAL TIME: 20 MINUTES **MAKES:** 4 SERVINGS

- 4 teaspoons instant coffee granules
- 1 tablespoon boiling water
- 1½ cups cold fat-free milk
- 1 package (1.4 ounces) sugar-free instant chocolate pudding mix
- ½ teaspoon ground cinnamon
- 1 cup reduced-fat whipped topping
  Additional whipped topping and chocolate wafer crumbs, optional

1. Dissolve coffee in boiling water; set aside. In a large bowl, combine the milk, pudding mix and cinnamon. Beat on low speed for 2 minutes. Let stand for 2 minutes or until set.
2. Stir in coffee. Fold in whipped topping. Spoon into serving dishes. Garnish with additional whipped topping and wafer crumbs if desired.
Nutrition Facts: ½ cup (calculated without optional ingredients) equals 105 calories, 2 g fat (0 saturated fat), 2 mg cholesterol, 48 mg sodium, 17 g carbohydrate, 0 fiber, 3 g protein.
Diabetic Exchanges: ½ starch, ½ fat-free milk.

Italian Steaks

PREP/TOTAL TIME: 25 MINUTES **MAKES:** 4 SERVINGS

- 1 egg
- ½ cup seasoned bread crumbs
- ½ teaspoon dried basil
- ½ teaspoon dried oregano
- ⅛ teaspoon salt
- ⅛ teaspoon pepper
- 1 beef top sirloin steak (1 pound)
- 1 tablespoon canola oil
- 1 cup pizza sauce
- ¼ cup shredded Italian cheese blend

1. In a shallow bowl, whisk egg. In another shallow bowl, combine the bread crumbs, basil, oregano, salt and pepper. Cut steak into four pieces; dip each piece in egg, then coat with bread crumb mixture.
2. In a large skillet, cook steaks in oil over medium-high heat for 2-4 minutes on each side or until meat reaches desired doneness (for medium-rare, a thermometer should read 145°; medium, 160°; well-done, 170°).
3. Meanwhile, heat sauce in a small saucepan. Spoon over steaks; sprinkle with cheese.
Nutrition Facts: 1 steak with ¼ cup sauce and 1 tablespoon cheese equals 264 calories, 11 g fat (3 g saturated fat), 104 mg cholesterol, 435 mg sodium, 9 g carbohydrate, 1 g fiber, 29 g protein. **Diabetic Exchanges:** 4 lean meat, 1 fat, ½ starch.

Sauteed Squash Medley

My sauteed veggies never last long on our dinner table. I usually pair them with an Italian-style entree, but they would go well with just about any main course.

—**KAY AYOTTE** ALBION, MICHIGAN

PREP/TOTAL TIME: 25 MINUTES
MAKES: 6 SERVINGS

- 1 small yellow summer squash, halved and sliced
- 1 small zucchini, halved and sliced
- 1½ cups sliced fresh mushrooms
- 1 medium onion, sliced
- 1 medium sweet red pepper, cut into ¼-inch strips
- 2 tablespoons butter
- ½ teaspoon garlic salt
- ¼ teaspoon pepper
- ½ cup grated Parmesan cheese

1. In a large skillet, saute the squash, zucchini, mushrooms, onion and red pepper in butter for 8-10 minutes or until tender. Stir in the garlic salt and pepper; sprinkle with cheese.
Nutrition Facts: ⅔ cup equals 91 calories, 6 g fat (4 g saturated fat), 16 mg cholesterol, 285 mg sodium, 6 g carbohydrate, 2 g fiber, 4 g protein. **Diabetic Exchanges:** 1 vegetable, 1 fat.

SAVORY SALAD IN THE MIX

If you think salad can't make a satisfying main course, you'll change your mind when you try this one! Create a complete menu with rustic rye muffins and family-friendly cereal bars.

> 66 Refreshing cucumber, garlic and jalapeno pepper give this entree salad its flair. I like to heat up the tangy dressing a bit before tossing it with the greens. 99

—JANET DINGLER CEDARTOWN, GEORGIA

Spinach Beef Salad

PREP/TOTAL TIME: 30 MINUTES **MAKES:** 4 SERVINGS

- ½ pound beef top sirloin steak, cut into thin strips
- 1 jalapeno pepper, seeded and chopped
- 1 garlic clove, minced
- 1 large sweet red pepper, julienned
- ½ medium cucumber, peeled and julienned
- ¼ cup lime juice
- 2 tablespoons brown sugar
- 2 tablespoons reduced-sodium soy sauce
- 1 teaspoon minced fresh mint or ½ teaspoon dried mint
- 1 teaspoon dried basil
- 1 teaspoon minced fresh gingerroot
- 6 cups torn fresh spinach

1. In a large nonstick skillet coated with cooking spray, saute the beef, jalapeno pepper and garlic until the beef reaches the desired doneness. Remove from the heat. Stir in the red pepper and cucumber.

2. In a small bowl, combine the lime juice, brown sugar, soy sauce, mint, basil and ginger. Place the spinach in a large bowl; add beef mixture and dressing. Toss to coat.

Editor's Note: *Wear disposable gloves when cutting hot peppers; the oils can burn skin. Avoid touching your face.*

Nutrition Facts: *2 cups equals 136 calories, 3 g fat (1 g saturated fat), 31 mg cholesterol, 367 mg sodium, 15 g carbohydrate, 2 g fiber, 13 g protein.* **Diabetic Exchanges:** *2 lean meat, 1 vegetable, ½ fruit.*

Quick Crisp Snack Bars

My daughters have loved peanutty, crispy cereal bars since they were in grade school. Now, both are adults and can whip up their own whenever they want a quick snack or treat.

—URSULA MAURER WAUWATOSA, WISCONSIN

PREP/TOTAL TIME: 30 MINUTES   **MAKES:** 1 DOZEN

- ½ cup honey
- ½ cup reduced-fat chunky peanut butter
- ½ cup nonfat dry milk powder
- 4 cups Rice Krispies

1. In a large saucepan, combine the honey, peanut butter and milk powder. Cook and stir over low heat until blended.
2. Remove from the heat; stir in cereal. Press into an 8-in. square dish coated with cooking spray. Let stand until set. Cut into bars.

Nutrition Facts: *1 bar equals 144 calories, 4 g fat (1 g saturated fat), 1 mg cholesterol, 144 mg sodium, 25 g carbohydrate, 1 g fiber, 5 g protein.* **Diabetic Exchanges:** *1½ starch, ½ fat.*

Raisin Rye Muffins

These yummy muffins spiced with cinnamon and sweetened with honey are egg-, wheat- and milk-free...but they don't taste like it!

—EDNA HOFFMAN HEBRON, INDIANA

PREP/TOTAL TIME: 30 MINUTES   **MAKES:** 6 MUFFINS

- 1 cup rye flour
- 2 teaspoons baking powder
- ½ teaspoon ground cinnamon
- ¼ teaspoon salt
- ½ cup water
- 2 tablespoons honey
- 2 tablespoons canola oil
- ½ cup raisins

1. In a large bowl, combine flour, baking powder, cinnamon and salt. Combine the water, honey and oil; stir into the dry ingredients just until moistened. Fold in raisins.
2. Fill six muffin cups coated with cooking spray two-thirds full. Bake at 400° for 15-20 minutes or until a toothpick comes out clean. Cool for 5 minutes before removing from pan to a wire rack. Serve warm.

Nutrition Facts: *1 muffin equals 160 calories, 5 g fat (trace saturated fat), 0 cholesterol, 234 mg sodium, 29 g carbohydrate, 3 g fiber, 2 g protein.* **Diabetic Exchanges:** *1 starch, 1 fruit, 1 fat.*

top tip — A Honey of a Hint

When I need to measure honey for baking or other recipes, I first oil the inside of the measuring cup. This way, the honey comes out easily, and I get the full measure without the messy process of scraping the cup.
—BARBARA R. PORTLAND, OREGON

FROM-THE-SEA SENSATION

Pair a delicious main course of shrimp and pasta with a well-dressed side salad, then serve fruity shakes as a refreshing finale. It's a meal your family will fall for hook, line and sinker!

Ginger-Peach Milk Shakes

PREP/TOTAL TIME: 5 MINUTES
MAKES: 3 SERVINGS

1 cup fat-free milk
1 cup reduced-fat vanilla ice cream
1 cup frozen unsweetened sliced peaches
¼ teaspoon ground ginger
    Unsweetened chopped peaches

1. In a blender, combine all ingredients; cover and process until smooth. Pour into chilled glasses; garnish with chopped peaches. Serve immediately.

Nutrition Facts: *¾ cup (calculated without garnish) equals 121 calories, 2 g fat (1 g saturated fat), 14 mg cholesterol, 67 mg sodium, 20 g carbohydrate, 1 g fiber, 5 g protein.* **Diabetic Exchanges:** *1 starch, ½ fat.*

What's better than a cool, creamy milk shake? Peaches and ginger result in a delightfully different combination.
—TASTE OF HOME TEST KITCHEN

top tip

Whenever I whip up a batch of milk shakes for a dessert or snack, I freeze a few extra servings separately. They make great, quick treats when my grandchildren pop in. It takes just 30 seconds in the microwave to soften the shakes to the right consistency.
—BONNIE BRAUN NAPA, CALIFORNIA

Springtime Tossed Salad

I first sampled a version of this distinctive medley at a restaurant. I liked the salad so much that I experimented in my own kitchen until I came up with a similar dressing that was lighter. The pecans lend a nice crunch, while cranberry-raspberry juice and mandarin oranges give fruity flavor to the mixed greens. It all adds up to one of my family's favorite summertime dishes.

—LAURA KOPP SHIOCTON, WISCONSIN

PREP/TOTAL TIME: 10 MINUTES **MAKES:** 6 SERVINGS

- 8 ounces spring mix salad greens
- 2 cans (11 ounces each) mandarin oranges, drained
- ½ cup crumbled blue cheese
- ¼ cup chopped pecans, toasted
- ½ cup cranberry-raspberry juice
- 3 tablespoons white wine vinegar
- 1 tablespoon olive oil

1. In a salad bowl, combine the greens, oranges, blue cheese and pecans. In a small bowl, whisk the cranberry-raspberry juice, vinegar and oil. Drizzle over the salad and toss to coat. Serve immediately.

Nutrition Facts: *1 cup equals 151 calories, 9 g fat (3 g saturated fat), 8 mg cholesterol, 173 mg sodium, 15 g carbohydrate, 2 g fiber, 4 g protein.*

Mediterranean Shrimp and Linguine

Toss together shrimp, linguine and veggies for a low-fat entree that looks like it came from an Italian eatery. The recipe can be prepared ahead of time and reheated for convenience.

—NANCY DEANS ACTON, MAINE

PREP/TOTAL TIME: 30 MINUTES **MAKES:** 6 SERVINGS

- 9 ounces uncooked linguine
- 1 pound uncooked medium shrimp, peeled and deveined
- 1 cup sliced fresh mushrooms
- 2 tablespoons olive oil
- 3 medium tomatoes, chopped
- 1 can (14 ounces) water-packed artichoke hearts, rinsed, drained and halved
- 1 can (6 ounces) pitted ripe olives, drained and halved
- 2 garlic cloves, minced
- 1 teaspoon dried oregano
- ½ teaspoon dried basil
- ½ teaspoon salt
- ⅛ teaspoon pepper

1. Cook the linguine according to the package directions. Meanwhile, in a large nonstick skillet, saute the shrimp and mushrooms in oil for 2 minutes. Add the remaining ingredients; cook and stir for 5 minutes or until the shrimp turn pink and sauce is heated through.

2. Drain the linguine; serve with the shrimp mixture.

Nutrition Facts: *1 cup shrimp mixture with ¾ cup linguine equals 328 calories, 9 g fat (1 g saturated fat), 112 mg cholesterol, 748 mg sodium, 41 g carbohydrate, 3 g fiber, 21 g protein.* **Diabetic Exchanges:** *2 starch, 2 lean meat, 1½ fat, 1 vegetable.*

TIME TO CHOOSE TURKEY

A healthier-for-you menu gets a great head start with an entree of turkey, pasta and veggies. Add a refreshing side salad and cool, fruity dessert for an unforgettable dinner.

Yogurt-Herb Salad Dressing

We enjoy this creamy, made-from-scratch salad dressing served with baby spinach greens, sliced tomatoes and onions. It's even good drizzled over fat-free cottage cheese.
—**GWEN KLAWUNDER** KENAI, ALASKA

PREP: 10 MINUTES + CHILLING **MAKES:** 1 CUP

> 1 **cup (8 ounces) fat-free plain yogurt**
> 1 **tablespoon white vinegar**
> 1 **tablespoon cider vinegar**
> 1 **teaspoon honey**
> 1 **tablespoon dried minced onion**
> 1½ **teaspoons Dijon mustard**
> ¾ **teaspoon dill weed**
> ¾ **teaspoon Italian seasoning**
> ¾ **teaspoon prepared mustard**
> ¼ **teaspoon seasoned salt**
> ⅛ **teaspoon pepper**

1. In a small bowl, whisk the yogurt, vinegars and honey. Stir in the remaining ingredients. Cover and refrigerate for at least 1 hour before serving.

Nutrition Facts: *2 tablespoons equals 19 calories, trace fat (trace saturated fat), 1 mg cholesterol, 94 mg sodium, 4 g carbohydrate, trace fiber, 1 g protein.*

Strawberry Rhubarb Sauce

You'll love how this strawberry-rhubarb sauce turns plain vanilla ice cream into an extra-special treat. Try the topping on your morning pancakes, waffles or French toast, too.
—**MIA WERNER** WAUKEGAN, ILLINOIS

PREP/TOTAL TIME: 15 MINUTES **MAKES:** 1¾ CUPS

> 2 **cups halved fresh strawberries**
> 1 **cup sliced fresh or frozen rhubarb**
> ⅔ **cup sugar**
> 1 **tablespoon cornstarch**
> 2 **tablespoons cold water**

1. In a small saucepan, combine the strawberries, rhubarb and sugar. Bring to a boil over medium heat. Combine cornstarch and water until smooth; stir into fruit mixture. Cook and stir for 1-2 minutes or until thickened. Serve warm or chilled.

Editor's Note: *If using frozen rhubarb, measure rhubarb while still frozen, then thaw completely. Drain in a colander, but do not press liquid out.*

Nutrition Facts: *¼ cup equals 96 calories, trace fat (trace saturated fat), 0 cholesterol, 1 mg sodium, 24 g carbohydrate, 1 g fiber, trace protein.*

Here is one of my family's favorite turkey dishes. It's quick, light and delicious. I never have to worry about leftovers!
—**PAULA MARCHESI** LENHARTSVILLE, PENNSYLVANIA

Creamy Turkey Fettuccine

PREP/TOTAL TIME: 30 MINUTES
MAKES: 6 SERVINGS

- 12 ounces uncooked fettuccine
- ¾ cup fat-free milk
- 4 ounces fat-free cream cheese, cubed
- ½ cup reduced-fat garlic-herb spreadable cheese
- 2 cups cubed cooked turkey breast
- 3 cups frozen chopped broccoli, thawed
- ½ cup chopped roasted sweet red peppers
- ½ cup shredded Parmesan cheese, divided
- ¼ teaspoon pepper

1. Cook the fettuccine according to the package directions. Meanwhile, in a large saucepan, combine milk, cream cheese and spreadable cheese. Cook and stir over medium heat until cheeses are melted and mixture is smooth. Stir in the turkey, broccoli, roasted peppers, ¼ cup Parmesan cheese and pepper; heat through.

2. Drain fettuccine and place in a large serving bowl. Top with turkey mixture; toss gently to coat. Sprinkle with remaining Parmesan cheese.

Nutrition Facts: *1⅓ cups equals 376 calories, 7 g fat (4 g saturated fat), 59 mg cholesterol, 461 mg sodium, 46 g carbohydrate, 4 g fiber, 32 g protein.*
Diabetic Exchanges: *3 lean meat, 2½ starch, 1 vegetable, 1 fat.*

Food Scale Solution

To measure out the correct amounts of foods listed in a recipe or on a diet plan, I use a food scale that is accurate to the ounce. It's really easy to get the right amount of an ingredient, such as pasta, if you need to use only part of the package or if the package is partially empty.
— **BETTY K.** FLORRISANT, MISSOURI

176

179

173

All-In-One Dinners

"The best part of making this zippy stir-fry is that it's a complete dinner all by itself—no side dishes are needed. My family is filled up with one recipe, and I'm out of the kitchen with time to spare!"

PATRICIA SWART GALLOWAY, NEW JERSEY
about her recipe, Mexican Fiesta Steak Stir-Fry, on page 185

Pronto Penne Pasta

PREP/TOTAL TIME: 30 MINUTES
MAKES: 6 SERVINGS

- 2¼ cups uncooked whole wheat penne pasta
- 1 pound Italian turkey sausage links, casings removed
- 1 medium red onion, chopped
- 1 medium green pepper, chopped
- 1 can (14½ ounces) no-salt-added diced tomatoes, undrained
- 1 can (14½ ounces) reduced-sodium chicken broth
- 2 garlic cloves, minced
- 2 teaspoons dried tarragon
- 2 teaspoons dried basil
- ¼ teaspoon cayenne pepper
- ¼ cup all-purpose flour
- ½ cup fat-free milk
- ½ cup shredded reduced-fat cheddar cheese
- ¼ cup grated Parmesan cheese

1. Cook the pasta according to package directions. Meanwhile, crumble sausage into a large nonstick skillet coated with cooking spray. Add the onion and green pepper; cook and stir over medium heat until meat is no longer pink. Drain. Stir in the tomatoes, broth, garlic, tarragon, basil and cayenne.

2. In a small bowl, combine flour and milk until smooth; stir into the sausage mixture. Bring to a boil; cook and stir for 2 minutes or until thickened.

3. Remove from the heat. Stir in the cheddar cheese until melted. Drain the pasta; toss with the sausage mixture. Sprinkle each serving with 2 teaspoons Parmesan cheese.

Nutrition Facts: *1 cup equals 373 calories, 11 g fat (3 g saturated fat), 55 mg cholesterol, 800 mg sodium, 45 g carbohydrate, 4 g fiber, 24 g protein.* **Diabetic Exchanges:** *2½ starch, 2 medium-fat meat, 1 vegetable.*

“My four sons have to be tricked into eating healthy! It's not easy to find foods they like, but this dinner always goes over well.”

—**TOMISSA HUART** UNION, ILLINOIS

Sausage Zucchini Skillet

I began serving a version of my skillet recipe as a side with grilled salmon. Adding Italian turkey sausage and rice created a complete meal-in-one dish. If you prefer, replace the rice with noodles.
—**DEBBY ABEL** FLAT ROCK, NORTH CAROLINA

PREP/TOTAL TIME: 25 MINUTES **MAKES:** 4 SERVINGS

- 1 **pound Italian turkey sausage links, casings removed**
- 2 **large zucchini, chopped**
- 1 **large sweet onion, chopped**
- 2 **garlic cloves, minced**
- 1 **can (14½ ounces) no-salt-added diced tomatoes, undrained**
- ¼ **teaspoon pepper**
- 2 **cups hot cooked rice**

1. In a large nonstick skillet coated with cooking spray, combine the sausage, zucchini and onion; cook and stir over medium heat until the meat is no longer pink. Add garlic; cook 1 minute longer. Drain.

2. Stir in the tomatoes and pepper; bring to a boil. Reduce heat; simmer, uncovered, for 4-5 minutes or until the liquid is evaporated. Serve with rice.

Nutrition Facts: *1¼ cups sausage mixture with ½ cup rice equals 329 calories, 11 g fat (2 g saturated fat), 68 mg cholesterol, 724 mg sodium, 36 g carbohydrate, 5 g fiber, 23 g protein.* **Diabetic Exchanges:** *3 lean meat, 2 vegetable, 1½ starch.*

Shrimp and Asparagus Penne

It's a breeze to whip up this special main course of asparagus, shrimp and penne pasta. We used to prepare it using heavy cream, but I substituted half-and-half to cut the fat. It's just as good!
—**DIANE SHIPLEY** MENTOR, OHIO

PREP/TOTAL TIME: 30 MINUTES **MAKES:** 4 SERVINGS

- 3 **cups uncooked penne pasta**
- 1 **pound fresh asparagus, trimmed and cut into 1-inch pieces**
- 1 **tablespoon butter**
- 1 **pound uncooked medium shrimp, peeled and deveined**
- 2 **teaspoons all-purpose flour**
- ¼ **teaspoon salt**
- ½ **cup half-and-half cream**
- ½ **cup grated Parmesan cheese, divided**

1. Cook pasta according to package directions. Meanwhile, in a large nonstick skillet, saute the asparagus in butter for 4 minutes. Add shrimp; cook and stir for 3-4 minutes or until shrimp turn pink. Remove and keep warm.

2. In a small bowl, combine the flour, salt and cream until smooth; gradually add to the skillet. Bring to a boil; cook and stir for 1-2 minutes or until thickened. Stir in ¼ cup cheese.

3. Remove from the heat. Drain pasta; toss with shrimp mixture and sauce. Sprinkle with remaining cheese.

Nutrition Facts: *2 cups equals 417 calories, 11 g fat (6 g saturated fat), 199 mg cholesterol, 580 mg sodium, 46 g carbohydrate, 3 g fiber, 32 g protein.* **Diabetic Exchanges:** *4 lean meat, 2½ starch, 2 fat, 1 vegetable.*

Chicken Orzo Skillet

As a busy homemaker with a home-based business, I try to serve my husband and children dinners that are quick yet healthy. I combined two recipes to come up with a skillet meal of chicken and orzo pasta.

—KATHLEEN FARRELL
ROCHESTER, NEW YORK

PREP/TOTAL TIME: 30 MINUTES
MAKES: 6 SERVINGS

- 1 **cup uncooked orzo pasta**
- 1 **pound boneless skinless chicken breasts, cubed**
- 3 **teaspoons olive oil, divided**
- 3 **garlic cloves, minced**
- 2 **cans (14½ ounces each) stewed tomatoes, cut up**
- 1 **can (15 ounces) white kidney or cannellini beans, rinsed and drained**
- 1½ **teaspoons Italian seasoning**
- ½ **teaspoon salt**
- 1 **package (16 ounces) frozen broccoli florets, thawed**

1. Cook orzo according to package directions. Meanwhile, in a large nonstick skillet coated with cooking spray, cook chicken in 2 teaspoons oil for 6-7 minutes or until no longer pink. Remove and keep warm.

2. In the same skillet, cook the garlic in the remaining oil for 1 minute or until tender. Stir in the tomatoes, beans, Italian seasoning and salt. Bring to a boil. Stir in the broccoli and chicken; heat through. Drain the orzo; stir into the chicken mixture.

Nutrition Facts: *1½ cup equals 342 calories, 5 g fat (1 g saturated fat), 42 mg cholesterol, 589 mg sodium, 49 g carbohydrate, 7 g fiber, 25 g protein.*
Diabetic Exchanges: *2 lean meat, 3 vegetable, 2 starch, ½ fat.*

Hamburger Chop Suey

Hearty and colorful, this beef chop suey with rice is a great way to please your family while using up homegrown peppers, spinach and other excess produce from the garden. If you have a bag of pea pods, consider tossing in some of those as well.

—BETH PISULA FREEPORT, ILLINOIS

PREP/TOTAL TIME: 30 MINUTES   **MAKES:** 6 SERVINGS

- 1 **tablespoon cornstarch**
- 2 **teaspoons minced fresh gingerroot**
- 1 **teaspoon reduced-sodium beef bouillon granules**
- ¾ **cup water**
- ⅓ **cup reduced-sodium soy sauce**

CHOP SUEY
- 1 **pound lean ground beef (90% lean)**
- 2 **celery ribs, sliced**
- 1 **cup sliced fresh mushrooms**
- 1 **medium green pepper, sliced**
- 1 **medium sweet red pepper, sliced**
- 1 **medium onion, halved and thinly sliced**
- 1 **can (14 ounces) bean sprouts, drained**
- 1 **can (8 ounces) sliced water chestnuts, drained**
- 1 **cup fresh spinach, torn**
- 3 **cups hot cooked rice**

1. In a small bowl, combine the cornstarch, ginger and bouillon; stir in water and soy sauce until blended. Set aside.

2. In a large nonstick skillet or wok, stir-fry the beef, celery, mushrooms, peppers and onion until meat is no longer pink and vegetables are tender. Drain. Stir in the bean sprouts, water chestnuts and spinach.

3. Stir the reserved sauce mixture; add to the pan. Bring to a boil; cook and stir for 1-2 minutes or until thickened. Serve with rice.

Nutrition Facts: *1⅓ cups chop suey with ½ cup rice equals 287 calories, 6 g fat (2 g saturated fat), 37 mg cholesterol, 679 mg sodium, 37 g carbohydrate, 4 g fiber, 20 g protein.* **Diabetic Exchanges:** *2 lean meat, 2 vegetable, 1½ starch.*

Did you know?

Cannellini beans are large white kidney beans and are generally available dry and canned. Some canned products will list both cannellini beans and large white kidney beans on the label. If you can't find cannellini beans in your area, substitute navy beans or great northern beans.

Shrimp 'n' Noodle Bowls

Here's a simple meal that tastes like it came from a restaurant. Cooked shrimp, bagged coleslaw mix and bottled salad dressing reduce the time needed to get it on the table.

—**MARY BERGFELD** EUGENE, OREGON

PREP/TOTAL TIME: 25 MINUTES **MAKES:** 6 SERVINGS

- 8 **ounces uncooked angel hair pasta**
- 1 **pound cooked small shrimp**
- 2 **cups broccoli coleslaw mix**
- 6 **green onions, thinly sliced**
- ½ **cup minced fresh cilantro**
- ⅔ **cup reduced-fat sesame ginger salad dressing**

1. Cook the pasta according to package directions; drain and rinse in cold water. Transfer to a large bowl. Add the shrimp, coleslaw mix, onions and cilantro. Drizzle with dressing; toss to coat. Cover and refrigerate until serving.

Nutrition Facts: *1⅓ cups equals 260 calories, 3 g fat (trace saturated fat), 147 mg cholesterol, 523 mg sodium, 36 g carbohydrate, 2 g fiber, 22 g protein.* **Diabetic Exchanges:** *2 starch, 2 lean meat, 1 vegetable.*

Cran-Apple Turkey Skillet

PREP/TOTAL TIME: 20 MINUTES **MAKES:** 6 SERVINGS

- 2 **medium apples, peeled and thinly sliced**
- ¾ **cup apple cider or unsweetened apple juice**
- ¾ **cup reduced-sodium chicken broth**
- ⅓ **cup dried cranberries**
- ⅛ **teaspoon ground nutmeg**
- 3 **cups cubed cooked turkey breast**
- 1 **package (6 ounces) corn bread stuffing mix**

1. In a large skillet, combine the apples, apple cider, broth, cranberries and nutmeg. Bring to a boil. Reduce heat; cover and simmer for 4-5 minutes or until apples are tender, stirring occasionally.

2. Stir in turkey and stuffing mix. Cover and cook for 2-3 minutes or until heated through.

Nutrition Facts: *1 cup equals 267 calories, 2 g fat (trace saturated fat), 60 mg cholesterol, 630 mg sodium, 36 g carbohydrate, 2 g fiber, 25 g protein.* **Diabetic Exchanges:** *3 lean meat, 1 starch, 1 fruit.*

❝Featuring the flavors of Thanksgiving dinner, this quick and easy dish is bound to become one of your go-to recipes.❞

—**LISA RENSHAW** KANSAS CITY, MISSOURI

Curry Turkey Stir-Fry

I've found that my spiced-up turkey stir-fry works well with leftover chicken, too. If you're in a hurry, use instant brown rice.

—LAUREEN RUSH ELK RIVER, MINNESOTA

PREP/TOTAL TIME: 25 MINUTES   **MAKES:** 4 SERVINGS

- ½ teaspoon cornstarch
- 2 tablespoons reduced-sodium soy sauce
- 1 tablespoon minced fresh cilantro
- 1 tablespoon honey
- 1 teaspoon curry powder
- 1 teaspoon sesame or canola oil
- 1 garlic clove, minced
- ⅛ teaspoon crushed red pepper flakes, optional
- 1 large sweet red pepper, julienned
- 1 tablespoon canola oil
- 3 green onions, cut into 3-inch pieces
- 2 cups cubed cooked turkey breast
- 2 cups cooked brown rice

1. In a small bowl, combine cornstarch, soy sauce, cilantro, honey, curry, sesame oil, garlic and pepper flakes if desired until blended; set aside.

2. In a large skillet or wok, stir-fry the red pepper in oil for 2 minutes or until crisp-tender. Add green onions; stir-fry 1-2 minutes longer or until vegetables are tender.

3. Stir cornstarch mixture and add to the pan. Bring to a boil; cook and stir for 2 minutes or until thickened. Add turkey; heat through. Serve with rice.

Nutrition Facts: *¾ cup stir-fry with ½ cup rice equals 287 calories, 7 g fat (1 g saturated fat), 60 mg cholesterol, 351 mg sodium, 31 g carbohydrate, 3 g fiber, 25 g protein.* **Diabetic Exchanges:** *3 lean meat, 1½ starch, 1 fat.*

Skillet Beef Tamales

Is your family in the mood for Mexican? These skillet tamales are beefy, cheesy and delicious—they don't taste light at all! Top off each serving with a dollop of fat-free sour cream.

—DEB WILLIAMS PEORIA, ARIZONA

PREP/TOTAL TIME: 30 MINUTES   **MAKES:** 5 SERVINGS

- 1 pound lean ground beef (90% lean)
- ⅓ cup chopped green pepper
- ⅓ cup chopped sweet red pepper
- 2 cups salsa
- ¾ cup frozen corn
- 2 tablespoons water
- 6 corn tortillas (6 inches), halved and cut into ½-inch strips
- ¾ cup shredded reduced-fat cheddar cheese
- 5 tablespoons fat-free sour cream

1. In a large nonstick skillet coated with cooking spray, cook beef and peppers over medium heat until meat is no longer pink; drain. Stir in the salsa, corn and water; bring to a boil.

2. Stir in tortilla strips. Reduce heat; cover and simmer for 10-15 minutes or until tortillas are softened. Sprinkle with cheese; cover and cook 2-3 minutes longer or until cheese is melted. Serve with sour cream.

Nutrition Facts: *1 cup beef mixture with 1 tablespoon sour cream equals 329 calories, 11 g fat (5 g saturated fat), 59 mg cholesterol, 679 mg sodium, 28 g carbohydrate, 6 g fiber, 25 g protein.* **Diabetic Exchanges:** *3 lean meat, 1½ starch, 1 vegetable, ½ fat.*

Stir-Fried Scallops and Asparagus

PREP/TOTAL TIME: 25 MINUTES
MAKES: 4 SERVINGS

- 1 package (3 ounces) chicken ramen noodles
- 1 pound fresh asparagus, trimmed and cut into 1-inch pieces
- 1 medium sweet red pepper, julienned
- 1 tablespoon olive oil
- 3 green onions, thinly sliced
- 1 garlic clove, minced
- 1 pound sea scallops, halved horizontally
- 1 tablespoon lime juice
- 2 tablespoons reduced-sodium soy sauce
- 1 teaspoon sesame oil
- 1 teaspoon hot pepper sauce

1. Discard the seasoning package from the ramen noodles or save for another use. Cook ramen noodles according to package directions; keep warm.

2. Meanwhile, in a nonstick skillet or wok, stir-fry asparagus and red pepper in oil for 2 minutes or until vegetables are crisp-tender. Add green onions and garlic, stir fry 1 minute longer. Stir in scallops. Stir-fry for 3 minutes or until scallops are firm and opaque.

3. Combine the lime juice, soy sauce, sesame oil and hot pepper sauce; stir into skillet. Serve with ramen noodles.

Nutrition Facts: *1 cup scallop mixture and ¼ cup noodles equals 269 calories, 9 g fat (3 g saturated fat), 37 mg cholesterol, 578 mg sodium, 22 g carbohydrate, 2 g fiber, 24 g protein.* **Diabetic Exchanges:** *3 lean meat, 1 starch, 1 vegetable, 1 fat.*

top tip If you ever use ramen noodles for recipes, you probably have a few of those seasoning packets left over. To use one up, try this simple rice dish. Heat 1 tablespoon of oil or butter in a saucepan, then stir in ⅓ cup uncooked long grain rice and the contents of the seasoning packet. Add ⅔ cup chicken broth and cover the pan. Simmer the rice for 15 minutes without lifting the lid, then turn off the heat and let it sit until the liquid is absorbed. It makes one serving of nicely seasoned rice.
—**BILL HILBRICH** ST. CLOUD, MINNESOTA

Served over quick-cooking ramen noodles, this seafood stir-fry is perfect for families on busy weekdays. It comes together in about half an hour. —**BARBARA SCHINDLER** NAPOLEON, OHIO

Sweet-and-Sour Pork

Why drive to a restaurant to get Chinese takeout when you can whip up your own in just 30 minutes? Red currant jelly gives my traditional dish of pork, pineapple and veggies a tangy kick. It's a colorful, satisfying dinner that's special enough for guests.

—JOANNE ALBERS GARDEN GROVE, CALIFORNIA

PREP/TOTAL TIME: 30 MINUTES **MAKES:** 4 SERVINGS

- 4 teaspoons cornstarch
- ½ teaspoon salt
- ½ teaspoon ground ginger
- ⅛ teaspoon pepper
- 1 can (8 ounces) unsweetened pineapple chunks
- ¼ cup cider vinegar
- 1 pork tenderloin (1 pound), cut into 1-inch cubes
- 5 teaspoons canola oil, divided
- 1 medium green pepper, cut into 1-inch pieces
- 1 medium sweet red pepper, cut into 1-inch pieces
- 1 small onion, cut into 1-inch pieces
- ⅓ cup red currant jelly
  Hot cooked rice, optional

1. In a small bowl, combine the cornstarch, salt, ginger and pepper. Drain pineapple, reserving juice; set pineapple aside. Stir juice and vinegar into cornstarch mixture until smooth; set aside.

2. In a large nonstick skillet or wok, stir-fry the pork in 3 teaspoons oil until no longer pink. Remove and keep warm. In the same pan, stir-fry peppers and onion in remaining oil until crisp-tender. Stir in the pork, pineapple and jelly.

3. Stir cornstarch mixture and add to the pan. Bring to a boil; cook and stir for 2 minutes or until thickened. Serve with rice if desired.

Nutrition Facts: 1¼ cups (calculated without rice) equals 311 calories, 10 g fat (2 g saturated fat), 63 mg cholesterol, 347 mg sodium, 33 g carbohydrate, 2 g fiber, 23 g protein. **Diabetic Exchanges:** 3 lean meat, 1 starch, 1 vegetable, 1 fat, ½ fruit.

Veggie Cheese Ravioli

PREP/TOTAL TIME: 20 MINUTES **MAKES:** 3 SERVINGS

- 1 package (9 ounces) refrigerated cheese ravioli
- 2 small zucchini, julienned
- 1 medium onion, chopped
- 1 can (14½ ounces) diced tomatoes, undrained
- 2 tablespoons chopped ripe olives
- ¾ teaspoon Italian seasoning
- 3 tablespoons shredded Parmesan cheese

1. Cook the ravioli according to the package directions. Meanwhile, in a large nonstick skillet coated with cooking spray, cook and stir zucchini and onion until tender. Stir in the tomatoes, olives and Italian seasoning. Bring to a boil. Reduce heat; simmer, uncovered, for 5 minutes.

2. Drain the ravioli and add to the pan; stir gently to combine. Sprinkle with cheese.

Nutrition Facts: 1½ cups equals 322 calories, 8 g fat (4 g saturated fat), 37 mg cholesterol, 649 mg sodium, 48 g carbohydrate, 6 g fiber, 17 g protein. **Diabetic Exchanges:** 2 starch, 2 vegetable, 1 lean meat, 1 fat.

"Have the best of both worlds with this fuss-free pasta meal. It tastes really light and refreshing, but the cheese ravioli makes it hearty and filling."

—GERTRUDIS MILLER EVANSVILLE, INDIANA

Black Bean Pasta

Want to skip the meat without sacrificing flavor? This satisfying vegetarian dish is a great choice. Plenty of beans, mushrooms and fettuccine will please everyone at the table.

—**ASHLYNN AZAR** ALBUQUERQUE, NEW MEXICO

PREP/TOTAL TIME: 25 MINUTES **MAKES:** 6 SERVINGS

    9 ounces uncooked whole wheat fettuccine
 1¾ cups sliced baby portobello mushrooms
    1 tablespoon olive oil
    1 garlic clove, minced
    1 can (15 ounces) black beans, rinsed and drained
    1 can (14½ ounces) diced tomatoes
    1 teaspoon dried rosemary, crushed
  ½ teaspoon dried oregano
    2 cups fresh baby spinach

1. Cook the fettuccine according to the package directions. Meanwhile, in a large skillet, saute mushrooms in oil until tender; add garlic, cook 2 minutes longer.
2. Stir in the black beans, tomatoes, rosemary and oregano. Cook and stir until heated through. Stir in the spinach until wilted. Drain fettuccine. Serve with bean mixture.
Nutrition Facts: *⅔ cup bean mixture with ⅔ cup pasta equals 255 calories, 3 g fat (trace saturated fat), 0 cholesterol, 230 mg sodium, 45 g carbohydrate, 9 g fiber, 12 g protein.* **Diabetic Exchanges:** *3 starch, 1 lean meat, ½ fat.*

Asian Pork Linguine

Peanut butter, ginger and honey make a delectable, Asian-style sauce for my pork and pasta toss. If I have fresh ginger on hand, I grate ¼ teaspoon to use in place of the ground version.

—**LISA VARNER** EL PASO, TEXAS

PREP/TOTAL TIME: 30 MINUTES **MAKES:** 5 SERVINGS

    6 ounces uncooked linguine
    2 teaspoons cornstarch
  ½ cup water
  ¼ cup reduced-fat creamy peanut butter
    2 tablespoons reduced-sodium soy sauce
    1 tablespoon honey
  ½ teaspoon garlic powder
  ⅛ teaspoon ground ginger
    1 pound boneless pork loin chops, cubed
    3 teaspoons sesame oil, divided
    2 medium carrots, sliced
    1 medium onion, halved and sliced

1. Cook linguine according to package directions. For sauce, in a small bowl, combine cornstarch and water until smooth. Whisk in the peanut butter, soy sauce, honey, garlic powder and ginger until blended; set aside.
2. In a large nonstick skillet or wok coated with cooking spray, stir-fry pork in 2 teaspoons oil until no longer pink. Remove and keep warm. Stir-fry carrots and onion in remaining oil until crisp-tender. Stir the sauce and add to the pan. Bring to a boil; cook and stir for 2 minutes or until thickened.
3. Return pork to the pan. Drain linguine; add to the pan and stir to coat.
Nutrition Facts: *1 cup equals 376 calories, 13 g fat (3 g saturated fat), 44 mg cholesterol, 358 mg sodium, 39 g carbohydrate, 3 g fiber, 27 g protein.*

Pepper Shrimp Scampi

Bright veggies, angel hair pasta and shrimp create an eye-catching combination that always wins raves. Just try it and see!
—**LINDA LASHLEY** REDGRANITE, WISCONSIN

PREP/TOTAL TIME: 30 MINUTES **MAKES:** 6 SERVINGS

- 6 ounces uncooked angel hair pasta
- 1 small zucchini, quartered and sliced
- 1 medium onion, chopped
- 1 medium green pepper, chopped
- 1 small sweet red pepper, chopped
- 4 garlic cloves, minced
- 1½ pounds uncooked medium shrimp, peeled and deveined
- ¼ cup reduced-fat butter, cubed
- 2 teaspoons dried oregano
- 1 teaspoon dried basil
- 2 tablespoons grated Parmesan cheese

1. Cook pasta according to package directions. Meanwhile, in a large nonstick skillet coated with cooking spray, saute the zucchini, onion, peppers and garlic until tender.
2. Add the shrimp; cook and stir for 2-4 minutes or until the shrimp turn pink. Stir in the butter, oregano and basil. Drain the pasta; add to the skillet and toss to coat. Sprinkle with Parmesan cheese.

Editor's Note: *This recipe was tested with Land O'Lakes light stick butter.*

Nutrition Facts: *1⅓ cups equals 258 calories, 6 g fat (3 g saturated fat), 183 mg cholesterol, 275 mg sodium, 27 g carbohydrate, 2 g fiber, 24 g protein.* **Diabetic Exchanges:** *3 lean meat, 1½ starch, 1 vegetable, 1 fat.*

Easy Chicken and Dumplings

Perfect for a cool autumn or winter evening, this meal-in-one recipe gives you all the comfort you're craving without all the fat, sodium and calories. Plus, it comes together in just half an hour.
—**NANCY TUCK** ELK FALLS, KANSAS

PREP/TOTAL TIME: 30 MINUTES **MAKES:** 6 SERVINGS

- 3 celery ribs, chopped
- 1 cup sliced fresh carrots
- 3 cans (14½ ounces each) reduced-sodium chicken broth
- 3 cups cubed cooked chicken breast
- ½ teaspoon poultry seasoning
- ⅛ teaspoon pepper
- 1⅔ cups reduced-fat biscuit/baking mix
- ⅔ cup fat-free milk

1. In a Dutch oven coated with cooking spray, saute celery and carrots for 5 minutes. Stir in the chicken broth, chicken, poultry seasoning and pepper. Bring to a boil; reduce heat to a gentle simmer.
2. For dumplings, combine biscuit mix and milk. Drop by tablespoonfuls onto simmering broth. Cover and simmer for 10-15 minutes or until a toothpick inserted in a dumpling comes out clean (do not lift cover while simmering).

Nutrition Facts: *1 cup chicken mixture with 3 dumplings equals 282 calories, 5 g fat (1 g saturated fat), 60 mg cholesterol, 1,022 mg sodium, 29 g carbohydrate, 1 g fiber, 28 g protein.* **Diabetic Exchanges:** *3 lean meat, 1½ starch, 1 vegetable, ½ fat.*

"Here's a restaurant-quality dish everyone will love. Pineapple gives the fried rice a tropical twist, while shrimp makes it a meal."

—LYNNE VAN WAGENEN SALT LAKE CITY, UTAH

Shrimp and Pineapple Fried Rice

PREP/TOTAL TIME: 30 MINUTES
MAKES: 6 SERVINGS

- 2 eggs
- 1 small onion, chopped
- 1 teaspoon canola oil
- 3 garlic cloves, minced
- 3 cups cooked instant brown rice
- 1 can (20 ounces) unsweetened pineapple chunks, drained
- ½ pound cooked medium shrimp, peeled and deveined
- ½ cup chopped cashews
- ½ cup frozen peas, thawed
- 2 green onions, sliced
- 3 tablespoons reduced-sodium soy sauce
- 1 tablespoon hoisin sauce
- 1 teaspoon sugar
- 1 teaspoon sesame oil
- ¼ teaspoon pepper

1. In a small bowl, whisk eggs. Heat a large nonstick skillet coated with cooking spray over medium heat. Add eggs; cook and stir until set; remove from the skillet and keep warm.

2. In the same skillet, saute onion in oil until tender. Add garlic; cook 1 minute longer. Stir in rice, pineapple, shrimp, cashews, peas and green onions; heat through. Combine the soy sauce, hoisin sauce, sugar, sesame oil and pepper; stir into rice mixture. Stir in eggs.

Nutrition Facts: *1⅓ cups equals 342 calories, 10 g fat (2 g saturated fat), 128 mg cholesterol, 521 mg sodium, 46 g carbohydrate, 4 g fiber, 16 g protein.*

top tip

Peeling Shrimp

Start on the underside by the head area to remove the shell from the shrimp. Pull the legs and first section of the shell to one side, then continue pulling the shell up around the top and to the other side. Pull off the shell by the tail of the shrimp if desired.

Fettuccine with Mushrooms and Tomatoes

I can toss together my fettuccine-and-vegetable recipe in just 30 minutes. It's a popular vegetarian choice I find myself relying on time and time again.
—**PHYLLIS SCHMALZ** KANSAS CITY, KANSAS

PREP/TOTAL TIME: 30 MINUTES **MAKES:** 6 SERVINGS

- 1 package (12 ounces) fettuccine
- 1 pound fresh mushrooms, halved
- 1 large onion, chopped
- 1 large green pepper, chopped
- 1 teaspoon olive oil
- 4 garlic cloves, minced
- 3 tablespoons all-purpose flour
- 3 cups 1% milk
- 1 teaspoon salt
- ¼ teaspoon pepper
- ½ cup sun-dried tomatoes (not packed in oil), thinly sliced
- 1 cup (4 ounces) shredded reduced-fat Swiss cheese
- ¼ cup grated Parmesan cheese

1. Cook fettuccine according to package directions. Meanwhile, in a large nonstick skillet, saute the mushrooms, onion and green pepper in oil for 4-6 minutes or until vegetables are tender. Add garlic; cook 1 minute longer.

2. In a small bowl, combine the flour, milk, salt and pepper until smooth; gradually stir into mushroom mixture. Add tomatoes. Bring to a boil; cook and stir for 2 minutes or until thickened. Stir in cheeses. Drain fettuccine; toss with sauce.

Nutrition Facts: *1⅓ cups equals 387 calories, 8 g fat (4 g saturated fat), 17 mg cholesterol, 662 mg sodium, 60 g carbohydrate, 5 g fiber, 23 g protein.*

Thai Restaurant Chicken

Treat everyone to a restaurant-style dinner featuring a taste of the Far East. Feel free to toss in any additional vegetables you like, creating your own Thai specialty.

—TRISHA KRUSE EAGLE, IDAHO

PREP/TOTAL TIME: 30 MINUTES
MAKES: 4 SERVINGS

- 2 **tablespoons cornstarch**
- 1 **tablespoon brown sugar**
- ¼ **teaspoon pepper**
- 1 **can (14½ ounces) reduced-sodium chicken broth**
- 2 **tablespoons rice vinegar**
- 2 **tablespoons reduced-sodium soy sauce**
- 2 **tablespoons reduced-fat peanut butter**
- 1 **pound boneless skinless chicken breasts, cut into 1-inch cubes**
- 2 **teaspoons sesame oil, divided**
- 1 **large onion, halved and sliced**
- 1 **medium sweet red pepper, julienned**
- 1 **cup sliced fresh mushrooms**
- 2 **garlic cloves, minced**
- 2 **cups hot cooked rice**

1. In a large bowl, combine cornstarch, brown sugar and pepper. Add chicken broth; stir until smooth. Stir in vinegar, soy sauce and peanut butter; set aside.

2. In a large nonstick skillet or wok, stir-fry chicken in 1 teaspoon oil until no longer pink. Remove and keep warm.

3. Stir-fry the onion and red pepper in the remaining oil for 2 minutes. Add the mushrooms; stir-fry 2-3 minutes or until crisp-tender. Add the garlic; cook 1 minute longer.

4. Stir cornstarch mixture and add to the pan. Bring to a boil; cook and stir for 1-2 minutes or until thickened. Add chicken; heat through. Serve with rice.

Nutrition Facts: *1 cup stir-fry with ½ cup rice equals 359 calories, 8 g fat (2 g saturated fat), 63 mg cholesterol, 704 mg sodium, 40 g carbohydrate, 2 g fiber, 31 g protein.*
Diabetic Exchanges: *3 lean meat, 2 starch, 1 vegetable, 1 fat.*

> This flavorful entree with chicken and pasta is hearty enough to be a one-dish meal. My family loves it—even with the spinach! —SARAH NEWMAN MAHTOMEDI, MINNESOTA

Italian Spinach and Chicken Skillet

PREP/TOTAL TIME: 30 MINUTES
MAKES: 4 SERVINGS

- 2 cups uncooked yolk-free whole wheat noodles
- 2 cups sliced fresh mushrooms
- 2 teaspoons olive oil
- 1 garlic clove, minced
- 1 can (14½ ounces) no-salt-added diced tomatoes, undrained
- 1 can (10¾ ounces) reduced-fat reduced-sodium condensed cream of chicken soup, undiluted
- ¾ cup spaghetti sauce
- 2 cups cubed cooked chicken breast
- 1 package (10 ounces) frozen chopped spinach, thawed and squeezed dry
- ¼ cup shredded Parmesan cheese
- 1½ teaspoons Italian seasoning
- ½ cup shredded part-skim mozzarella cheese

1. Cook the noodles according to the package directions. Meanwhile, in a large skillet, saute mushrooms in oil until tender. Add garlic; cook 1 minute longer. Stir in tomatoes, soup, spaghetti sauce, chicken, spinach, Parmesan cheese and Italian seasoning. Cook for 5-8 minutes or until heated through, stirring occasionally.
2. Drain the noodles; toss with the chicken mixture. Sprinkle with mozzarella cheese.

Nutrition Facts: *1½ cups equals 389 calories, 12 g fat (4 g saturated fat), 73 mg cholesterol, 821 mg sodium, 38 g carbohydrate, 7 g fiber, 35 g protein.*

top tip Cooking time varies with the variety of pasta. Dried pasta can take from 5 to 15 minutes to cook. To test for doneness, use a fork to remove a piece of pasta from the boiling water. Rinse it in cold water and taste. Pasta should be cooked until "al dente," or firm yet tender. Test often while cooking to avoid overcooking, which can result in a soft or mushy texture.

Black Bean Chicken with Rice

Enjoy a family favorite that dresses up chicken with beans, spices, rice and a handful of other pantry staples. It's a great go-to dinner when you're short on time.

—MOLLY NEWMAN PORTLAND, OREGON

PREP/TOTAL: 25 MINUTES
MAKES: 4 SERVINGS

- 3 teaspoons chili powder
- 1 teaspoon ground cumin
- 1 teaspoon pepper
- ¼ teaspoon salt
- 4 boneless skinless chicken breast halves (4 ounces each)
- 2 teaspoons canola oil
- 1 can (15 ounces) black beans, rinsed and drained
- 1 cup frozen corn
- 1 cup salsa
- 2 cups cooked brown rice

1. Combine the chili powder, cumin, pepper and salt; rub over the chicken. In a large nonstick skillet coated with cooking spray, brown the chicken in oil on both sides. Stir in the black beans, corn and salsa. Cover and cook over medium heat for 10-15 minutes or until a thermometer reads 170°.

2. Slice chicken; serve with rice and bean mixture.

Nutrition Facts: *1 chicken breast half with ¾ cup bean mixture and ½ cup rice equals 400 calories, 7 g fat (1 g saturated fat), 63 mg cholesterol, 670 mg sodium, 52 g carbohydrate, 8 g fiber, 32 g protein.*

Tortellini Primavera

Sprinkled with Parmesan cheese, this decadent tortellini with spinach, mushrooms and tomatoes always brings compliments. No one even notices that it's meatless!

—SUSIE PIETROWSKI BELTON, TEXAS

PREP/TOTAL TIME: 30 MINUTES   **MAKES:** 5 SERVINGS

- 1 package (19 ounces) frozen cheese tortellini
- ½ pound sliced fresh mushrooms
- 1 small onion, chopped
- 2 teaspoons butter
- 2 garlic cloves, minced
- ⅔ cup fat-free milk
- 1 package (8 ounces) fat-free cream cheese, cubed
- 1 package (10 ounces) frozen chopped spinach, thawed and squeezed dry
- 1 teaspoon Italian seasoning
- 1 large tomato, chopped
- ¼ cup shredded Parmesan cheese

1. Cook tortellini according to package directions. Meanwhile, in a large nonstick skillet coated with cooking spray, saute mushrooms and onion in butter until tender. Add garlic; cook 1 minute longer. Stir in milk; heat through. Stir in cream cheese until blended. Add spinach and Italian seasoning; heat through.

2. Drain tortellini; toss with sauce and tomato. Sprinkle with Parmesan cheese.

Nutrition Facts: *1¼ cups equals 341 calories, 10 g fat (5 g saturated fat), 28 mg cholesterol, 671 mg sodium, 41 g carbohydrate, 4 g fiber, 23 g protein.* **Diabetic Exchanges:** *2½ starch, 2 lean meat, 1 vegetable.*

---

top tip

Squeezing Spinach Dry

When a recipe calls for frozen spinach that is thawed and squeezed dry, I put the spinach in my salad spinner instead of squeezing it with my hands. The salad spinner makes it easy to get rid of the excess water without straining my fingers.

—EDITH L. LONGWOOD, FLORIDA

Asparagus Ham Dinner

I've been fixing my asparagus-ham combo for years, and it's always well received. Tomatoes, spiral pasta and cayenne pepper create a tempting and nutritious blend of flavors and textures.

—**RHONDA ZAVODNY** DAVID CITY, NEBRASKA

PREP/TOTAL TIME: 25 MINUTES **MAKES:** 6 SERVINGS

- 2 **cups uncooked spiral pasta**
- ¾ **pound fresh asparagus, cut into 1-inch pieces**
- 1 **medium sweet yellow pepper, julienned**
- 1 **tablespoon olive oil**
- 3 **cups diced fresh tomatoes (about 6 medium)**
- 6 **ounces boneless fully cooked ham, cubed**
- ¼ **cup minced fresh parsley**
- ½ **teaspoon salt**
- ½ **teaspoon dried oregano**
- ½ **teaspoon dried basil**
- ⅛ to ¼ **teaspoon cayenne pepper**
- ¼ **cup shredded Parmesan cheese**

1. Cook pasta according to package directions. Meanwhile, in a large nonstick skillet, saute asparagus and yellow pepper in oil until tender. Add tomatoes and ham; heat through.
2. Drain pasta; add to the vegetable mixture. Stir in seasonings. Sprinkle with cheese.

Nutrition Facts: *1⅓ cups equals 198 calories, 5 g fat (1 g saturated fat), 17 mg cholesterol, 559 mg sodium, 27 g carbohydrate, 3 g fiber, 12 g protein.* **Diabetic Exchanges:** *1 starch, 1 lean meat, 1 vegetable, ½ fat.*

Easy Mediterranean Chicken

Everyone's happy when this delicious chicken goes on the table. I lightened up the ingredients a bit, and it tastes just as good!

—**KARA ZILIS** OAK FOREST, ILLINOIS

PREP/TOTAL TIME: 30 MINUTES **MAKES:** 4 SERVINGS

- 4 **boneless skinless chicken breast halves (4 ounces each)**
- 1 **tablespoon olive oil**
- 1 **can (14½ ounces) no-salt-added stewed tomatoes**
- 1 **can (14½ ounces) cut green beans, drained**
- 1 **cup water**
- 1 **teaspoon dried oregano**
- ¼ **teaspoon garlic powder**
- 1½ **cups instant brown rice**
- 12 **pitted Greek olives, halved**
- ½ **cup crumbled feta cheese**

1. In a large nonstick skillet, brown the chicken in oil on each side. Stir in the tomatoes, green beans, water, oregano and garlic powder. Bring to a boil; reduce heat. Cover and simmer for 10 minutes.
2. Stir in the rice. Return to a boil. Cover and simmer 8-10 minutes longer or until a thermometer reads 170° and rice is tender. Stir in olives; sprinkle with cheese.

Nutrition Facts: *1 chicken breast half with 1 cup rice mixture and 2 tablespoons cheese equals 394 calories, 12 g fat (3 g saturated fat), 70 mg cholesterol, 724 mg sodium, 37 g carbohydrate, 6 g fiber, 30 g protein.* **Diabetic Exchanges:** *3 lean meat, 2 starch, 2 vegetable, 1 fat.*

Pork and Noodles

Savor a satisfying meal in just 30 minutes with this quick stovetop choice. It's the perfect way to use up leftover pork loin—or those extra cooked chops sitting in the refrigerator.

—**JANICE KENNEDY** SAYVILLE, NEW YORK

PREP/TOTAL TIME: 30 MINUTES **MAKES:** 2 SERVINGS

- 3 ounces uncooked angel hair pasta
- ½ pound boneless pork loin chops, cut into thin strips
- ¼ teaspoon salt
- ¼ teaspoon pepper
- 1 teaspoon canola oil, divided
- 1½ cups cut fresh green beans
- 2 celery ribs, sliced
- 4½ teaspoons chopped onion
- 3 tablespoons water
- 4 teaspoons reduced-sodium soy sauce
- 1 teaspoon butter

1. Cook pasta according to package directions. Meanwhile, sprinkle pork with salt and pepper. In a large nonstick skillet or wok coated with cooking spray, stir-fry pork in ½ teaspoon oil until no longer pink. Remove and keep warm.

2. In the same pan, stir-fry the beans, celery and onion in remaining oil until crisp-tender. Add the water, soy sauce and reserved pork; heat through. Drain pasta; stir in butter until melted. Add pork mixture and toss to coat.

Nutrition Facts: *2 cups equals 389 calories, 11 g fat (4 g saturated fat), 60 mg cholesterol, 783 mg sodium, 40 g carbohydrate, 5 g fiber, 30 g protein.* **Diabetic Exchanges:** *3 lean meat, 2 starch, 1 vegetable, 1 fat.*

Mexican Fiesta Steak Stir-Fry

The best part of making this zippy stir-fry is that it's a complete dinner all by itself—no side dishes are needed. My family is filled up with one recipe, and I'm out of the kitchen with time to spare!

—**PATRICIA SWART** GALLOWAY, NEW JERSEY

PREP/TOTAL TIME: 30 MINUTES **MAKES:** 4 SERVINGS

- 1 pound boneless beef top loin steak, trimmed and cut into thin strips
- 3 garlic cloves, minced
- 1 to 2 tablespoons canola oil
- 1 package (14 ounces) frozen pepper strips, thawed
- 1⅓ cups chopped sweet onion
- 2 plum tomatoes, chopped
- 1 can (4 ounces) chopped green chilies
- ½ teaspoon salt
- ½ teaspoon dried oregano
- ¼ teaspoon pepper
  Hot cooked rice

1. In a large skillet or wok, stir-fry beef and garlic in oil until meat is no longer pink. Remove and keep warm.

2. Add peppers and onion to pan; stir-fry until tender. Stir in the tomatoes, chilies, salt, oregano, pepper and beef; heat through. Serve with rice.

Nutrition Facts: *1½ cups (calculated without rice) equals 247 calories, 9 g fat (2 g saturated fat), 50 mg cholesterol, 473 mg sodium, 13 g carbohydrate, 3 g fiber, 26 g protein.* **Diabetic Exchanges:** *3 lean meat, 2 vegetable, 1 fat.*

Favorite Skillet Lasagna

PREP/TOTAL TIME: 30 MINUTES
MAKES: 5 SERVINGS

- ½ **pound Italian turkey sausage links, casings removed**
- 1 **small onion, chopped**
- 1 **jar (14 ounces) spaghetti sauce**
- 2 **cups uncooked whole wheat egg noodles**
- 1 **cup water**
- ½ **cup chopped zucchini**
- ½ **cup fat-free ricotta cheese**
- 2 **tablespoons grated Parmesan cheese**
- 1 **tablespoon minced fresh parsley or 1 teaspoon dried parsley flakes**
- ½ **cup shredded part-skim mozzarella cheese**

1. In a large nonstick skillet, cook sausage and onion over medium heat until no longer pink; drain. Stir in the spaghetti sauce, egg noodles, water and zucchini. Bring to a boil. Reduce heat; cover and simmer for 8-10 minutes or until the pasta is tender, stirring occasionally.

2. Combine the ricotta cheese, Parmesan cheese and parsley. Drop by tablespoonfuls over pasta mixture. Sprinkle with mozzarella cheese; cover and cook 3-5 minutes longer or until cheese is melted.

Nutrition Facts: *1 cup equals 250 calories, 10 g fat (3 g saturated fat), 41 mg cholesterol, 783 mg sodium, 24 g carbohydrate, 3 g fiber, 17 g protein.* **Diabetic Exchanges:** *2 lean meat, 1½ starch, 1 fat.*

Whole wheat pasta and zucchini pump up the nutrition in my 30-minute skillet lasagna. Topped off with dollops of ricotta cheese and a sprinkling of mozzarella, it's a light meal that tastes decadent. —**LORIE MINER** KAMAS, UTAH

top tip Handle zucchini carefully; they're thin-skinned and easily damaged. To pick the freshest zucchini, look for a firm, heavy squash with a moist stem end and a shiny skin. Smaller squash are generally sweeter and more tender than larger ones. Store zucchini in a plastic bag in the refrigerator crisper for 4 to 5 days. Do not wash zucchini until you are ready to use it.

Asian Chicken with Pasta

With its mild flavors, this dinner will please even the pickiest eaters at the table. Broccoli coleslaw mix adds a pleasant crunch.

—REBECCA SAMS OAK HARBOR, OHIO

PREP/TOTAL TIME: 25 MINUTES **MAKES:** 6 SERVINGS

- ½ pound uncooked angel hair pasta
- 1 pound chicken tenderloins, cut into 1-inch cubes
- ⅓ cup prepared balsamic vinaigrette
- ⅓ cup prepared Italian salad dressing
- 1 package (12 ounces) broccoli coleslaw mix
- ½ pound sliced fresh mushrooms
- ¾ cup julienned sweet red pepper
- ½ cup sliced onion
- ½ teaspoon garlic powder
- ½ teaspoon ground ginger
- ¼ teaspoon salt
- ⅛ teaspoon pepper

1. Cook pasta according to package directions. Meanwhile, in a large skillet, saute chicken in vinaigrette and salad dressing until no longer pink. Remove and keep warm.

2. In the same skillet, saute the coleslaw mix, mushrooms, red pepper and onion until tender. Add the seasonings. Stir in the chicken; heat through. Drain pasta. Add to chicken mixture; toss to coat.

Nutrition Facts: *1½ cups equals 320 calories, 8 g fat (1 g saturated fat), 44 mg cholesterol, 474 mg sodium, 38 g carbohydrate, 4 g fiber, 25 g protein.* **Diabetic Exchanges:** *3 lean meat, 2 starch, 1 vegetable, 1 fat.*

Beef 'n' Asparagus Pasta

I like to serve my beef-and-asparagus stir-fry over penne, but feel free to use whatever pasta you have on hand. The recipe can also make a filling meatless dish if you skip the beef strips.

—ELAINE NORGAARD PENN VALLEY, CALIFORNIA

PREP/TOTAL TIME: 30 MINUTES **MAKES:** 4 SERVINGS

- 3 cups uncooked bow tie pasta
- 1 tablespoon cornstarch
- ¾ cup reduced-sodium beef broth, divided
- 1 beef top sirloin steak (1 pound), cut into 2-inch strips
- 1 tablespoon olive oil
- 1 pound fresh asparagus, trimmed and cut into 1-inch pieces
- 4 green onions, chopped
- 4 garlic cloves, minced
- 1 cup sliced fresh mushrooms
- 1 large tomato, diced
- 1 teaspoon dried basil
- ½ teaspoon dried oregano
- ½ cup dry red wine or additional reduced-sodium beef broth
- 2 tablespoons sliced ripe olives, drained
- ½ teaspoon salt
- ¼ teaspoon pepper

1. Cook the pasta according to the package directions. In a small bowl, combine cornstarch and ¼ cup beef broth until smooth; set aside.

2. Meanwhile, in a large nonstick skillet or wok, stir-fry beef in oil for 1 minute or until the meat is no longer pink. Add the asparagus, onions and garlic; stir-fry for 2 minutes. Add the mushrooms, tomato, basil and oregano; stir-fry 2 minutes longer or until vegetables are crisp-tender.

3. Add the wine, olives, salt, pepper and remaining broth. Stir cornstarch mixture and gradually stir into skillet. Bring to a boil; cook and stir for 2 minutes or until thickened. Drain pasta; serve with beef mixture.

Nutrition Facts: *1 cup equals 451 calories, 11 g fat (3 g saturated fat), 64 mg cholesterol, 477 mg sodium, 51 g carbohydrate, 4 g fiber, 32 g protein.*

Gingered Beef Stir-Fry

Stir-fry is always popular in our home. My oldest son especially enjoys the combination of flank steak, fresh ginger, sweet red peppers and whole baby corn.

—DEBBIE WILLIAMS ASHLAND, OHIO

PREP/TOTAL TIME: 20 MINUTES **MAKES:** 4 SERVINGS

- 1½ teaspoons sugar
- 1 teaspoon cornstarch
- ¼ cup cold water
- 3 tablespoons reduced-sodium soy sauce
- 2 teaspoons sesame oil, divided
- 1 beef flank steak (1 pound), cut into thin strips
- 1 jar (8 ounces) whole baby corn, drained
- ¼ cup julienned sweet red pepper
- 2 teaspoons minced fresh gingerroot
- 2 teaspoons minced garlic
- ¼ pound fresh sugar snap peas
- 3 cups hot cooked rice

1. In a small bowl, combine sugar and cornstarch. Stir in the water, soy sauce and 1 teaspoon oil until smooth; set aside. In a large nonstick skillet or wok, stir-fry beef in remaining oil for 4-5 minutes or until no longer pink.

2. Add the corn, red pepper, ginger and garlic; stir-fry for 2-3 minutes or until the vegetables are crisp-tender. Add the peas; stir-fry 30 seconds longer. Stir soy sauce mixture and add to the pan. Bring to a boil; cook and stir for 2 minutes or until thickened. Serve with rice.

Nutrition Facts: *1 cup beef mixture with ¾ cup rice equals 377 calories, 12 g fat (4 g saturated fat), 48 mg cholesterol, 618 mg sodium, 41 g carbohydrate, 2 g fiber, 25 g protein.* **Diabetic Exchanges:** *3 lean meat, 2 starch, 1 vegetable, ½ fat.*

Italian Beef and Shells

PREP/TOTAL TIME: 30 MINUTES
MAKES: 4 SERVINGS

- 1½ cups uncooked medium pasta shells
- 1 pound lean ground beef (90% lean)
- 1 small onion, chopped
- 1 garlic clove, minced
- 1 jar (23 ounces) marinara sauce
- 1 small yellow summer squash, quartered and sliced
- 1 small zucchini, quartered and sliced
- ¼ cup dry red wine or reduced-sodium beef broth
- ½ teaspoon salt
- ½ teaspoon Italian seasoning
- ½ teaspoon pepper

1. Cook pasta according to package directions.

2. Meanwhile, in a Dutch oven, cook the beef, onion and garlic over medium heat until the meat is no longer pink; drain. Stir in the marinara sauce, squash, zucchini, wine and seasonings. Bring to a boil. Reduce heat; simmer, uncovered, for 10-15 minutes or until thickened. Drain pasta; stir into beef mixture and heat through.

Nutrition Facts: *1¾ cups equals 396 calories, 10 g fat (4 g saturated fat), 71 mg cholesterol, 644 mg sodium, 45 g carbohydrate, 5 g fiber, 29 g protein.*
Diabetic Exchanges: *3 starch, 3 lean meat.*

Slicing Beef for Stir-Fry

I like to use flank steak (London broil) for stir-fry dishes and fajitas, but it can be difficult to cut the meat into thin, uniform slices when it's fresh. I've found it's much faster and easier to do if the meat is partially frozen.

—ELIZABETH W. VEAZIE, MAINE

"A hearty dinner comes easy when you prepare this Italian pasta recipe. A little wine lends extra flavor to the sauce."

—**MIKE TCHOU** PEPPER PIKE, OHIO

Colorful Crab Stir-Fry

My love for seafood has carried over from childhood, when we used to fish together as a family. So I was happy to discover a change-of-pace recipe that combines stir-fry with seafood.

—**LEE DENEAU** LANSING, MICHIGAN

PREP/TOTAL TIME: 30 MINUTES **MAKES:** 4 SERVINGS

- 2 teaspoons cornstarch
- 1 teaspoon chicken bouillon granules
- ¾ cup water
- ½ teaspoon reduced-sodium soy sauce
- 1 cup sliced fresh carrots
- 1 tablespoon canola oil
- 1 cup fresh or frozen snow peas
- ½ cup julienned sweet red pepper
- 1 teaspoon minced fresh gingerroot
- 1 teaspoon minced garlic
- 1 package (8 ounces) imitation crabmeat
  Hot cooked rice, optional

1. In a small bowl, combine the cornstarch, chicken bouillon, water and soy sauce until smooth; set aside. In a large skillet or wok, stir-fry carrots in oil. Add the peas, red pepper, ginger and garlic; stir-fry 1-2 minutes longer or until vegetables are crisp-tender.

2. Stir cornstarch mixture and gradually add to the pan. Bring to a boil; cook and stir for 2 minutes or until thickened. Add crab; heat through. Serve with rice if desired.

Nutrition Facts: *¾ cup (calculated without rice) equals 126 calories, 4 g fat (trace saturated fat), 7 mg cholesterol, 562 mg sodium, 16 g carbohydrate, 2 g fiber, 7 g protein.* **Diabetic Exchanges:** *3 vegetable, 1 lean meat.*

Asian Vegetable Pasta

Peanut butter and a sprinkling of peanuts give this Asian-inspired dish plenty of flavor. While red pepper flakes provide a little kick, brown sugar balances it out with a touch of sweetness.

—**MITZI SENTIFF** ANNAPOLIS, MARYLAND

PREP/TOTAL TIME: 20 MINUTES **MAKES:** 5 SERVINGS

- 4 quarts water
- 1 pound fresh asparagus, trimmed and cut into 1-inch pieces
- 8 ounces uncooked angel hair pasta
- ¾ cup julienned carrots
- ⅓ cup reduced-fat creamy peanut butter
- 3 tablespoons rice vinegar
- 3 tablespoons reduced-sodium soy sauce
- 2 tablespoons brown sugar
- ½ teaspoon crushed red pepper flakes
- ¼ cup unsalted peanuts, chopped

1. In a Dutch oven, bring the water to a boil. Add asparagus and pasta; cook for 3 minutes. Stir in carrots; cook for 1 minute or until pasta is tender. Drain and keep warm.

2. In a small saucepan, combine the peanut butter, vinegar, soy sauce, brown sugar and pepper flakes. Bring to a boil over medium heat, stirring constantly. Pour over pasta mixture; toss to coat. Sprinkle with peanuts.

Nutrition Facts: *1 cup equals 358 calories, 10 g fat (2 g saturated fat), 0 cholesterol, 472 mg sodium, 54 g carbohydrate, 5 g fiber, 15 g protein.*

Stir-Fried Steak & Veggies

Want a dinner that's done in less than half an hour? Convenience products such as frozen stir-fry vegetables combine with simple seasonings for a delicious, healthful meal you're sure to enjoy.

—VICKY PRIESTLEY
ALUM CREEK, WEST VIRGINIA

PREP/TOTAL TIME: 25 MINUTES
MAKES: 6 SERVINGS

- 1½ cups uncooked instant brown rice
- 1 tablespoon cornstarch
- 1 tablespoon brown sugar
- ¾ teaspoon ground ginger
- ½ teaspoon chili powder
- ¼ teaspoon garlic powder
- ¼ teaspoon pepper
- ½ cup cold water
- ¼ cup reduced-sodium soy sauce
- 1 pound beef top sirloin steak, cut into ½-inch cubes
- 2 tablespoons canola oil, divided
- 1 package (16 ounces) frozen stir-fry vegetable blend, thawed

1. Cook rice according to package directions. Meanwhile, in a small bowl, combine the cornstarch, brown sugar and seasonings. Stir in water and soy sauce until smooth; set aside.

2. In a large nonstick skillet or wok coated with cooking spray, stir-fry beef in 1 tablespoon oil until no longer pink. Remove and keep warm. Stir-fry the vegetables in the remaining oil until crisp-tender.

3. Stir cornstarch mixture and add to the pan. Bring to a boil; cook and stir for 2 minutes or until thickened. Add beef; heat through. Serve with rice.

Nutrition Facts: *¾ cup stir-fry with ½ cup rice equals 304 calories, 8 g fat (2 g saturated fat), 42 mg cholesterol, 470 mg sodium, 37 g carbohydrate, 3 g fiber, 19 g protein.* **Diabetic Exchanges:** *2 lean meat, 2 vegetable, 1½ starch, 1 fat.*

194

202

210

Decadent Desserts

❝ You'll love the tangy combination of berry and lemon in these pretty little tartlets. Quick and easy, they're ideal for a bridal shower or as a fun dessert anytime. **❞**

PAM JAVOR NORTH HUNTINGDON, PENNSYLVANIA
about her recipe, Lemon Burst Tartlets, on page 215

Angel Food Trifle

A ricotta-vanilla "custard" cuts calories and boosts calcium in this light take on an English classic. Try the refreshing trifle for a spring or summer get-together.

—MERWYN GARBINI TUCSON, ARIZONA

PREP/TOTAL TIME: 15 MINUTES
MAKES: 8 SERVINGS

- 2 cups fat-free vanilla yogurt
- 1 cup part-skim ricotta cheese
- 1 cup fresh blueberries
- 1 cup sliced fresh strawberries
- 4 cups cubed angel food cake
- ½ cup reduced-fat whipped topping

1. In a blender, combine the yogurt and ricotta cheese; cover and process until combined.
2. In a small bowl, combine blueberries and strawberries. Place half the angel food cake cubes in a 2-qt. glass bowl. Layer with 1 cup berries and half the yogurt mixture. Top with the remaining cake cubes, ¾ cup berries and the remaining yogurt mixture. Garnish with the remaining berries. Top with whipped topping. Refrigerate leftovers.
Nutrition Facts: *¾ cup equals 182 calories, 3 g fat (2 g saturated fat), 11 mg cholesterol, 248 mg sodium, 30 g carbohydrate, 1 g fiber, 8 g protein.* **Diabetic Exchanges:** *1½ starch, ½ fat-free milk, ½ fat.*

Chocolate Biscuit Puffs

I know these treats are fun for children because I dreamed them up when I was 9 years old! Made with convenient refrigerated biscuit dough, the easy puffs are filled with chocolate, sprinkled with cinnamon-sugar and baked until golden brown.

—JOY CLARK SEABECK, WASHINGTON

PREP/TOTAL TIME: 20 MINUTES **MAKES:** 10 SERVINGS

- 1 package (7½ ounces) refrigerated flaky buttermilk biscuits
- 1 milk chocolate candy bar (1.55 ounces)
- 2 teaspoons cinnamon-sugar

1. Flatten each biscuit into a 3-in. circle. Break candy bar into 10 pieces; place a piece on each biscuit. Bring up edges to enclose candy and pinch to seal.
2. Place on an ungreased baking sheet. Sprinkle with cinnamon-sugar. Bake at 450° for 8-10 minutes or until golden brown.
Nutrition Facts: *1 puff equals 78 calories, 2 g fat (1 g saturated fat), 1 mg cholesterol, 185 mg sodium, 14 g carbohydrate, trace fiber, 2 g protein.* **Diabetic Exchange:** *1 starch.*

Did you know?

When a cheese maker separates milk or cream into curds and whey, the curds are used to make cottage cheese and the whey is used to make ricotta. That's why these two cheeses, although similarly soft and mild in flavor, have such different textures.

Summertime Fruit Cones

PREP/TOTAL TIME: 20 MINUTES
MAKES: 4 SERVINGS

- 2 medium nectarines, chopped
- 1 cup whole small fresh strawberries
- 1 cup fresh blueberries
- 2 tablespoons mashed fresh strawberries
- 1 teaspoon finely chopped crystallized ginger
- ¼ teaspoon ground cinnamon
- 1 cup reduced-fat whipped topping
- 4 ice cream waffle cones

1. In a small bowl, combine nectarines, whole strawberries and blueberries. In another bowl, combine the mashed strawberries, ginger and cinnamon. Fold in whipped topping.

2. Fill each waffle cone with ¼ cup fruit mixture; top with 2 tablespoons whipped topping mixture. Repeat layers. Serve immediately.

Nutrition Facts: *1 fruit cone equals 162 calories, 4 g fat (2 g saturated fat), 1 mg cholesterol, 18 mg sodium, 31 g carbohydrate, 3 g fiber, 2 g protein.* **Diabetic Exchanges:** *1 starch, 1 fruit, ½ fat.*

Here's a simple summer treat that appeals to both children and adults. If you like, serve the fruit mixture and whipped topping in parfait glasses instead of ice cream cones.
—TASTE OF HOME TEST KITCHEN

Apple Skewers

These spiced-up apple chunks are lightly coated with cinnamon and sugar before going on the grill. They're wonderful for dessert when you're having a cookout!

—**DORIS SOWERS** HUTCHINSON, KANSAS

PREP/TOTAL TIME: 30 MINUTES
MAKES: 4 SERVINGS

- 4 medium apples, peeled and quartered
- 4 teaspoons sugar
- 1¼ teaspoons ground cinnamon

1. Thread the apples on four metal or soaked wooden skewers. Lightly spray with cooking spray. Combine sugar and cinnamon; sprinkle over apples.

2. Using long-handled tongs, moisten a paper towel with cooking oil and lightly coat the grill rack. Grill, covered, over medium heat or broil 4 in. from the heat for 6-8 minutes or until golden. Turn; cook 8-10 minutes longer or until golden and tender. Serve warm.

Nutrition Facts: *1 skewer equals 80 calories, trace fat (trace saturated fat), 0 cholesterol, trace sodium, 21 g carbohydrate, 2 g fiber, trace protein.*
Diabetic Exchange: *1 fruit.*

top tip
My children and husband love having cinnamon toast for breakfast. To save time, I mix together a big batch of cinnamon-sugar and keep it in a large shaker. This way, my family can have their favorite treat whenever they want without me preparing a brand-new batch of cinnamon-sugar every morning.

—**HEATHER TUCKER** SHELLEY, IDAHO

Berries with Sour Cream Sauce

A dollop of honey-sweetened sour cream makes a yummy finishing touch for fresh-picked berries. Try it—you'll love it!

—LINDA FRANCESCHI ELDRED, NEW YORK

PREP/TOTAL TIME: 10 MINUTES **MAKES:** 10 SERVINGS

- 1 **quart fresh strawberries, halved**
- 1 **pint fresh raspberries**
- 1 **pint fresh blueberries**
- 1 **pint fresh blackberries**
- 2 **cups (16 ounces) reduced-fat sour cream**
- ¼ **cup honey**

1. In a large bowl, combine the first four ingredients. In another bowl, combine the sour cream and honey. Serve with the berries.

Nutrition Facts: *¾ cup fruit with 3 tablespoons sauce equals 147 calories, 4 g fat (3 g saturated fat), 15 mg cholesterol, 32 mg sodium, 25 g carbohydrate, 6 g fiber, 4 g protein.* **Diabetic Exchanges:** *1 fruit, ½ starch, ½ fat.*

Banana Chocolate Parfaits

Smooth chocolate pudding, sliced bananas, whipped topping and crunchy wafer crumbs are an irresistible combination. Layer the ingredients to create parfaits, then watch them disappear!

—TASTE OF HOME TEST KITCHEN

PREP/TOTAL TIME: 20 MINUTES **MAKES:** 8 SERVINGS

- 3 **medium bananas, sliced**
- ¼ **cup lemon juice**
- 2 **cups cold fat-free milk**
- 1 **package (1.4 ounces) sugar-free instant chocolate pudding mix**
- 1 **cup (8 ounces) reduced-fat sour cream**
- 1½ **cups reduced-fat whipped topping**
- 8 **chocolate wafers, crushed**

1. In a small bowl, combine the bananas and lemon juice; let stand for 5 minutes. In another bowl, whisk the milk and pudding mix for 2 minutes. Refrigerate for 5 minutes. Stir in the sour cream.

2. Drain the bananas. Place half of the banana slices in eight parfait glasses; layer with the pudding mixture, whipped topping, chocolate wafer crumbs and remaining banana slices. Refrigerate until serving.

Nutrition Facts: *1 parfait equals 183 calories, 6 g fat (5 g saturated fat), 11 mg cholesterol, 236 mg sodium, 27 g carbohydrate, 2 g fiber, 5 g protein.* **Diabetic Exchanges:** *1 starch, 1 fat, ½ fruit.*

Angel Food Cake with Fruit

I get so many compliments when I serve this dessert, and no one guesses how simple it is to prepare. A mixture of fruit and peach pie filling really dresses up the prepared angel food cake.
—**JENNIFER DRAKE** EVANS, GEORGIA

PREP/TOTAL TIME: 10 MINUTES **MAKES:** 8 SERVINGS

- 1 **can (21 ounces) peach pie filling**
- 1 **package (16 ounces) frozen unsweetened strawberries, thawed and drained or 1½ cups fresh strawberries, halved**
- 1 **can (11 ounces) mandarin oranges, drained**
- 2 **medium apples, chopped**
- 2 **medium firm bananas, sliced**
- 1 **prepared angel food cake (8 to 10 ounces), cut into 8 slices**
   Whipped topping, optional

1. In a large bowl, combine the peach pie filling, strawberries, oranges and apples. Fold in the bananas. Spoon a heaping ½ cupful over each slice of angel food cake. Garnish with whipped topping if desired.

Nutrition Facts: *1 serving equals 231 calories, 1 g fat (trace saturated fat), 0 cholesterol, 229 mg sodium, 56 g carbohydrate, 4 g fiber, 3 g protein.*

Double Chocolate Pudding

In the mood for something comforting? Whip up your own rich, creamy pudding from scratch. You'll never want to settle for a store-bought mix again! Using both German chocolate and baking cocoa is a doubly delightful way to keep the fat content in check.
—**TASTE OF HOME TEST KITCHEN**

PREP/TOTAL TIME: 25 MINUTES **MAKES:** 8 SERVINGS

- ¾ **cup sugar**
- ⅓ **cup baking cocoa**
- ¼ **cup cornstarch**
- ⅛ **teaspoon salt**
- 3 **cups fat-free milk**
- 1 **can (5 ounces) evaporated milk**
- 1 **ounce German sweet chocolate, grated**
- 1 **teaspoon vanilla extract**
- ¼ **cup whipped topping**

1. In a large heavy saucepan, combine the sugar, cocoa, cornstarch and salt. Gradually add the milks. Bring to a boil over medium heat; cook and stir for 2 minutes or until thickened. Remove from the heat.

2. Stir in grated chocolate and vanilla. Spoon into individual serving dishes. Serve warm or cold with whipped topping.

Nutrition Facts: *½ cup equals 166 calories, 2 g fat (1 g saturated fat), 4 mg cholesterol, 72 mg sodium, 33 g carbohydrate, 1 g fiber, 5 g protein.* **Diabetic Exchanges:** *1½ starch, ½ fat-free milk.*

With toasted angel food cake and chocolate syrup, this recipe makes fruit seem decadent. It's the perfect treat for a backyard party. —**MELISSA HASS** GILBERT, SOUTH CAROLINA

Grilled Fruit Skewers with Chocolate Syrup

PREP/TOTAL TIME: 25 MINUTES
MAKES: 8 SERVINGS

- 2 cups cubed angel food cake
- 1 cup fresh strawberries
- 1 cup cubed fresh pineapple
- 1 cup cubed cantaloupe
- 1 large banana, cut into 1-inch slices
- 2 medium plums, pitted and quartered
  Butter-flavored cooking spray
- ½ cup packed brown sugar
- 8 teaspoons chocolate syrup

1. On eight metal or soaked wooden skewers, alternately thread the angel food cake cubes and fruits. Spritz each skewer with butter-flavored spray and roll in brown sugar.

2. Place the skewers on a piece of heavy-duty foil. Place foil on grill rack. Grill, covered, over medium heat for 4-5 minutes on each side or until fruits are tender, turning once. Drizzle each skewer with 1 teaspoon chocolate syrup.

Nutrition Facts: *1 skewer equals 131 calories, 1 g fat (trace saturated fat), 0 cholesterol, 93 mg sodium, 30 g carbohydrate, 2 g fiber, 2 g protein.*
Diabetic Exchanges: *1 starch, 1 fruit.*

Grilled Peach Crisps

Much of the fat and sugar found in traditional peach cobbler is missing from my campfire version. The tender fruit is sprinkled with cinnamon and sugar, cooked on the grill, then topped off with crunchy granola and a scoop of vanilla ice cream. Yum!
—**MICHELLE SANDOVAL** ESCALON, CALIFORNIA

PREP/TOTAL TIME: 25 MINUTES   **MAKES:** 8 SERVINGS

- 2 tablespoons sugar
- 1 teaspoon ground cinnamon
- 4 medium peaches, halved and pitted
- 4 cups reduced-fat vanilla ice cream
- 1 cup reduced-fat granola

1. In a small bowl, combine sugar and cinnamon; sprinkle over cut sides of peaches. Let stand for 5 minutes.

2. Using long-handled tongs, moisten a paper towel with cooking oil and lightly coat the grill rack. Place peaches cut side down on grill rack. Grill, covered, over medium heat for 8-10 minutes or until peaches are tender and begin to caramelize.

3. Place peaches in dessert bowls. Serve with ice cream and granola.

Nutrition Facts: *1 serving equals 193 calories, 4 g fat (2 g saturated fat), 18 mg cholesterol, 83 mg sodium, 36 g carbohydrate, 2 g fiber, 5 g protein.*

Peachy Pointers

Purchase peaches that have an intense fragrance and that give slightly to palm pressure. Store ripe peaches in a plastic bag in the refrigerator for up to 5 days. To easily remove the pit, cut the fruit from stem to stem all the way around, then simply twist the peach halves in opposite directions and lift out the pit.

Berry-Marshmallow Trifle

My guests say this trifle is almost too pretty to eat! I love the fact that I can put it together a day ahead of time for convenience, and neither taste nor appearance is compromised.

—**SHANNON ALDRIDGE** SUWANEE, GEORGIA

PREP/TOTAL TIME: 25 MINUTES **MAKES:** 10 SERVINGS

- 1¾ cups cold fat-free milk
- 1 package (1 ounce) sugar-free instant vanilla pudding mix
- 1 carton (8 ounces) frozen fat-free whipped topping, thawed, divided
- 1 loaf (10¾ ounces) frozen reduced-fat pound cake, thawed and cut into 1-inch cubes
- 3 cups fresh strawberries, halved
- 2 cups miniature marshmallows
- 3 tablespoons sliced almonds

1. In a small bowl, whisk milk and pudding mix for 2 minutes. Let stand for 2 minutes or until soft-set. Fold in 2½ cups whipped topping; set aside.

2. Place half of the pound cake cubes in a 3-qt. trifle bowl; spoon half of the reserved pudding mixture over the top. Top with half of the strawberries and marshmallows. Repeat layers. Top with the remaining whipped topping; sprinkle with almonds. Chill until serving.

Nutrition Facts: *1 cup equals 230 calories, 6 g fat (1 g saturated fat), 18 mg cholesterol, 298 mg sodium, 40 g carbohydrate, 2 g fiber, 4 g protein.*

Broiled Fruit Dessert

Popped in the oven for a few minutes, the sugar-sprinkled halves of a peach and nectarine become bubbly and delicious. If you like, top them with whipped cream or vanilla ice cream.

—**JIM GALES** GLENDALE, WISCONSIN

PREP/TOTAL TIME: 15 MINUTES **MAKES:** 2 SERVINGS

- 1 medium peach
- 1 medium fresh nectarine
- 1 tablespoon brown sugar
  Whipped cream or vanilla ice cream, optional

1. Halve and pit the peach and nectarine. Line a shallow baking dish with foil; coat foil with cooking spray. Place fruit cut side down in prepared dish.

2. Broil 6 in. from the heat for 3 minutes; turn fruit over and sprinkle with brown sugar. Broil 2-3 minutes longer or until sugar is melted and bubbly. Serve warm with whipped cream or ice cream if desired.

Nutrition Facts: *1 serving (calculated without whipped cream or ice cream) equals 80 calories, trace fat (trace saturated fat), 0 cholesterol, 3 mg sodium, 20 g carbohydrate, 2 g fiber, 1 g protein.* **Diabetic Exchange:** *1 fruit.*

I turn to this simple recipe when I want a light yet special treat for company. Enjoy the parfaits not only for dessert, but also for breakfast. —**KARIN CHRISTIAN** PLANO, TEXAS

Fresh Fruit Parfaits

PREP/TOTAL TIME: 30 MINUTES
MAKES: 4 SERVINGS

- ½ cup mixed berry yogurt
- ¾ cup reduced-fat whipped topping
- 1 cup sliced ripe banana
- 1 cup sliced fresh strawberries
- 1 cup cubed fresh pineapple
- 1 cup fresh blueberries
- 4 whole strawberries

1. In a small bowl, combine yogurt and whipped topping; set aside 4 teaspoons for topping. Spoon half of the remaining yogurt mixture into four parfait glasses; layer with half of the banana, sliced strawberries, pineapple and blueberries. Repeat layers.

2. Top each parfait with the reserved yogurt mixture and a whole strawberry. Chill until serving.

Nutrition Facts: *1 parfait equals 149 calories, 2 g fat (2 g saturated fat), 2 mg cholesterol, 22 mg sodium, 31 g carbohydrate, 4 g fiber, 2 g protein.*
Diabetic Exchanges: *1½ fruit, ½ starch.*

Dark Chocolate Fondue

Indulge in the decadence of a chocolate dessert—without a lick of guilt! This lighter, melt-in-your-mouth fondue is rich, velvety and fun to share with family and friends. You could also serve it as a topping for ice cream or frozen yogurt.

—TASTE OF HOME TEST KITCHEN

PREP/TOTAL TIME: 20 MINUTES
MAKES: 2 CUPS

- 2 **tablespoons all-purpose flour**
- 1½ **cups 2% milk**
- 2 **dark chocolate candy bars (1.55 ounces each), chopped**
- 3 **ounces milk chocolate, chopped**
- 2 **tablespoons light corn syrup**
   Cubed angel food cake and assorted fresh fruit

1. In a small saucepan, combine flour and milk until smooth. Bring to a boil over medium-high heat; cook and stir for 1 minute or until thickened. Reduce heat to low. Stir in chocolate and corn syrup. Cook and stir until melted.

2. Transfer to a small fondue pot and keep warm. Serve with cake cubes and fresh fruit.

Nutrition Facts: *¼ cup (calculated without cake and fruit) equals 154 calories, 7 g fat (5 g saturated fat), 6 mg cholesterol, 29 mg sodium, 21 g carbohydrate, 1 g fiber, 2 g protein.* **Diabetic Exchanges:** *1½ fat, 1 starch.*

Double-Decker Banana Cups

I whip up little parfaits by layering a vanilla pudding mixture with sliced bananas and graham cracker crumbs. The yummy cups are ready to eat in just 20 minutes.

— PATRICIA KINSELLA CALGARY, ALBERTA

PREP/TOTAL TIME: 20 MINUTES **MAKES:** 4 SERVINGS

- 1 **cup cold fat-free milk**
- 1 **package (3.4 ounces) instant vanilla pudding mix**
- 1 **cup reduced-fat whipped topping**
- 1 **cup thinly sliced firm bananas**
- 4 **teaspoons graham cracker crumbs**
- 4 **maraschino cherries with stems**

1. In a bowl, whisk together milk and pudding for 2 minutes. Fold in whipped topping. Refrigerate for at least 5 minutes.

2. Divide half of the pudding mixture among four dessert dishes. Top with half of the banana slices and remaining pudding mixture. Sprinkle with crumbs. Top each with the remaining banana slices and garnish with a cherry. Serve immediately.

Nutrition Facts: *¾ cup equals 193 calories, 2 g fat (2 g saturated fat), 1 mg cholesterol, 350 mg sodium, 40 g carbohydrate, 1 g fiber, 3 g protein.* **Diabetic Exchanges:** *2 starch, ½ fruit.*

Delightful Dippers

Be creative when picking dippers for chocolate fondue. Consider marshmallows and pretzels in addition to cake cubes and fruit. Before serving fresh-cut fruit, you may want to brush it with lemon juice to prevent browning.

Ginger-Glazed Grilled Honeydew

I love the idea of cooking everything from appetizers to desserts on the grill. If you've never made fruit like this before, you're in for a treat! The glazed honeydew is sweet and really light.

—**JACQUELINE CORREA** LANDING, NEW JERSEY

PREP/TOTAL TIME: 25 MINUTES   **MAKES:** 6 SERVINGS

    ¼ cup peach preserves
    1 tablespoon lemon juice
    1 tablespoon finely chopped crystallized ginger
    2 teaspoons grated lemon peel
    ⅛ teaspoon ground cloves
    1 medium honeydew, cut into 2-inch cubes

1. In a small bowl, combine the first five ingredients. Thread honeydew onto six metal or soaked wooden skewers; brush with half the glaze.

2. Moisten a paper towel with cooking oil; using long-handled tongs, lightly coat the grill rack. Grill honeydew, covered, over medium-high heat or broil 4 in. from the heat for 4-6 minutes or just until melon begins to soften and brown, turning and basting frequently with remaining glaze.

Nutrition Facts: *1 skewer equals 101 calories, trace fat (trace saturated fat), 0 cholesterol, 18 mg sodium, 26 g carbohydrate, 1 g fiber, 1 g protein.*

Cheesecake Phyllo Cups

I've been whipping up little cheesecake bites in tart shells for years. Topped with oranges and kiwi, they're yummy and fun for parties.

—**LORRAINE CHEVALIER** MERRIMAC, MASSACHUSETTS

PREP/TOTAL TIME: 25 MINUTES   **MAKES:** 2½ DOZEN

    4 ounces reduced-fat cream cheese
    ½ cup reduced-fat sour cream
       Sugar substitute equivalent to 2 tablespoons sugar
    1 teaspoon vanilla extract
    2 packages (2.1 ounces each) frozen miniature phyllo tart shells, thawed
    1 can (11 ounces) mandarin oranges slices, drained
    1 kiwifruit, peeled, sliced and cut into quarters

1. In a large bowl, beat the cream cheese, sour cream, sugar substitute and vanilla until smooth.

2. Pipe or spoon into phyllo shells. Top each with an orange segment and kiwi piece. Refrigerate until serving.

Editor's Note: *This recipe was tested with Splenda sugar blend.*

Nutrition Facts: *1 each equals 46 calories, 2 g fat (1 g saturated fat), 4 mg cholesterol, 29 mg sodium, 5 g carbohydrate, trace fiber, 1 g protein.*

Green Tea Tiramisu

Put a luscious new twist on classic Italian tiramisu. Green tea and citrus give this version a delightfully different flavor, while mascarpone cheese and ladyfingers lend the taste of the original.

—TASTE OF HOME TEST KITCHEN

PREP/TOTAL TIME: 20 MINUTES **MAKES:** 8 SERVINGS

- ¾ cup mascarpone cheese
- 2 tablespoons sugar
- 2 teaspoons grated orange peel
- 2 cups fat-free whipped topping
- ¼ cup strong brewed green tea
- 1 tablespoon orange juice
- 1 package (3 ounces) ladyfingers, split
  - Mint sprigs and orange peel strips, optional

1. In a small bowl, combine the mascarpone cheese, sugar and orange peel. Fold in whipped topping; set aside. In another small bowl, combine tea and orange juice.

2. Arrange six ladyfinger halves, split side up, in an ungreased 8-in. x 4-in. loaf pan. Brush with a fourth of the tea mixture. Spread ½ cup cheese mixture just over the top of ladyfingers. Repeat layers three times.

3. Cover and refrigerate until serving. Cut into slices; garnish with mint and orange peel strips if desired.

Nutrition Facts: *1 slice equals 200 calories, 11 g fat (6 g saturated fat), 88 mg cholesterol, 47 mg sodium, 20 g carbohydrate, trace fiber, 3 g protein.*

Chocolate Mousse with Strawberries

PREP/TOTAL TIME: 5 MINUTES **MAKES:** 2½ CUPS

- 1 package (1.4 ounces) sugar-free instant chocolate fudge pudding mix
- 1 cup cold fat-free milk
- 1¾ cups reduced-fat whipped topping
  - Whole fresh strawberries

1. In a bowl, beat the pudding and milk until blended, about 2 minutes. Fold in whipped topping. Serve with strawberries for dipping.

Nutrition Facts: *2 tablespoons dip equals 24 calories, trace fat (0 saturated fat), trace cholesterol, 70 mg sodium, 4 g carbohydrate, 0 fiber, 1 g protein.* **Diabetic Exchange:** *1 free food.*

"Everyone in our family likes dipping berries in this easy yet irresistible mousse. Our son, who is diabetic, also enjoys it as a "frosting" on angel food cake."

—KIM MARIE VAN RHEENEN MENDOTA, ILLINOIS

Cinnamon Blueberry Sauce

Like to finish dinner with a scoop or two of frozen yogurt? Top it off with a yummy, cinnamon-spiced blueberry sauce that goes together in a snap on the stovetop.

—LINDA JOHNSON
MONTESANO, WASHINGTON

PREP/TOTAL TIME: 20 MINUTES
MAKES: 1 CUP

> **Sugar substitute equivalent to ¼ cup sugar**
> 2 **teaspoons cornstarch**
> 2 **cups frozen unsweetened blueberries**
> ¼ **cup water**
> 2 **tablespoons lemon juice**
> ½ **teaspoon ground cinnamon**

1. In a small saucepan, combine the sugar substitute and cornstarch. Add the blueberries, water, lemon juice and cinnamon. Cook and stir until mixture comes to a boil. Reduce heat; simmer, uncovered, for 5 minutes, stirring frequently. Serve warm. Refrigerate leftovers.

Editor's Note: This recipe was tested with Splenda no-calorie sweetener.

Nutrition Facts: ¼ cup equals 50 calories, 1 g fat (trace saturated fat), 0 cholesterol, 1 mg sodium, 12 g carbohydrate, 2 g fiber, trace protein. **Diabetic Exchange:** 1 fruit.

Did you know?

Sugar substitutes have different cooking properties than sugar. They usually work well in drinks, such as smoothies, and in other foods that contain a fair amount of liquid, like puddings, pie fillings and sauces. Keep in mind that, with prolonged heating, sugar substitutes lose sweetness and can even take on a bitter taste.

Grilled Pineapple Dessert

This refreshing grilled dessert is one of my very favorites. Vanilla ice cream slowly melts over the warm, sweet, buttery slices of pineapple, while granola adds a fun crunch.

—**KATIE SISSON** VALLEY PARK, MISSOURI

PREP/TOTAL TIME: 20 MINUTES **MAKES:** 6 SERVINGS

- 1 can (20 ounces) unsweetened sliced pineapple
- 1 tablespoon butter
- 1 teaspoon brown sugar
- ½ teaspoon vanilla extract
- ¼ teaspoon ground cinnamon
- 3 cups reduced-fat vanilla ice cream
- 6 tablespoons hot caramel ice cream topping
- 6 tablespoons granola without raisins

1. Drain pineapple, reserving ⅓ cup juice and six pineapple slices (save remaining juice and pineapple for another use).
2. In a small microwave-safe bowl, combine the butter, brown sugar, vanilla, cinnamon and reserved juice. Microwave, uncovered, on high for 1-2 minutes or until butter is melted. Brush half of the mixture on both sides of pineapple slices.
3. Grill, uncovered, over medium heat or broil 4 in. from the heat for 3-5 minutes or until lightly browned, turning once and basting with remaining butter mixture.
4. Place the pineapple in dessert bowls; top with ice cream. Drizzle with caramel topping; sprinkle with granola.

Editor's Note: *This recipe was tested in a 1,100-watt microwave.*

Nutrition Facts: *1 serving equals 246 calories, 6 g fat (3 g saturated fat), 23 mg cholesterol, 142 mg sodium, 45 g carbohydrate, 2 g fiber, 5 g protein.*

Buttermilk Chocolate Sauce

Our family received this wonderful chocolate sauce recipe from a dear friend. The thick, rich, not-too-sweet topping is luscious over everything from ice cream to cake and fruit.

—**LEAH RAMAGE** SASKATOON, SASKATCHEWAN

PREP/TOTAL TIME: 15 MINUTES **MAKES:** ¾ CUP

- ¾ cup sugar
- ¼ cup baking cocoa
- 1 tablespoon cornstarch
- ¾ cup buttermilk
- 1 teaspoon vanilla extract
   Reduced-fat ice cream

1. In a small saucepan, combine sugar, cocoa and cornstarch. Whisk in the buttermilk. Bring to a boil over medium heat, stirring constantly. Reduce heat; simmer, uncovered, for 5-7 minutes or until slightly thickened.
2. Remove from the heat; stir in vanilla. Serve warm over ice cream. Refrigerate leftovers.

Nutrition Facts: *One serving (1 tablespoon sauce, calculated without ice cream) equals 62 calories, trace fat (trace saturated fat), 1 mg cholesterol, 16 mg sodium, 15 g carbohydrate, trace fiber, 1 g protein.* **Diabetic Exchange:** *1 starch.*

Mocha Pudding Cakes

PREP/TOTAL TIME: 30 MINUTES
MAKES: 2 SERVINGS

- ¼ cup all-purpose flour
- 3 tablespoons sugar
- 1½ teaspoons baking cocoa
- ½ teaspoon baking powder
- ⅛ teaspoon salt
- 3 tablespoons 2% milk
- 1½ teaspoons butter, melted
- ¼ teaspoon vanilla extract

TOPPING

- 2 tablespoons brown sugar
- 1½ teaspoons baking cocoa
- 3 tablespoons hot brewed coffee
- 1 tablespoon hot water
  Whipped topping, optional

1. In a small bowl, combine the flour, sugar, cocoa, baking powder and salt. Stir in the milk, butter and vanilla until smooth. Spoon into two 4-oz. ramekins coated with cooking spray.

2. Combine the brown sugar and cocoa; sprinkle over the batter. Combine the coffee and water; pour over the topping. Bake at 350° for 15-20 minutes or until a knife inserted near the center comes out clean. Serve warm or at room temperature with whipped topping if desired.

Nutrition Facts: *1 serving (calculated without whipped topping) equals 227 calories, 4 g fat (2 g saturated fat), 9 mg cholesterol, 294 mg sodium, 47 g carbohydrate, 1 g fiber, 3 g protein.*

Fun Fruit Dessert

Here's a colorful, festive dessert you'll love for summer get-togethers. Fresh berries and peaches are served with a creamy yogurt dip and tempting slices of chocolate.

—TASTE OF HOME TEST KITCHEN

PREP/TOTAL TIME: 20 MINUTES   **MAKES:** 6 SERVINGS

- 1 cup vanilla yogurt
- 1 tablespoon honey
- 1 to 2 tablespoons minced fresh mint
- ¾ cup chopped peeled peaches or nectarines
- 1½ teaspoons orange juice
- ¾ cup chopped fresh strawberries
- ¾ cup fresh raspberries
- ¾ cup fresh blueberries
- 1 tablespoon sugar
- 1 package (3.78 ounces) curved chocolate slices (Swoops)

1. In a small bowl, combine the yogurt, honey and mint. Cover and refrigerate until serving.

2. Just before serving, place peaches in a large bowl; sprinkle with orange juice. Add the berries. Sprinkle with sugar; toss gently. Using a slotted spoon, transfer fruit to a serving bowl. Serve with yogurt sauce and chocolate slices.

Nutrition Facts: *½ cup fruit with 2 tablespoons yogurt sauce and 3 chocolate slices equals 191 calories, 7 g fat (4 g saturated fat), 4 mg cholesterol, 93 mg sodium, 29 g carbohydrate, 3 g fiber, 4 g protein.* **Diabetic Exchanges:** *1 starch, 1 fruit, 1 fat.*

Did you know?

Baking cocoa is the powdery residue produced when cocoa beans are processed. Most of the cocoa butter (the main fat in chocolate) is removed from this powder, making it an ideal ingredient for baking lighter treats without sacrificing the chocolaty flavor you love.

"These mini pudding cakes are perfect for a twosome. My mom used to make them when I was a little girl. Now I whip them up for a speedy treat."

—**DEBORA SIMMONS** EGLON, WEST VIRGINIA

Makeover Nutty Monkey Malts

Get all the appeal of the classic diner milk shake with only a fraction of the calories and fat. Brimming with peanut butter, bananas and chocolate, this is a treat kids will go crazy for!

—TASTE OF HOME TEST KITCHEN

PREP/TOTAL TIME: 5 MINUTES **MAKES:** 5 SERVINGS

- ¼ cup fat-free milk
- 1 small banana, cut into chunks
- ¼ cup chocolate malted milk powder
- 2 tablespoons reduced-fat creamy peanut butter
- 2 cups fat-free frozen chocolate yogurt
  Whipped cream, optional

1. Place the milk, banana, malted milk powder and peanut butter in a blender. Cover and process for 10 seconds or until smooth. Add frozen yogurt. Cover and process 10 seconds longer or until blended. Stir if necessary.

2. Pour into chilled glasses; garnish with whipped cream if desired. Serve immediately.

Nutrition Facts: *½ cup (calculated without whipped cream) equals 203 calories, 3 g fat (1 g saturated fat), 1 mg cholesterol, 190 mg sodium, 39 g carbohydrate, 3 g fiber, 8 g protein.*

Maple Baked Apple

Craving something warm and comforting? Pull out this simple, autumn-flavored recipe. It dresses up a tart apple with dried fruit, maple syrup, brown sugar, nuts and spices.

— MARY KELLEY MINNEAPOLIS, MINNESOTA

PREP/TOTAL TIME: 10 MINUTES **MAKES:** 1 SERVING

- 2 teaspoons maple syrup
- 1 teaspoon brown sugar
- 1 teaspoon chopped walnuts
- 1 teaspoon raisins, dried cranberries or dried currants
- ⅛ teaspoon ground cinnamon
- ⅛ teaspoon ground nutmeg
- 1 medium tart apple

1. In a small bowl, combine the first six ingredients. Core apple and peel the top third. Place in a small microwave-safe dish. Fill apple with walnut mixture. Microwave, uncovered, on high for 3-4 minutes or until apple is tender. Serve warm.

Nutrition Facts: *1 serving equals 151 calories, 2 g fat (trace saturated fat), 0 cholesterol, 5 mg sodium, 36 g carbohydrate, 4 g fiber, 1 g protein.*

Special Ladyfinger Dessert

Everyone will think you fussed when you serve a platter of pretty ladyfinger sandwiches filled with strawberry preserves and sweetened cheeses. For an extra-special finishing touch, add a dusting of baking cocoa and a garnish of fresh berries.

— TASTE OF HOME TEST KITCHEN

PREP/TOTAL TIME: 10 MINUTES **MAKES:** 2 SERVINGS

    2 ounces fat-free cream cheese
    1 tablespoon mascarpone cheese
    1 tablespoon confectioners' sugar
    6 ladyfingers, split
    2 tablespoons reduced-sugar strawberry preserves
    ¼ teaspoon baking cocoa
    2 fresh strawberries

1. In a small bowl, combine the cheeses and confectioners' sugar. Split ladyfingers; spread cheese mixture over top halves and preserves over bottom halves. Sandwich halves together. Dust with cocoa. Garnish with strawberries.

Nutrition Facts: *3 pieces equal 178 calories, 5 g fat (2 g saturated fat), 56 mg cholesterol, 307 mg sodium, 27 g carbohydrate, 1 g fiber, 7 g protein.* **Diabetic Exchanges:** *2 starch, ½ fat.*

Gingered Melon

I like to let guests spoon chunks of spiced honeydew from a large bowl and choose their own toppings, such as whipped cream and raspberries. You could also combine the fruit with frozen yogurt and ginger ale to make a melon float instead.

— PATRICIA RICHARDSON VERONA, ONTARIO

PREP/TOTAL TIME: 15 MINUTES **MAKES:** 4 SERVINGS

    ½ medium honeydew, cut into 1-inch cubes
    ¼ cup orange juice
    1½ teaspoons ground ginger
    ½ to 1 cup whipped cream
    ¼ cup fresh or frozen unsweetened raspberries

1. In a small bowl, combine the melon, orange juice and ginger; cover and refrigerate for 5-10 minutes. Spoon into tall dessert glasses or bowls. Top with whipped cream and raspberries.

Nutrition Facts: *1 cup equals 76 calories, 2 g fat (1 g saturated fat), 6 mg cholesterol, 22 mg sodium, 15 g carbohydrate, 1 g fiber, 1 g protein.*

Makeover Coconut Cookies

Grab a cookie guilt-free! These scrumptious coconut goodies have just two-thirds the calories, half the fat and a quarter of the saturated fat of the original recipe. Enjoy one with a cup of coffee after dinner or with a glass of milk in the afternoon.

—TASTE OF HOME TEST KITCHEN

PREP: 15 MINUTES **BAKE:** 10 MINUTES/BATCH
MAKES: 3½ DOZEN

- ¼ **cup butter, softened**
- ¼ **cup canola oil**
- ½ **cup packed brown sugar**
- ¼ **cup sugar**
- 1 **egg**
- 3 **egg whites**
- 3 **teaspoons vanilla extract**
- 2 **teaspoons coconut extract**
- 1¾ **cups all-purpose flour**
- 3 **teaspoons baking powder**
- ½ **teaspoon salt**
- 4 **cups cornflakes**

1. In a large bowl, combine the butter, oil and sugars. Beat in the egg, egg whites and extracts. Combine the flour, baking powder and salt; gradually add to the egg mixture. Stir in cornflakes.

2. Drop by tablespoonfuls 2 in. apart onto baking sheets coated with cooking spray. Bake at 375° for 10-12 minutes or until lightly browned. Remove to wire racks.

Nutrition Facts: *1 cookie equals 69 calories, 3 g fat (1 g saturated fat), 8 mg cholesterol, 94 mg sodium, 10 g carbohydrate, trace fiber, 1 g protein.* **Diabetic Exchanges:** *½ starch, ½ fat.*

Rhubarb Sauce

Five ingredients are all you need to dress up scoops of reduced-fat vanilla ice cream with a tongue-tingling rhubarb topping. We also like the sauce served warm over oven-fresh biscuits with a dash of cinnamon and a dollop of whipped cream.

—EVELYN GEBHARDT KASILOF, ALASKA

PREP/TOTAL TIME: 20 MINUTES **MAKES:** 5 SERVINGS

- 3 **cups sliced fresh or frozen rhubarb**
  Sugar substitute equivalent to ½ cup sugar
- ¼ **cup water**
- ⅛ **teaspoon ground nutmeg**
- ¼ **teaspoon vanilla extract**
  Reduced-fat no-sugar-added vanilla ice cream

1. In a saucepan, combine the rhubarb, sugar substitute, water and nutmeg. Bring to a boil. Reduce heat; simmer, uncovered, for 6-8 minutes or until the rhubarb is tender. Remove from the heat; stir in the vanilla. Serve warm or cold over ice cream.

Editor's Note: *This recipe was tested with Splenda no-calorie sweetener.*

Nutrition Facts: *¼ cup sauce (calculated without ice cream) equals 26 calories, trace fat (trace saturated fat), 0 cholesterol, 3 mg sodium, 6 g carbohydrate, 1 g fiber, 1 g protein.* **Diabetic Exchange:** *½ fruit.*

Lemon Burst Tartlets

You'll love the tangy combination of berry and lemon in these pretty little tartlets. Quick and easy, they're ideal for a bridal shower or as a fun dessert anytime.

—PAM JAVOR
NORTH HUNTINGDON, PENNSYLVANIA

PREP/TOTAL TIME: 20 MINUTES
MAKES: 2½ DOZEN.

- 1 jar (10 ounces) lemon curd
- 1 carton (8 ounces) frozen whipped topping, thawed
- 5 to 6 drops yellow food coloring, optional
- ⅔ cup raspberry cake and pastry filling
- 2 packages (1.9 ounces each) frozen miniature phyllo tart shells
- 30 fresh raspberries

1. In a large bowl, combine lemon curd, whipped topping and food coloring if desired until smooth. Spoon 1 teaspoon raspberry filling into each tart shell. Pipe or spoon the lemon mixture over filling. Garnish each with a raspberry. Refrigerate leftovers.

Editor's Note: *This recipe was tested with Solo brand cake and pastry filling. Look for it in the baking aisle.*

Nutrition Facts: *1 tartlet equals 89 calories, 3 g fat (1 g saturated fat), 7 mg cholesterol, 21 mg sodium, 14 g carbohydrate, trace fiber, trace protein.* **Diabetic Exchange:** *1 starch.*

top tip Popular in England, lemon curd is a soft custard that's often used as a tart filling. It's made from lemon juice, sugar, eggs and butter. The flavor and texture are similar to lemon meringue pie filling. Commercially prepared lemon curd is available in larger grocery stores, usually alongside the jams and jellies or with the baking supplies.

218

221

227

Holidays & Parties

❝My mom always put her burger on top of a salad. I adjusted her idea and created these unusual sandwiches featuring red peppers and Brie cheese. They make an extra-special treat for a cookout.❞

DEVON DELANEY WESTPORT, CONNECTICUT
about her recipe, Beefstro Bruschetta Burgers, on page 232

Autumn Turkey Tenderloins

Enjoy an autumn-flavored turkey entree that's special enough for Thanksgiving. Brown sugar and cinnamon lend a touch of spicy sweetness, while walnuts add a pleasant, toasty crunch.

—**BRENDA LION** WARREN, PENNSYLVANIA

PREP/TOTAL TIME: 30 MINUTES   **MAKES:** 10 SERVINGS

- 1¼ pounds turkey breast tenderloins
- 1 tablespoon butter
- 1 cup unsweetened apple juice
- 1 medium apple, sliced
- 1 tablespoon brown sugar
- 2 teaspoons chicken bouillon granules
- ¼ teaspoon ground cinnamon
- ¼ teaspoon ground nutmeg
- 1 tablespoon cornstarch
- 2 tablespoons cold water
- ½ cup chopped walnuts, toasted

1. In a large skillet, brown turkey in butter. Add apple juice, apple, brown sugar, bouillon, cinnamon and nutmeg. Bring to a boil. Reduce heat; cover and simmer for 10-12 minutes or until a thermometer reads 170°.

2. Using a slotted spoon, remove turkey and apple slices to a serving platter; keep warm.

3. Combine the cornstarch and water until smooth; stir into the pan juices. Bring to a boil; cook and stir for 2 minutes or until thickened. Spoon over the turkey and apple. Sprinkle with walnuts.

Nutrition Facts: *1 serving equals 274 calories, 11 g fat (2 g saturated fat), 62 mg cholesterol, 423 mg sodium, 16 g carbohydrate, 2 g fiber, 30 g protein.* **Diabetic Exchanges:** *4 lean meat, 2 fat, 1 fruit.*

Prosciutto-Wrapped Asparagus with Raspberry Sauce

What a delightful way to kick off a spring party! Fresh asparagus spears are wrapped with prosciutto and served with a tangy sauce. Guests are always impressed with these simply elegant appetizers.

—**NOELLE MYERS** GRAND FORKS, NORTH DAKOTA

PREP/TOTAL TIME: 30 MINUTES   **MAKES:** 16 APPETIZERS

- ⅓ pound thinly sliced prosciutto or deli ham
- 16 fresh asparagus spears, trimmed
- ½ cup seedless raspberry jam
- 2 tablespoons balsamic vinegar

1. Cut the prosciutto slices in half. Wrap a prosciutto piece around each asparagus spear; secure ends with toothpicks. Moisten a paper towel with cooking oil; using long-handled tongs, lightly coat the grill rack.

2. Grill asparagus, covered, over medium heat for 6-8 minutes or until prosciutto is crisp, turning once. Discard toothpicks.

3. In a small microwave-safe bowl, microwave raspberry jam and vinegar on high for 15-20 seconds or until jam is melted. Serve with asparagus.

Nutrition Facts: *1 asparagus spear with 1½ teaspoons sauce equals 50 calories, 1 g fat (trace saturated fat), 8 mg cholesterol, 184 mg sodium, 7 g carbohydrate, trace fiber, 3 g protein.* **Diabetic Exchange:** *½ starch.*

This potluck-perfect dish layers some of the best produce of summer gardens and comes together in only 20 minutes. Presented in a glass bowl, the salad is almost too pretty to eat—almost! —JODI ANDERSON OVERBROOK, KANSAS

Favorite Layered Salad

PREP/TOTAL TIME: 20 MINUTES
MAKES: 8 SERVINGS

- 2 cups torn romaine
- 2 cups fresh baby spinach
- 1 cup sliced fresh mushrooms
- 1 cup grape tomatoes
- ½ cup shredded carrot
- 1 medium red onion, halved and sliced
- 1 medium sweet red pepper, chopped
- 1 medium cucumber, sliced
- 1 cup frozen peas, thawed
- ½ cup Miracle Whip Light
- 3 tablespoons sugar
- ½ cup shredded cheddar cheese
- 3 tablespoons crumbled cooked bacon

1. In a 3-qt. trifle bowl or glass bowl, combine the romaine and spinach. Layer with the mushrooms, tomatoes, carrot, onion, pepper, cucumber and peas. Combine Miracle Whip and sugar; spread over peas. Sprinkle with cheese and bacon. Chill until serving.

Nutrition Facts: *1½ cups equals 131 calories, 6 g fat (2 g saturated fat), 14 mg cholesterol, 293 mg sodium, 16 g carbohydrate, 3 g fiber, 5 g protein.* **Diabetic Exchanges:** *1 vegetable, 1 fat, ½ starch.*

top tip

I store crumbled cooked bacon in the freezer to use later for recipes.
I also like to sprinkle a little into my scrambled eggs—I feel like I've enjoyed "bacon and eggs" for breakfast with only a fraction of the fat and calories. Before cooking the bacon, I cut the strips into small pieces so they cook faster.
—K.K.M. MAPLEWOOD, MINNESOTA

Heavenly Filled Strawberries

Celebrate strawberry season—and share the bounty with your guests—by serving these juicy gems stuffed with sweetened cream cheese and sprinkled with grated chocolate. They make the perfect bite-size dessert for a summer party.

—STEPHEN MUNRO
BEAVERBANK, NOVA SCOTIA

PREP/TOTAL TIME: 20 MINUTES
MAKES: 3 DOZEN

- 3 dozen large fresh strawberries
- 2 packages (one 8 ounces, one 3 ounces) cream cheese, softened
- ½ cup confectioners' sugar
- ¼ teaspoon almond extract
  Grated chocolate

1. Remove stems from strawberries; cut a deep "X" in the tip of each berry. Gently spread berries open.

2. In a small bowl, beat cream cheese, confectioners' sugar and almond extract until light and fluffy. Pipe or spoon about 2 teaspoons into each berry; sprinkle with chocolate. Chill until serving.

Nutrition Facts: *1 filled strawberry (calculated without chocolate) equals 41 calories, 3 g fat (2 g saturated fat), 10 mg cholesterol, 26 mg sodium, 3 g carbohydrate, trace fiber, 1 g protein.* **Diabetic Exchange:** *½ fat.*

Strawberry Smarts

Purchase strawberries that are shiny, firm and very fragrant. A strawberry should be almost completely red, though some whiteness near the leafy cap is acceptable. Refrigerate the unwashed strawberries with the caps on until you are ready to use them. Just before using, wash and hull the berries.

Party Tortellini Salad

Wondering what to bring to a cookout or picnic? Here's an easy-to-assemble pasta salad that requires only cheese tortellini, broccoli, red pepper and a few other basic ingredients. Full of crowd-pleasing flavors, it's a favorite with people of all ages.

—MARY WILT IPSWICH, MASSACHUSETTS

PREP/TOTAL TIME: 25 MINUTES **MAKES:** 10 SERVINGS

- 1 package (19 ounces) frozen cheese tortellini
- 2 cups fresh broccoli florets
- 1 medium sweet red pepper, chopped
- ½ cup pimiento-stuffed olives, halved
- ¾ cup reduced-fat red wine vinaigrette
- ½ teaspoon salt

1. Cook the cheese tortellini according to the package directions; drain and rinse in cold water.

2. In a large bowl, combine the tortellini, broccoli, red pepper and olives. Drizzle with dressing and sprinkle with salt; toss to coat. Cover and refrigerate until serving.

Nutrition Facts: *¾ cup equals 156 calories, 7 g fat (2 g saturated fat), 8 mg cholesterol, 596 mg sodium, 19 g carbohydrate, 1 g fiber, 6 g protein.* **Diabetic Exchanges:** *1 starch, 1 lean meat, ½ fat.*

Holiday Peas

When I was a child, my mother would dress up peas with a cheesy, buttery topping. That side dish of hers is still one of my favorites. Just about any type of savory cracker, including herb-flavored varieties, can be substituted for the wheat crackers.
—SUE GRONHOLZ BEAVER DAM, WISCONSIN

PREP/TOTAL TIME: 20 MINUTES **MAKES:** 12 SERVINGS

- 2 packages (16 ounces each) frozen peas
- 2 teaspoons salt
- 1 cup finely crushed wheat crackers
- 2 tablespoons grated Parmesan cheese
- 2 tablespoons butter, melted

1. Place peas in a large saucepan; add salt. Cover with water. Bring to a boil. Reduce heat; cover and simmer for 5-6 minutes or until tender.

2. Meanwhile, toss the cracker crumbs, Parmesan cheese and butter. Drain the peas and place in a serving bowl; top with the crumb mixture.

Nutrition Facts: *¾ cup equals 87 calories, 3 g fat (1 g saturated fat), 6 mg cholesterol, 523 mg sodium, 12 g carbohydrate, 4 g fiber, 4 g protein.* **Diabetic Exchanges:** *1 starch, ½ fat.*

Goat Cheese Crostini

My husband received a crostini recipe from a friend at work. I was skeptical at first because I thought the ingredients wouldn't work well together. Was I wrong—they blend deliciously!
—REBECCA EBELING NEVADA CITY, CALIFORNIA

PREP/TOTAL TIME: 10 MINUTES **MAKES:** 32 APPETIZERS

- 1 cup crumbled goat cheese
- 1 teaspoon minced fresh rosemary
- 1 French bread baguette (10½ ounces), cut into ½-inch slices and toasted
- 3 tablespoons honey
- ¼ cup slivered almonds, toasted

1. In a small bowl, combine cheese and rosemary; spoon over toast slices. Drizzle with honey; sprinkle with almonds.

Bacon-Almond Crostini: *Combine 2 cups shredded Monterey Jack cheese, ⅔ cup mayonnaise, ½ cup toasted sliced almonds, 6 slices crumbled cooked bacon, 1 chopped green onion and a dash of salt. Spread over toast. Bake for 5-7 minutes or until cheese is melted. Sprinkle with additional almonds if desired.*

Nutrition Facts: *1 piece equals 76 calories, 4 g fat (2 g saturated fat), 6 mg cholesterol, 92 mg sodium, 9 g carbohydrate, 1 g fiber, 3 g protein.* **Diabetic Exchanges:** *½ starch, ½ fat.*

Blue Cheese-Topped Steaks

These juicy tenderloin steaks, lightly crusted with blue cheese and bread crumbs, are special enough for holidays. With a drizzle of the accompanying wine sauce, the beef melts in your mouth.

—**TIFFANY VANCIL** SAN DIEGO, CALIFORNIA

PREP/TOTAL TIME: 30 MINUTES **MAKES:** 4 SERVINGS

- 2 tablespoons crumbled blue cheese
- 4½ teaspoons dry bread crumbs
- 4½ teaspoons minced fresh parsley
- 4½ teaspoons minced chives
  Dash pepper
- 4 beef tenderloin steaks (4 ounces each)
- 1½ teaspoons butter
- 1 tablespoon all-purpose flour
- ½ cup reduced-sodium beef broth
- 1 tablespoon Madeira wine
- ⅛ teaspoon browning sauce, optional

1. In a small bowl, combine the blue cheese, bread crumbs, parsley, chives and pepper. Press onto one side of each steak.
2. In a large nonstick skillet coated with cooking spray, cook the steaks over medium-high heat for 2 minutes on each side. Transfer to a 15-in. x 10-in. x 1-in. baking pan coated with cooking spray.
3. Bake at 350° for 6-8 minutes or until meat reaches desired doneness (for medium-rare, a thermometer should read 145°; medium, 160°; well-done, 170°).
4. Meanwhile, in a small saucepan, melt the butter. Whisk in flour until smooth. Gradually whisk in broth and wine. Bring to a boil; cook and stir for 2 minutes or until thickened. Stir in browning sauce if desired. Serve with steaks.

Nutrition Facts: *1 steak equals 228 calories, 11 g fat (5 g saturated fat), 78 mg cholesterol, 197 mg sodium, 4 g carbohydrate, trace fiber, 26 g protein.* **Diabetic Exchanges:** *3 lean meat, 1½ fat, ½ fat-free milk.*

Easy Party Bruschetta

My fuss-free bruschetta piles on the fresh flavor and gets a little bit of heat from jalapeno peppers. I frequently serve this appetizer for casual summer buffets when tomatoes are at their best.

—**DEL MASON** MARTENSVILLE, SASKATCHEWAN

PREP/TOTAL TIME: 25 MINUTES **MAKES:** 2½ DOZEN

- 1½ cups chopped seeded tomatoes
- ⅔ cup finely chopped red onion
- 2 tablespoons minced seeded jalapeno pepper
- 2 garlic cloves, minced
- ½ teaspoon dried basil
- ¼ teaspoon salt
- ¼ teaspoon coarsely ground pepper
- 2 tablespoons olive oil
- 1 tablespoon cider vinegar
- 1 tablespoon red wine vinegar
- 3 dashes hot pepper sauce
- 1 loaf (8 ounces) French bread, cut into ¼-inch slices
- 2 tablespoons grated Parmesan cheese

1. In a small bowl, combine the first seven ingredients. In another bowl, whisk the oil, vinegars and pepper sauce; stir into tomato mixture.
2. Place bread slices on an ungreased baking sheet. Broil 3-4 in. from the heat for 1-2 minutes or until golden brown. With a slotted spoon, top each slice with tomato mixture. Sprinkle with cheese.

Editor's Note: *Wear disposable gloves when cutting hot peppers; the oils can burn skin. Avoid touching your face.*

Nutrition Facts: *1 appetizer equals 34 calories, 1 g fat (trace saturated fat), trace cholesterol, 73 mg sodium, 5 g carbohydrate, trace fiber, 1 g protein.* **Diabetic Exchange:** *½ starch.*

Cranberry Fudge

PREP: 20 MINUTES + CHILLING
MAKES: 1⅓ POUNDS (81 PIECES)

- 2 **cups (12 ounces) semisweet chocolate chips**
- ¼ **cup light corn syrup**
- ½ **cup confectioners' sugar**
- ¼ **cup reduced-fat evaporated milk**
- 1 **teaspoon vanilla extract**
- 1 **package (5 ounces) dried cranberries**
- ⅓ **cup chopped walnuts**

1. Line a 9-in. square pan with foil. Coat the foil with cooking spray; set aside.
2. In a heavy saucepan, combine chocolate chips and corn syrup. Cook and stir over low heat until smooth. Remove from the heat. Stir in the confectioners' sugar, milk and vanilla. Beat with a wooden spoon until thickened and glossy, about 5 minutes. Stir in cranberries and walnuts. Spread into prepared pan; refrigerate until firm.
3. Using the foil, lift the fudge out of the pan; discard foil. Cut fudge into 1-in. squares. Store in an airtight container in the refrigerator.

Nutrition Facts: *1 piece equals 36 calories, 2 g fat (1 g saturated fat), trace cholesterol, 3 mg sodium, 6 g carbohydrate, trace fiber, trace protein.* **Diabetic Exchange:** *½ starch.*

Warm Strawberry Fondue

Delight guests by whipping up a smooth, refreshing fondue. It's easy to do with just four basic ingredients—strawberries, cream, cornstarch and lemon juice. I like to use additional strawberries plus grapes, bananas and cubes of angel food cake as dippers.
—**SHARON MENSING** GREENFIELD, IOWA

PREP/TOTAL TIME: 15 MINUTES **MAKES:** 1½ CUPS

- 1 **package (10 ounces) frozen sweetened sliced strawberries, thawed**
- ¼ **cup fat-free half-and-half cream**
- 1 **teaspoon cornstarch**
- ½ **teaspoon lemon juice**
  Angel food cake cubes and fresh fruit

1. In a food processor, combine the strawberries, cream, cornstarch and lemon juice; cover and process until smooth.
2. Pour into saucepan. Bring to a boil; cook and stir for 2 minutes or until slightly thickened. Transfer to a fondue pot or 1½-qt. slow cooker; keep warm. Serve with cake and fruit.

Nutrition Facts: *2 tablespoons (calculated without cake and fruit) equals 27 calories, trace fat (0 saturated fat), 0 cholesterol, 6 mg sodium, 7 g carbohydrate, trace fiber, trace protein.* **Diabetic Exchanges:** *½ fruit.*

Did you know?
Evaporated milk is made when milk is condensed to about half of its original volume in a heating process using a vacuum evaporator, which removes 60% of the water in milk. Once evaporated milk is opened, treat it as you would fresh milk. Store leftover evaporated milk in a sealed container in the refrigerator for up to 5 days.

"With this lightened-up fudge recipe, you can satisfy your sweet tooth guilt-free. Each decadent bite is packed with crunchy walnuts and tangy dried cranberries."

—**DELIA KENNEDY** DEER PARK, WASHINGTON

Asparagus with Tarragon Lemon Sauce

With its fresh-picked taste and minimal prep work, this is a side dish you're sure to love. It makes an elegant addition to Easter feasts or other special menus.

—PATRICIA SWART GALLOWAY, NEW JERSEY

PREP/TOTAL TIME: 15 MINUTES
MAKES: 6 SERVINGS

- 2 **pounds fresh asparagus, trimmed**
- 3 **tablespoons olive oil**
- 1 **teaspoon all-purpose flour**
- 3 **tablespoons fat-free milk**
- 1 **tablespoon lemon juice**
- 2 **teaspoons minced fresh tarragon**
  Dash salt

1. Place the asparagus in a steamer basket; place in a large saucepan over 1 in. of water. Bring to a boil; cover and steam for 3-5 minutes or until crisp-tender. Drain.

2. Meanwhile, in a small saucepan, combine olive oil and flour. Gradually stir in the milk until smooth. Bring to a boil; cook and stir for 1 minute or until thickened. Remove from the heat. Stir in the lemon juice, tarragon and salt. Serve with asparagus.

Nutrition Facts: *1 serving equals 83 calories, 7 g fat (1 g saturated fat), trace cholesterol, 36 mg sodium, 4 g carbohydrate, 1 g fiber, 2 g protein.* **Diabetic Exchanges:** *1 vegetable, 1 fat.*

Did you know?

An herb with slender, green leaves and a distinctive anise-like flavor, tarragon is widely used in French cooking and pairs well with chicken, fish and vegetables. Tarragon is most well-known for flavoring Bearnaise sauce and for making flavored vinegar.

Looking for can't-miss appetizers to serve at your next party? You can't go wrong offering warm-from-the-oven stuffed shrimp. For a main course instead, serve them with rice or pasta. —**KAROLEE PLOCK** BURWELL, NEBRASKA

Mushroom-Stuffed Shrimp

PREP/TOTAL TIME: 25 MINUTES
MAKES: 1 DOZEN

- 12 uncooked shell-on jumbo shrimp (about 1 pound)
- ½ teaspoon chicken bouillon granules
- 1 tablespoon hot water
- ¾ cup soft bread crumbs
- 2 tablespoons finely chopped fresh mushrooms
- 2 tablespoons finely chopped celery
- 1 teaspoon reduced-fat butter
- ¼ teaspoon garlic powder
- 4 drops hot pepper sauce

1. Peel and devein shrimp, leaving the tails on. Butterfly each shrimp along the outside curve. Open shrimp flat and place with tails up in an 8-in. square baking dish coated with cooking spray.

2. In a small bowl, dissolve bouillon in hot water. Stir in the remaining ingredients. Spoon about 1 teaspoon onto each shrimp. Bake at 375° for 5-8 minutes or until the shrimp turn pink. Serve warm.

Editor's Note: *This recipe was tested with Land O'Lakes light stick butter.*

Nutrition Facts: *1 serving (3 each) equals 115 calories, 2 g fat (1 g saturated fat), 170 mg cholesterol, 353 mg sodium, 5 g carbohydrate, trace fiber, 19 g protein.*
Diabetic Exchange: *3 lean meat.*

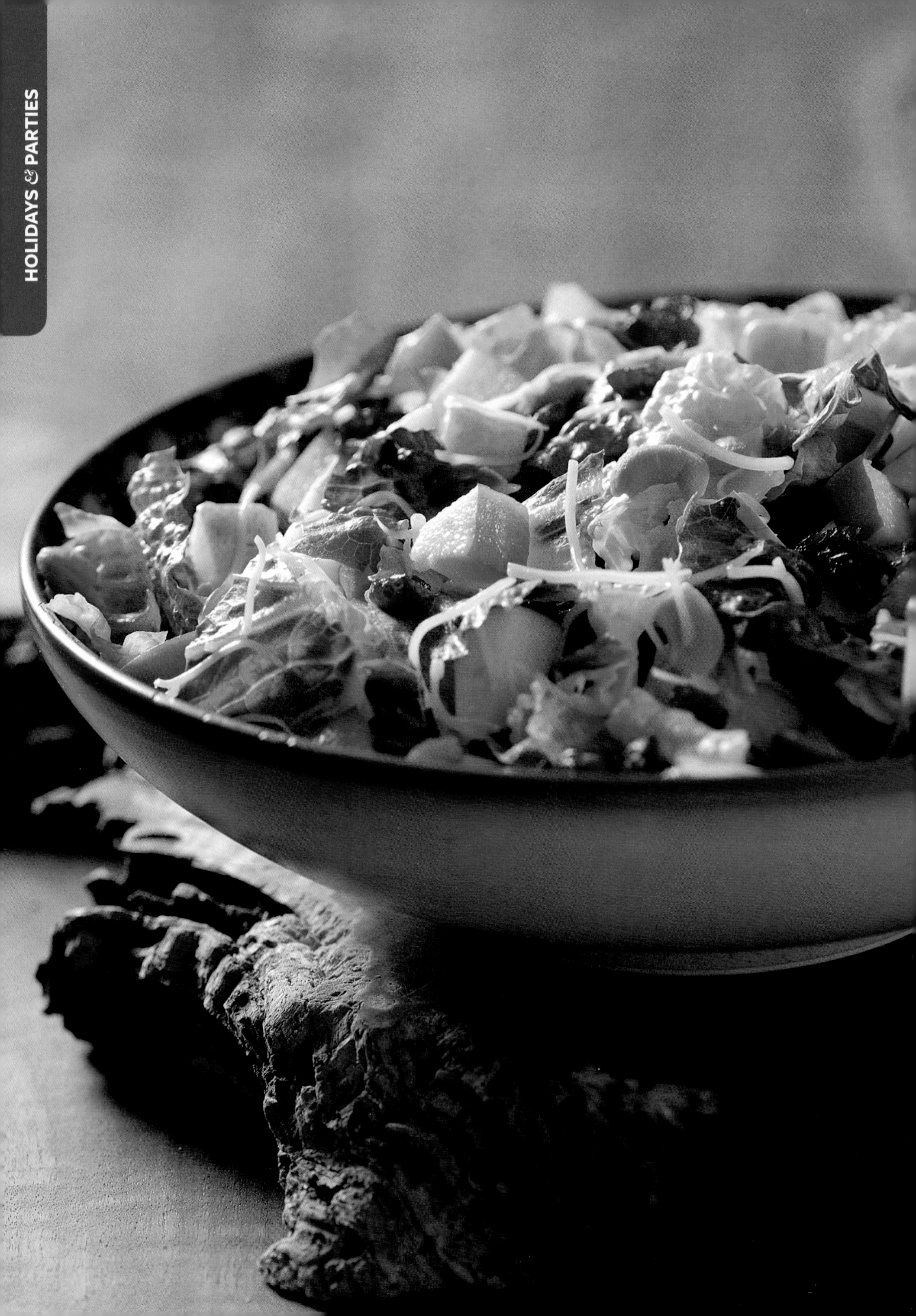

Holiday Lettuce Salad

Family members always request that I bring my fruity romaine salad to get-togethers. I top it off with a tangy homemade dressing and a sprinkling of cashews.

—**BRYAN BRAACK** ELDRIDGE, IOWA

PREP/TOTAL TIME: 20 MINUTES
MAKES: 14 SERVINGS

- 10 **cups torn romaine**
- 2 **medium red apples, cubed**
- 2 **medium pears, cubed**
- 1 **cup (4 ounces) shredded Swiss cheese**
- ½ **cup dried cranberries**
- 6 **tablespoons lemon juice**
- 3 **tablespoons canola oil**
- 3 **tablespoons light corn syrup**
- 1½ **teaspoons grated onion**
- 1½ **teaspoons Dijon mustard**
- ½ **teaspoon salt**
- ½ **cup chopped lightly salted cashews**

1. In a salad bowl, combine the first five ingredients.

2. For the dressing, in a small bowl, whisk the lemon juice, oil, corn syrup, onion, mustard and salt. Pour over the romaine mixture; toss to coat. Sprinkle with cashews.

Nutrition Facts: *1 cup equals 144 calories, 8 g fat (2 g saturated fat), 7 mg cholesterol, 134 mg sodium, 17 g carbohydrate, 3 g fiber, 4 g protein.* **Diabetic Exchanges:** *1½ fat, 1 starch, 1 vegetable.*

Sirloin Steak with Rich Mushroom Gravy

Toasting the flour to a light tan color gives this gravy a rich taste and thickness—without overloading on fat. The thick gravy can be thinned to taste with additional broth.

—**TASTE OF HOME TEST KITCHEN**

PREP/TOTAL TIME: 30 MINUTES **MAKES:** 4 SERVINGS

- ¼ **cup all-purpose flour**
- 1 **cup reduced-sodium beef broth**
- 1 **beef top sirloin steak (1¼ pounds)**
- ½ **teaspoon salt**
- ¼ **teaspoon pepper**
- 1 **tablespoon canola oil**
- ½ **pound sliced fresh mushrooms**
- 1 **garlic clove, minced**
- ½ **teaspoon dried rosemary, crushed**
- ⅛ **teaspoon salt**
- ¼ **cup sherry or additional reduced-sodium beef broth**
- 1 **tablespoon butter**

1. In a large skillet over medium-high heat, cook and stir flour for 4-5 minutes or until light tan in color. Immediately transfer to a small bowl; whisk in broth until smooth. Set aside.

2. Sprinkle the beef with salt and pepper. In the same skillet, cook beef in oil over medium heat for 5-6 minutes on each side or until meat reaches desired doneness (for medium-rare, a thermometer should read 145°; medium, 160°; well-done, 170°). Remove and keep warm.

3. In the same skillet, saute mushrooms until tender. Add the garlic, rosemary and salt; saute 1 minute longer. Stir in the sherry. Stir flour mixture; add to the pan. Bring to a boil; cook and stir for 1 minute or until thickened. Stir in butter until melted. Serve with steak.

Nutrition Facts: *4 ounces cooked beef with ½ cup gravy equals 289 calories, 12 g fat (4 g saturated fat), 66 mg cholesterol, 565 mg sodium, 9 g carbohydrate, 1 g fiber, 33 g protein.* **Diabetic Exchanges:** *4 lean meat, 1 vegetable, 1 fat.*

Lemon Juice In a Jiffy

I like to keep fresh lemon juice on hand because it's such an easy way to add a burst of refreshing flavor to recipes. After juicing the lemons, I freeze the juice in ice cube trays. Then I simply defrost the number of cubes I need and use them in poultry recipes, lemon desserts, iced or hot teas and many other dishes.

—**JUDY M.** SOUTH BEND, INDIANA

Chilly-Day Hot Cocoa Mix

This easy-to-assemble blend makes the perfect gift for teachers, friends and neighbors at Christmastime or any time at all. You'll want to keep a batch for yourself, too!

—**MARIE WIERSMA** ST. JOHNS, MICHIGAN

PREP/TOTAL TIME: 15 MINUTES
MAKES: 10 SERVINGS (2½ CUPS HOT COCOA MIX)

- 2 **cups nonfat dry milk powder**
- 6 **tablespoons baking cocoa**
- 5 **tablespoons confectioners' sugar**
- 5 **tablespoons sugar**
  ADDITIONAL INGREDIENTS (FOR EACH SERVING)
- ½ **cup hot fat-free milk**
- ½ **cup hot water**

1. In a small airtight container, combine the milk powder, cocoa, confectioners' sugar and sugar. Store in a cool dry place for up to 2 months.

To prepare hot cocoa: *Place ¼ cup mix in a mug; stir in hot milk and water until blended.*

Nutrition Facts: *1 cup hot cocoa equals 137 calories, trace fat (trace saturated fat), 5 mg cholesterol, 127 mg sodium, 25 g carbohydrate, 1 g fiber, 10 g protein.* **Diabetic Exchanges:** *1 fat-free milk, ½ starch.*

Banana Cream Pie

Here's a luscious, home-style pie everyone enjoys. The no-bake treat is full of old-fashioned flavor but requires only a fraction of the work. Best of all, you can indulge guilt-free.

— **PERLENE HOEKEMA** LYNDEN, WASHINGTON

PREP/TOTAL TIME: 10 MINUTES **MAKES:** 8 SERVINGS

- 1 **cup fat-free milk**
- ½ **teaspoon vanilla extract**
- 1 **package (3.4 ounces) sugar-free instant vanilla pudding mix**
- 1 **carton (12 ounces) frozen reduced-fat whipped topping, thawed, divided**
- 1 **reduced-fat graham cracker crust (9 inches)**
- 2 **medium firm bananas, sliced**
  Additional banana slices, optional

1. In a large bowl, whisk the milk, vanilla and pudding mix for 2 minutes (mixture will be thick). Fold in 3 cups whipped topping.

2. Pour 1⅓ cups of pudding mixture into the pie crust. Layer with banana slices and remaining pudding mixture. Top with remaining whipped topping. Garnish with additional banana slices if desired. Refrigerate until serving.

Nutrition Facts: *One piece equals 274 calories, 8 g fat (6 g saturated fat), 1 mg cholesterol, 612 mg sodium, 43 g carbohydrate, 1 g fiber, 3 g protein.* **Diabetic Exchanges:** *2 starch, 1 fruit, 1 fat.*

Eggnog Shakes

I like to serve this yummy drink as a healthier alternative to the classic holiday beverage. Although made with fat-free ingredients, the fast-to-fix shakes have the same thick, creamy consistency of traditional eggnog. I sprinkle each serving with a little nutmeg.

—**DALE HARTMAN** COVENTRY, RHODE ISLAND

PREP/TOTAL TIME: 10 MINUTES **MAKES:** 1½ CUPS

- 1½ cups fat-free sugar-free vanilla ice cream
- ½ cup fat-free milk
- 1 tablespoon fat-free whipped topping
    Sugar substitute equivalent to ½ teaspoon sugar
- ⅛ teaspoon rum extract
- ⅛ teaspoon brandy extract or vanilla extract
    Dash ground nutmeg

1. In a blender, combine the first six ingredients; cover and process until smooth. Pour into chilled glasses; sprinkle with nutmeg.

Editor's Note: *This recipe was tested with Splenda sugar blend.*

Nutrition Facts: *¾ cup equals 163 calories, 7 g fat (4 g saturated fat), 0 cholesterol, 109 mg sodium, 21 g carbohydrate, 0 fiber, 7 g protein.* **Diabetic Exchanges:** *1 starch, 1 fat, ½ milk.*

Fruit-Filled Angel Food Torte

Tired of eating plain angel food cake or fruit as a low-fat dessert, I decided to combine the two with a little whipped topping. The result was a refreshing torte that satisfied my sweet tooth.

—**HETTIE JOHNSON** JACKSONVILLE, FLORIDA

PREP/TOTAL TIME: 15 MINUTES **MAKES:** 12 SERVINGS

- 1 carton (12 ounces) frozen reduced-fat whipped topping, thawed, divided
- 1 can (15 ounces) reduced-sugar fruit cocktail, drained
- 1 prepared angel food cake (8 to 10 ounces)
- 1 can (11 ounces) mandarin oranges, drained
- 1 large navel orange, sliced, optional
    Fresh mint, optional

1. Fold 1½ cups whipped topping into fruit cocktail just until blended. Split cake horizontally into three layers; place one layer on a serving plate. Spread with half of the fruit mixture. Repeat layers. Top with remaining cake layer.

2. Frost the top and sides with remaining whipped topping. Arrange mandarin oranges on top. Refrigerate until serving. Serve with orange slices and mint if desired.

Nutrition Facts: *1 piece equals 177 calories, 4 g fat (4 g saturated fat), 0 cholesterol, 218 mg sodium, 32 g carbohydrate, 1 g fiber, 2 g protein.* **Diabetic Exchanges:** *1½ starch, ½ fruit, ½ fat.*

Beefstro Bruschetta Burgers

PREP/TOTAL TIME: 30 MINUTES
MAKES: 4 SERVINGS

- 3 tablespoons Dijon mustard
- 3 tablespoons reduced-sugar apricot preserves
- 1 tablespoon prepared horseradish
- 2 thin slices prosciutto or deli ham, chopped
- 1 pound lean ground beef (90% lean)
- ¾ teaspoon salt-free lemon-pepper seasoning
- 8 slices French bread (½ inch thick)
- 1 cup fresh arugula or baby spinach
- 2 ounces Brie cheese, cut into eight thin slices
- ¼ cup julienned roasted sweet red peppers

1. In a small bowl, combine mustard, preserves and horseradish. In a small skillet coated with cooking spray, cook and stir prosciutto over medium heat until lightly browned. Set aside.

2. In a large bowl, combine the ground beef and lemon-pepper seasoning. Shape into eight patties.

3. Moisten a paper towel with cooking oil; using long-handled tongs, lightly coat the grill rack. Grill burgers, covered, over medium heat or broil 4 in. from heat for 3-4 minutes on each side or until a thermometer reads 160° and juices run clear. Remove and keep warm.

4. Grill or broil bread for 1-2 minutes on each side or until toasted. Spread each slice of toast with 1¼ teaspoons reserved mustard sauce. Layer each with arugula, a burger, a Brie cheese slice and 1¼ teaspoons additional sauce. Garnish with red peppers and prosciutto. Serve immediately.

Nutrition Facts: *2 bruschetta burgers equals 329 calories, 14 g fat (6 g saturated fat), 76 mg cholesterol, 767 mg sodium, 20 g carbohydrate, 1 g fiber, 29 g protein.*

My mom always put her burger on top of a salad. I adjusted her idea and created these unusual sandwiches featuring red peppers and Brie cheese. They make an extra- special treat for a cookout. **—DEVON DELANEY** WESTPORT, CONNECTICUT

Sweet-Tart Rhubarb Crepes

When you want a festive dish for a holiday brunch, look here. The delicate crepes are filled with a tangy combination of rhubarb and citrus. For a pretty finish, sprinkle on confectioners' sugar and orange peel.

—ELIZABETH KING DULUTH, MINNESOTA

PREP/TOTAL TIME: 25 MINUTES
MAKES: 8 SERVINGS

- 5 cups finely chopped fresh or frozen rhubarb, thawed
- ¾ cup sugar
- 2 tablespoons all-purpose flour
- 2 tablespoons orange juice
- 1 tablespoon butter
- 1 teaspoon grated orange peel
- 16 prepared crepes (9 inches)
  Confectioners' sugar and additional grated orange peel, optional

1. In a large saucepan, combine the first five ingredients. Cook, stirring occasionally, over medium heat for 15-18 minutes or until tender. Remove from the heat; stir in orange peel.

2. Spread 2 tablespoons filling down the center of each crepe; roll up. Sprinkle with confectioners' sugar and additional orange peel if desired.

Editor's Note: *If using frozen rhubarb, measure rhubarb while still frozen, then thaw completely. Drain in a colander, but do not press liquid out.*

Nutrition Facts: *2 filled crepes (calculated without confectioners' sugar) equals 200 calories, 4 g fat (2 g saturated fat), 15 mg cholesterol, 175 mg sodium, 40 g carbohydrate, 1 g fiber, 3 g protein.*

Oven-Fried Chicken with Cranberry Sauce

PREP/TOTAL TIME: 30 MINUTES
MAKES: 4 SERVINGS (1 CUP SAUCE)

- ½ cup dry bread crumbs
- 2 tablespoons grated Parmesan cheese
- 2 tablespoons toasted wheat germ
- 2 garlic cloves, minced
- ½ teaspoon paprika
- ¼ teaspoon each dried oregano, thyme and rosemary, crushed
- ¼ teaspoon pepper
- 4 boneless skinless chicken breast halves (4 ounces each)

SAUCE

- 1 cup jellied cranberry sauce
- 2 tablespoons lime juice
- 1 tablespoon balsamic vinegar
- 1½ teaspoons Dijon mustard

1. In a large resealable plastic bag, combine the bread crumbs, cheese, wheat germ, garlic and seasonings. Add the chicken, one piece at a time, and shake to coat. Place on a baking sheet coated with cooking spray.

2. Bake at 375° for 20-25 minutes or until a thermometer reads 170°, turning once.

3. Meanwhile, in a small saucepan, bring cranberry sauce to a boil. Remove from the heat; whisk in the lime juice, vinegar and mustard. Serve with chicken.

Nutrition Facts: *1 chicken breast half with ¼ cup sauce equals 268 calories, 4 g fat (1 g saturated fat), 64 mg cholesterol, 182 mg sodium, 34 g carbohydrate, 2 g fiber, 25 g protein.* **Diabetic Exchanges:** *3 lean meat, 2 starch.*

❝Fried chicken isn't off limits when it's prepared with a light coating and baked in the oven. Adding a tangy cranberry sauce results in an entree that's truly memorable.❞

—DONNA NOEL GRAY, MAINE

Mashed Potato Casserole

Be sure to leave room on your plate for a helping of this delicious potato casserole. Dressed up with green onions and melted cheddar cheese, it gets its richness from reduced-fat sour cream.

—DONNA NOEL GRAY, MAINE

PREP/TOTAL TIME: 30 MINUTES   **MAKES:** 5 SERVINGS

- 4 medium potatoes, peeled and quartered
- ½ cup reduced-fat sour cream
- ½ cup cream-style cottage cheese
- ¼ cup fat-free milk
- 2 to 3 green onions, thinly sliced
- ¼ cup shredded reduced-fat cheddar cheese

1. Place the potatoes in a large saucepan and cover with water. Bring to a boil. Reduce heat; cover and simmer for 15-20 minutes or until tender. Drain.

2. In a large bowl, mash potatoes with sour cream, cottage cheese and milk; stir in onions. Transfer to an 8-in. square baking dish coated with cooking spray; sprinkle with cheddar cheese. Bake at 375° for 5-10 minutes or until heated through and cheese is melted.

Nutrition Facts: *¾ cup equals 177 calories, 4 g fat (3 g saturated fat), 16 mg cholesterol, 153 mg sodium, 27 g carbohydrate, 2 g fiber, 8 g protein.* **Diabetic Exchanges:** *2 starch, 1 fat.*

Special Green Beans

With bright color and fresh flavor, this simple yet tasty side dish can round out just about any meal. It's a recipe you'll want to keep handy for holidays and busy weekdays, too.

—DONNA NOEL GRAY, MAINE

PREP/TOTAL TIME: 20 MINUTES   **MAKES:** 4 SERVINGS

- 1 pound fresh green beans, trimmed
- 2 green onions, thinly sliced
- 2 tablespoons minced fresh parsley
- 2 tablespoons olive oil
- 1 tablespoon red wine vinegar
- 1 garlic clove, minced
- 1 teaspoon Dijon mustard
- ¼ teaspoon salt
- ¼ teaspoon pepper

1. Place the green beans in a large saucepan and cover with water. Bring to a boil. Cover and cook for 4-7 minutes or until crisp-tender.

2. Meanwhile, in a small bowl, combine the remaining ingredients. Drain green beans; stir in the onion mixture and heat through.

Nutrition Facts: *¾ cup equals 97 calories, 7 g fat (1 g saturated fat), 0 cholesterol, 186 mg sodium, 9 g carbohydrate, 4 g fiber, 2 g protein.* **Diabetic Exchanges:** *1 vegetable, 1 fat.*

Sugarplums

Grab one of these sweet-spicy treats early—they'll be gone before you can lick the sugar from your fingers! The moist, fruity goodies are fun to include on Christmas cookie trays.

—**CORLEEN HEIDGERKEN** MILWAUKEE, WISCONSIN

PREP/TOTAL TIME: 25 MINUTES   **MAKES:** 2½ DOZEN

> 1⅓ cups chopped walnuts
> 1 cup pitted dates
> 1 package (5 ounces) dried cherries
> ¼ cup honey
> 2 teaspoons grated orange peel
> 1 teaspoon ground cinnamon
> 1 teaspoon ground allspice
> ½ teaspoon ground nutmeg
> ¼ teaspoon ground ginger
> ½ cup coarse sugar

1. Place the walnuts, dates and cherries in a food processor; cover and process until finely chopped. Transfer to a small bowl; stir in the honey, orange peel and spices. Roll into 1-in. balls, then roll in coarse sugar. Store in an airtight container in the refrigerator.

Nutrition Facts: *1 sugarplum equals 84 calories, 3 g fat (trace saturated fat), 0 cholesterol, 1 mg sodium, 13 g carbohydrate, 1 g fiber, 1 g protein.* **Diabetic Exchange:** *1 starch.*

Pumpkin Mousse

Here's a wonderful dessert for special autumn meals. Guests savor every smooth, cool spoonful of this luscious mousse. It tastes so rich and creamy, no one guesses that it's low in fat.

—**PATRICIA SIDLOSKAS** ANNISTON, ALABAMA

PREP/TOTAL TIME: 15 MINUTES   **MAKES:** 4 SERVINGS

> 1½ cups cold fat-free milk
> 1 package (1 ounce) sugar-free instant butterscotch pudding mix
> ½ cup canned pumpkin
> ½ teaspoon ground cinnamon
> ¼ teaspoon ground ginger
> ¼ teaspoon ground allspice
> 1 cup fat-free whipped topping, divided

1. In a large bowl, whisk milk and pudding mix for 2 minutes. Let stand for 2 minutes or until soft-set. Combine pumpkin, cinnamon, ginger and allspice; fold into the pudding. Fold in ½ cup whipped topping.
2. Transfer to individual serving dishes. Refrigerate until serving. Garnish with remaining whipped topping.
Nutrition Facts: *⅔ cup mousse with 2 tablespoons whipped topping equals 96 calories, trace fat (trace saturated fat), 2 mg cholesterol, 360 mg sodium, 18 g carbohydrate, 1 g fiber, 4 g protein.* **Diabetic Exchanges:** *½ starch, ½ fat-free milk.*

Smoked Salmon Tomato Cups

To get a summer gathering off to a delicious start, I serve cherry tomatoes stuffed with a filling of smoked salmon, cottage cheese, green onion, celery and dill. The colorful little cups really stand out on an appetizer table—and disappear in a flash!

—**VICKI RAATZ** WATERLOO, WISCONSIN

PREP/TOTAL TIME: 30 MINUTES **MAKES:** 2 DOZEN

- 24 cherry tomatoes (about 1 pint)
- 1 package (3 ounces) smoked salmon or lox, finely chopped
- ¼ cup fat-free cottage cheese
- 2 tablespoons finely chopped celery
- 1 tablespoon finely chopped green onion
- ¼ teaspoon dill weed

1. Cut a thin slice off the top of each tomato. Scoop out and discard pulp; invert tomatoes onto paper towels to drain.
2. In a small bowl, combine the remaining ingredients; stuff into tomatoes. Refrigerate until serving.

Nutrition Facts: *1 tomato cup equals 9 calories, trace fat (trace saturated fat), 1 mg cholesterol, 81 mg sodium, 1 g carbohydrate, trace fiber, 1 g protein.* **Diabetic Exchange:** *Free food.*

Orange-Glazed Sweet Potatoes

Each bite of this healthier side dish bursts with tangy orange flavor. The glazed potatoes are easy to fix and make a holiday-worthy addition to a Thanksgiving or Christmas feast.

—**TASTE OF HOME TEST KITCHEN**

PREP/TOTAL TIME: 25 MINUTES **MAKES:** 3 SERVINGS

- 1 pound sweet potatoes, peeled and cut into ½-inch slices
- ½ cup orange juice
- 1 tablespoon butter
- ½ teaspoon grated orange peel
- ¼ teaspoon pumpkin pie spice

1. Place sweet potatoes in a small saucepan and cover with water. Bring to a boil. Reduce heat; cover and simmer for 4-6 minutes or just until tender.
2. Meanwhile, in a small skillet, bring the orange juice, butter, orange peel and pumpkin pie spice to a boil. Reduce heat; simmer, uncovered, for 3-4 minutes or until thickened. Drain sweet potatoes; return to pan. Pour glaze over potatoes and stir gently to coat.

Nutrition Facts: *⅔ cup equals 147 calories, 4 g fat (2 g saturated fat), 10 mg cholesterol, 48 mg sodium, 27 g carbohydrate, 3 g fiber, 2 g protein.* **Diabetic Exchanges:** *1½ starch, ½ fat.*

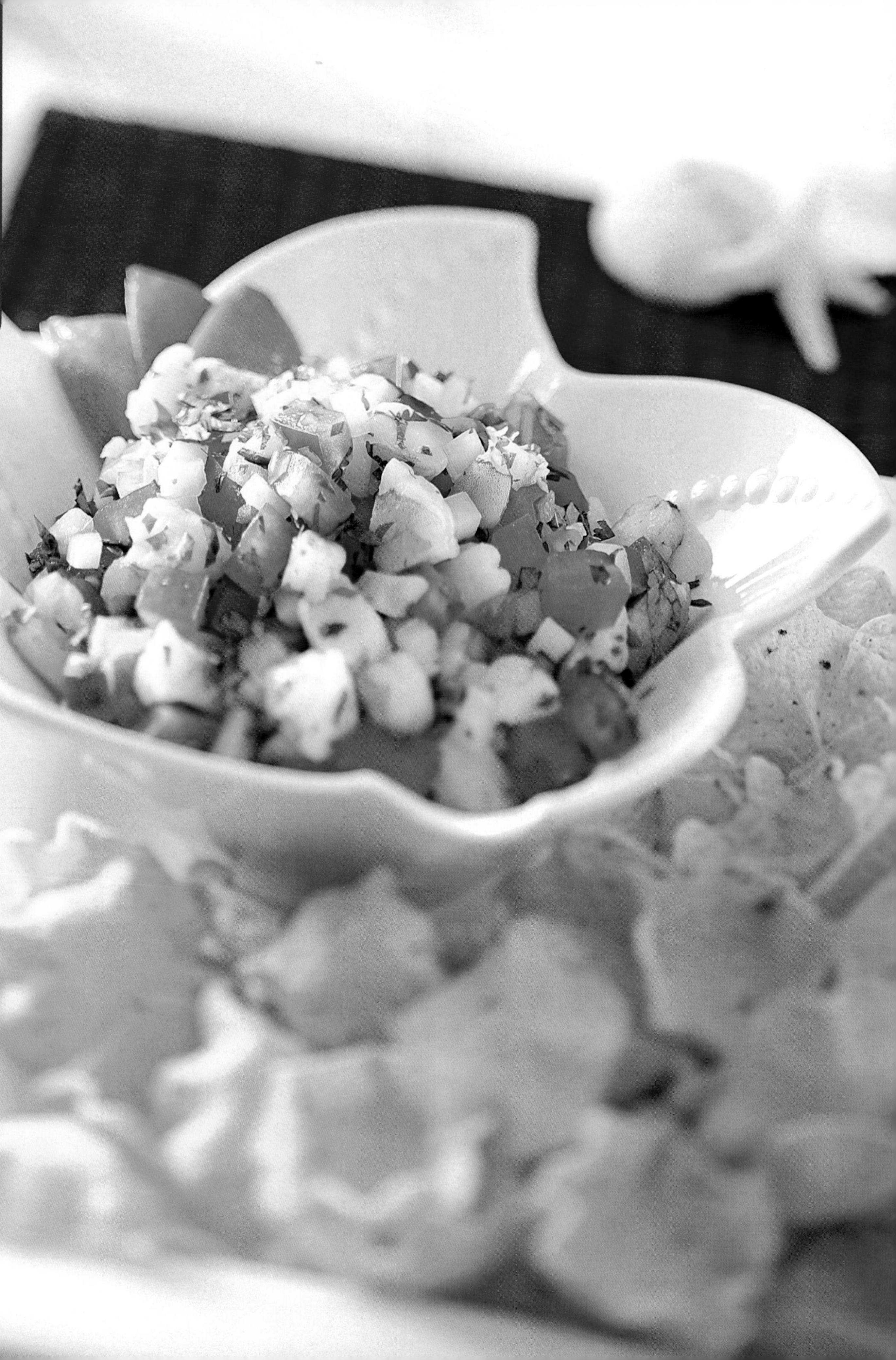

Spicy Shrimp Salsa

Radishes bring a wonderful crunch to this colorful seafood salsa. It's great not only with tortilla chips as a snack, but also served over grilled fish as an entree. The recipe has just enough jalapeno to enhance the flavor without adding too much heat.

—**MARY RELYEA** CANASTOTA, NEW YORK

PREP/TOTAL TIME: 15 MINUTES
MAKES: 2 CUPS

- ½ pound cooked shrimp, peeled, deveined and chopped
- 1 large tomato, chopped
- ¼ cup finely chopped onion
- 3 radishes, chopped
- ¼ cup minced fresh cilantro
- 2 tablespoons lime juice
- 1½ teaspoons finely chopped seeded jalapeno pepper
- ¼ teaspoon salt
  Baked tortilla chip scoops

1. In a small bowl, combine the first eight ingredients. Refrigerate until serving. Serve with chips.

Editor's Note: *Wear disposable gloves when cutting hot peppers; the oils can burn skin. Avoid touching your face.*

Nutrition Facts: *¼ cup (calculated without chips) equals 38 calories, 1 g fat (trace saturated fat), 43 mg cholesterol, 119 mg sodium, 2 g carbohydrate, trace fiber, 6 g protein.* **Diabetic Exchange:** *1 lean meat.*

Salmon Salad-Stuffed Endive Leaves

Bursting with a delicious filling of salmon, tartar sauce, capers and seasonings, little endive leaves create an elegant appetizer for dinner parties or other special occasions. Plus, you'll need just six ingredients and 15 minutes in the kitchen.

—**MELISSA CARAFA** BROOMALL, PENNSYLVANIA

PREP/TOTAL TIME: 15 MINUTES **MAKES:** 14 APPETIZERS

- 1 salmon fillet (6 ounces), cooked and flaked
- ¼ cup tartar sauce
- 2 teaspoons capers
- 1 teaspoon snipped fresh dill
- ¼ teaspoon lemon-pepper seasoning
- 1 head Belgian endive (about 5 ounces), separated into leaves
  Additional snipped fresh dill, optional

1. In a small bowl, combine the salmon, tartar sauce, capers, dill and lemon-pepper. Spoon about 2 teaspoonfuls onto each endive leaf. Garnish with additional dill if desired. Refrigerate until serving.

Nutrition Facts: *1 serving equals 42 calories, 3 g fat (trace saturated fat), 9 mg cholesterol, 60 mg sodium, 2 g carbohydrate, 1 g fiber, 3 g protein.* **Diabetic Exchange:** *½ fat.*

Did you know?

Capers are the immature buds from a small bush native to the Middle East and Mediterranean regions that are either brined in vinegar or packed in coarse salt to preserve. Best rinsed before using, capers are frequently used in French, Italian and Greek cooking. Enjoy them in Salmon Salad-Stuffed Endive Leaves (recipe above right).

Spinach & Black Bean Egg Rolls

PREP/TOTAL TIME: 30 MINUTES
MAKES: 20 EGG ROLLS

- 2 cups frozen corn, thawed
- 1 can (15 ounces) black beans, rinsed and drained
- 1 package (10 ounces) frozen chopped spinach, thawed and squeezed dry
- 1 cup (4 ounces) shredded reduced-fat Mexican cheese blend
- 1 can (4 ounces) chopped green chilies, drained
- 4 green onions, chopped
- 1 teaspoon ground cumin
- ½ teaspoon chili powder
- ½ teaspoon pepper
- 20 egg roll wrappers
  Cooking spray
  Salsa and reduced-fat ranch salad dressing, optional

1. In a large bowl, combine the first nine ingredients. Place ¼ cup mixture in the center of one egg roll wrapper. (Keep remaining wrappers covered with a damp paper towel until ready to use.) Fold bottom corner over filling. Fold sides toward center over filling. Moisten remaining corner with water; roll up tightly to seal. Repeat.

2. Place seam side down on baking sheets coated with cooking spray. Spray tops of egg rolls with cooking spray. Bake at 425° for 10-15 minutes or until lightly browned. Serve warm with salsa and dressing if desired. Refrigerate leftovers.

Nutrition Facts: *1 egg roll (calculated without salsa and salad dressing) equals 147 calories, 2 g fat (1 g saturated fat), 7 mg cholesterol, 298 mg sodium, 26 g carbohydrate, 2 g fiber, 7 g protein.* **Diabetic Exchanges:** *1½ starch, 1 lean meat.*

Wholesome black beans and spinach give these delicious baked egg rolls a burst of nutrition. Plus, assembling them couldn't be easier. **—MELANIE SCOTT** AMARILLO, TEXAS

Spiced Tangerine Ham

A real time-saver for busy holidays, this savory skillet ham is special enough to serve company but takes only 15 minutes to bring to the table. With a hint of sweetness from honey, the thick tangerine sauce is nicely seasoned with ginger and cloves.

—TASTE OF HOME TEST KITCHEN

PREP/TOTAL TIME: 15 MINUTES **MAKES:** 4 SERVINGS

- 8 medium tangerines
- 2 teaspoons cornstarch
- 1 tablespoon honey
- ¼ teaspoon ground ginger
- ¼ teaspoon ground cloves
- 4 slices fully cooked ham (1 pound)

1. Squeeze juice from six tangerines; strain pulp. Cut a thin slice off the bottom and top of the remaining tangerines. Place each tangerine cut side down on a cutting board. With a sharp knife, remove peel and white pith from fruit. Holding fruit over a bowl, slice between the membrane of each section and the fruit until the knife reaches the center; remove sections; set aside.

2. In a small bowl, combine cornstarch and tangerine juice until smooth; stir in the honey, ginger and cloves.

3. In a large nonstick skillet coated with cooking spray, brown ham slices on both sides; remove and keep warm. Stir the tangerine juice mixture and add to the skillet. Bring to a boil; cook and stir for 2 minutes or until thickened. Stir in the tangerine segments; heat through. Serve with the ham.

Nutrition Facts: *4 ounces cooked ham with 3 tablespoons sauce equals 232 calories, 6 g fat (2 g saturated fat), 53 mg cholesterol, 1,623 mg sodium, 22 g carbohydrate, 3 g fiber, 23 g protein.* **Diabetic Exchanges:** *3 lean meat, 1 fruit.*

Makeover Mini Bacon Quiches

My friends and family loved my original recipe for miniature bacon quiches, but I wanted to make them a little healthier. The solution? Replace some of the ingredients with their reduced-fat versions. Those substitutions slashed calories, fat and sodium, but left in all the mouthwatering bacon flavor we crave.

—**JULIE HIEGGELKE** GRAYSLAKE, ILLINOIS

PREP/TOTAL TIME: 30 MINUTES
MAKES: 2½ DOZEN

- 1 egg, lightly beaten
- ½ pound sliced bacon, cooked and crumbled
- ½ cup reduced-fat ricotta cheese
- ½ cup shredded part-skim mozzarella cheese
- ½ cup shredded reduced-fat cheddar cheese
- 1 small onion, finely chopped
- ¼ teaspoon garlic powder
  Dash cayenne pepper
  Dash pepper
- 2 packages (1.9 ounces each) frozen miniature phyllo tart shells

1. In a small bowl, combine the first nine ingredients. Place phyllo tart shells on an ungreased baking sheet; fill each with two teaspoons mixture.

2. Bake at 350° for 8-10 minutes or until filling is set and shells are lightly browned. Serve warm.

Nutrition Facts: *1 appetizer equals 54 calories, 3 g fat (1 g saturated fat), 13 mg cholesterol, 77 mg sodium, 3 g carbohydrate, trace fiber, 3 g protein.*

General Recipe Index

This handy index lists every recipe by food category, major ingredient and/or cooking method, so you can easily find recipes to suit your needs.

BANANAS

Banana Chocolate Parfaits, 198
Banana Cream Pie, 230
Bananas Foster Sundaes, 143
Cinnamon-Spiced Bananas, 154
Double-Decker Banana Cups, 205

BEANS

Beans & Spinach, 90
Black Bean and Beef Tostadas, 130
Black Bean Chicken with Rice, 182
Black Bean Pasta, 176
Blackened Chicken and Beans, 131
Gingered Green Bean Salad, 150
Refried Bean Nachos, 17
Roasted Parmesan Green Beans, 100
Salsa Black Bean Burgers, 66
Sausage Bean Soup, 74
Savory 'n' Saucy Baked Beans, 89
Special Green Beans, 234
Spinach & Black Bean Egg Rolls, 240

BEEF & CORNED BEEF (also see Ground Beef)

Beef 'n' Asparagus Pasta, 187
Beef Fajita Salad, 121
Blue Cheese-Topped Steaks, 223
Chili Steak & Peppers, 111
Gingered Beef Stir-Fry, 188
Italian Steaks, 158
Makeover Beef Stroganoff, 112
Makeover Hash and Eggs, 47
Mexican Fiesta Steak Stir-Fry, 185
Pastrami Deli Wraps, 65
Sirloin Steak with Rich Mushroom Gravy, 229
Spinach Beef Salad, 160
Stir-Fried Steak & Veggies, 191
Toasted Clubs with Dill Mayo, 60

BEVERAGES

A.M. Rush Espresso Smoothie, 35
Berry Best Smoothies, 33
Blueberry Orange Smoothies, 38
Chilly-Day Hot Cocoa Mix, 230
Eggnog Shakes, 231
Ginger-Peach Milk Shakes, 162
Iced Coffee, 34
Makeover Nutty Monkey Malts, 212
Sunrise Slushies, 45

BISCUITS & SCONES

Blueberry Orange Scones, 40
Cheddar Dill Biscuits, 80
Cherry-Almond Drop Scones, 52
Coconut-Glazed Orange Scones, 48
Green Onion Biscuits, 84
Makeover British Scones, 33
Onion Poppy Seed Biscuits, 149
Parmesan Sage Scones, 81
Sweet Potato Biscuits, 97

BLUEBERRIES

Angel Food Trifle, 194
Blueberry Orange Scones, 40
Blueberry Orange Smoothies, 38
Cinnamon Blueberry Sauce, 208

BREADS (see Biscuits & Scones; Corn & Corn Bread; French Toast & Waffles; Muffins; Pancakes & Crepes; Rolls & Breadsticks)

BREAKFAST

A.M. Rush Espresso Smoothie, 35
Baked Eggs with Cheddar and Bacon, 41
Berry Best Smoothies, 33
Bird's Nest Breakfast Cups, 52
Black Forest Crepes, 36
Blueberry Orange Scones, 40
Blueberry Orange Smoothies, 38
Cafe Mocha Mini Muffins, 39
Cherry-Almond Drop Scones, 52
Coconut-Glazed Orange Scones, 48
Easy Breakfast Quesadillas, 45
French Toast with Apple Topping, 48
Honey Wheat Pancakes, 51
Iced Coffee, 34
Makeover British Scones, 33
Makeover Hash and Eggs, 47
Makeover Waffles, 50
Morning Cinnamon Rolls, 39
Omelet Tortilla Wrap, 41
Puffy Apple Omelet, 42
Pumpkin Pancakes, 38
Roasted Red Pepper Omelets, 32
Sausage and Egg Pizza, 47
Savory Apple-Chicken Sausage, 32
Spicy Scrambled Egg Sandwiches, 42
Strawberry Puff Pancake, 44
Sunrise Slushies, 45
Sweet Berry Bruschetta, 44

Chicken Sausage Gyros, 70
Open-Faced Chicken Salad Sandwiches, 76
Spicy Chicken Tomato Pitas, 56
Soups
Simple Chicken Soup, 71
Zippy Chicken Soup, 73

CHOCOLATE
Banana Chocolate Parfaits, 198
Buttermilk Chocolate Sauce, 209
Cafe Mocha Mini Muffins, 39
Cappuccino Pudding, 158
Chilly-Day Hot Cocoa Mix, 230
Chocolate Biscuit Puffs, 194
Chocolate Mousse with Strawberries, 207
Dark Chocolate Fondue, 205
Double Chocolate Pudding, 199
Grilled Fruit Skewers with Chocolate Syrup, 201
Mocha Pudding Cakes, 210

COCONUT
Coconut-Crusted Turkey Strips, 126
Coconut-Glazed Orange Scones, 48
Makeover Coconut Cookies, 214

COOKIES & BARS
Cinnamon-Raisin Bites, 157
Makeover Coconut Cookies, 214
Quick Crisp Snack Bars, 161

CORN & CORN BREAD
Buttermilk Corn Bread, 87
Calico Corn Salsa, 9
Chive 'n' Garlic Corn, 144
Corn & Pepper Orzo, 102
Maple Syrup Corn Bread, 94
Quick Corn Dip, 22

CRANBERRIES
Cran-Apple Turkey Skillet, 172
Cranberry Chili Meatballs, 15
Cranberry Fudge, 224
Oven-Fried Chicken with Cranberry Sauce, 234

DESSERTS *(also see Cakes & Torte; Candy; Cookies & Bars; Mousse; Puddings & Parfaits; Sauces)*
Amaretto Cheese-Filled Apricots, 147
Angel Food Trifle, 194
Apple Skewers, 197

Banana Cream Pie, 230
Bananas Foster Sundaes, 143
Berries with Sour Cream Sauce, 198
Berry-Marshmallow Trifle, 202
Broiled Fruit Dessert, 202
Cheesecake Phyllo Cups, 206
Chocolate Biscuit Puffs, 194
Cinnamon-Spiced Bananas, 154
Creamy Peaches, 144
Dark Chocolate Fondue, 205
Fruit-Filled Quesadillas, 148
Fun Fruit Dessert, 210
Ginger-Glazed Grilled Honeydew, 206
Ginger-Peach Milk Shakes, 162
Gingered Melon, 213
Green Tea Tiramisu, 207
Grilled Fruit Skewers with Chocolate Syrup, 201
Grilled Peach Crisps, 201
Grilled Pineapple Dessert, 209
Heavenly Filled Strawberries, 221
Lemon Burst Tartlets, 215
Makeover Nutty Monkey Malts, 212
Maple Baked Apple, 212
Saucy Poached Pears, 150
Special Ladyfinger Dessert, 213
Sugarplums, 236
Summertime Fruit Cones, 196
Warm Strawberry Fondue, 224

DIPS & FONDUE
Calico Corn Salsa, 9
Cinnamon Chips 'n' Dip, 12
Dark Chocolate Fondue, 205
Easy Buffalo Chicken Dip, 26
Honey-Balsamic Goat Cheese Dip, 146
Makeover Hot Pizza Dip, 18
Pineapple Salsa, 18
Quick Corn Dip, 22
Spicy Shrimp Salsa, 239
Spinach & Crab Dip, 29
Tortellini with Roasted Red Pepper Dip, 14
Warm Spinach Dip, 153
Warm Strawberry Fondue, 224

EGGS & EGG SUBSTITUTE
Baked Eggs with Cheddar and Bacon, 41
Bird's Nest Breakfast Cups, 52
Deviled Eggs with Dill, 17
Easy Breakfast Quesadillas, 45
Makeover Hash and Eggs, 47

INDEXES

Alphabetical Index

This index lists every recipe alphabetically, so you can easily find the recipes you and your family enjoy most.